The Films of Wim Wenders traces the development of one of the most well known directors of the New German Cinema, which flourished in the seventies and early eighties. Examining Wenders' career from his early film-school productions through his mature works of the seventies, this book also analyzes his more recent films, as well as the themes and preoccupations that unite his oeuvre. As the authors note, Wenders' works have been profoundly influenced by American films, especially the "road movie" genre. They often feature characters who are always on the move in an attempt to capture a glimpse of their identity and place in the world. They also represent a generation of postwar Germans seeking to redeem themselves and the history of their country by turning to American popular culture, particularly its music and movies. In such films as *The Goalie's Anxiety at the Penalty Kick, Alice in the Cities, Kings of the Road,* and *The American Friend,* Wenders offers an articulate cinematic vision of the emotional landscape of postwar Germany. In his most recent films, such as *Paris, Texas, Wings of Desire,* and *Until the End of the World,* Wenders continues his quest for certainty, for a domestic and romantic haven, in a style that transforms modernism into postmodern pastiche and in which such elements as melodrama, fantasy, and desire are fused.

Providing close analyses of Wenders' most important works, *The Films of Wim Wenders* serves as a useful introduction to a serious filmmaker for whom cinema represents nothing less than the redemption of the imagination and the reclamation of history.

CAMBRIDGE FILM CLASSICS

General Editor: Raymond Carney, Boston University

The Films of Wim Wenders

"Double-crossed for the very last time, but now I'm finally free!" Robert Lander in *Kings of the Road*.

The Films of Wim Wenders

Cinema as Vision and Desire

ROBERT PHILLIP KOLKER
PETER BEICKEN

CAMBRIDGE
UNIVERSITY PRESS

Published by the Press Syndicate of the University of Cambridge
The Pitt Building, Trumpington Street, Cambridge CB2 1RP
40 West 20th Street, New York, NY 10011-4211, USA
10 Stamford Road, Oakleigh, Melbourne 3166, Australia

© Cambridge University Press 1993

First published 1993
Reprinted 1993, 1995

Printed in the United States of America

Library of Congress Cataloging-in-Publication Data is available.

A catalogue record for this book is available from the British Library.

ISBN 0-521-38064-2 hardback
ISBN 0-521-38976-3 paperback

Contents

Preface

Tell stories looking ahead, that is what I want to do. . . . This was the great
accomplishment of classical American cinema: that collective narrative came
about because of the studio system, not just storytelling in one voice. The
collective narrative was the one that created all those myths which, in fact,
connected the cinema back to the great storytelling of the past. Something the
European cinema never achieved nor the auteur film. None of us was able to
come up with such storytelling. Our stories have been subjective. Now, we
have to understand that this form of collective narrative can neither be imi-
tated nor ever be recuperated. That fact should not be lamented over. That's
done with forever. Nevertheless, there is an enormous need for stories: people
still want to experience connectedness – certainly not only in *Star Wars*, but
in stories in which they discover part of themselves. We must stop complaining
about the loss of the resounding voice of the old cinema.

Wim Wenders, *Die Logik der Bilder*

This book tells the story of a filmmaker who attempted to knit together the
broken weave of cinema and culture in the seventies and eighties. He began
making films as a student in Munich, collaborated with the Austrian novelist
Peter Handke on his first commercial feature, *The Goalie's Anxiety at the
Penalty Kick,* and went on to develop a moving variation of the American
road movie in such films as *Alice in the Cities* and *Kings of the Road*. With
his homage to fifties film noir, *The American Friend,* he became (along with
Rainer Werner Fassbinder and Werner Herzog) one of the best-known directors of the New German Cinema in the United States. He came to the
attention of Francis Ford Coppola, who invited him to come to America to
direct the ill-fated *Hammett*. Wenders' experience in Hollywood led him to
make a stark and contemplative film, *The State of Things,* a despairing
reflection on the possibilities and impossibilities of cinema today. In an
attempt to come to terms with filmmaking and the continuing influence of

vii

American culture on his imagination, he returned to America and made another English-language film, *Paris, Texas*. He then returned to Germany to make his postmodernist meditation on romance in Berlin, *Wings of Desire*, and went back on the road for *Until the End of the World*.

Throughout his work, Wim Wenders connects history and personality, Hollywood storytelling and the practices of modernism, the anxieties of postwar Europe and the desire to be saved by cinema. His films constitute an ongoing narrative in which self and style, hope and despair, the highway and the road to heaven find a common intersection. The story is a rich one because Wenders' films – themselves deeply emotional and visually eloquent meditations – are part of large cultural and aesthetic forces, complex and often contradictory.

The goal of this study is to expose the weave in the alternately rich and confused pattern of Wenders' life and work. We concentrate on an analysis of the films, read them closely in order to see what makes them work, how they structure intentions and meanings, how cinema and self intertwine in stories about modernity and disrupted identities. However, Wenders' work is intensely personal, and his personality is the result of many currents; we have therefore started with a chapter that mixes the biographic with the aesthetic. A childhood in postwar Germany, an early attraction to the movie camera and American rock and roll music, and a late adolescence in film school during the political upheavals of the sixties help explain the often conflicted elements in the later films.

The second chapter serves as a link between the discussion of the school films that ends the first chapter and the close analyses of the films in those that follow. Here we account for Wenders' place in the great movement of the New German Cinema of the seventies and eighties and his love of fifties American film, particularly the work of John Ford and Nicholas Ray. We explore some of the images and themes that recur, almost obsessively, in film after film. In so doing, we lay a base for discussing in detail *Kings of the Road, The State of Things, Paris, Texas,* and *Wings of Desire*. The second chapter also gives us an opportunity to look at such films as *The American Friend* and *Wrong Move*. Other films, especially the documentaries *Tokyo-Ga* and *Lightning over Water*, are discussed in later chapters where they help clarify the fictional works. *Until the End of the World*, released late during the writing of the book, is referred to throughout. (One film, Wenders' adaptation of Hawthorne's *The Scarlet Letter*, seems so much outside the concerns of the body of his work and so much the product of other intervention – it was done on assignment for a Spanish–German coproduction – that it gets only brief reference.)

With this structure in place, the reader can get a sense of the movement and interrelationship of Wenders' films, life, and cultural milieu, and then move to the analyses of specific works. And because all of the films (with the exception of the early school exercises) are available on videocassette, there is opportunity for the reader to look at the images as closely as they are examined here, enlarge upon our analyses, and even go beyond them.

Our hope, finally, is that this study will offer insight about the work of one important contemporary filmmaker, present some speculation about the relationships between history, subjectivity, and mass-mediated art, and provide some tools with which to examine the complex fabric of cinema.

Acknowledgments

We acknowledge with gratitude Jolanda Darbyshire, Road Movies (Berlin), Gerhard Ullmann, Filmmuseum München, and other companies and institutions for their help in providing materials for this book and granting permission to publish the illustrations.

The stills from *Der Stand der Dinge* (*The State of Things*), *Der amerikanische Freund* (*The American Friend*), *Paris, Texas,* and *Der Himmel über Berlin* (*Wings of Desire*) are copyrighted by Road Movies Filmproduktion, Berlin.

The stills from *Same Player Shoots Again, Silver City, Alabama: 2000 Light Years, Polizeifilm* (*Film about the Police*), *Summer in the City, Die Angst des Tormanns beim Elfmeter* (*The Goalie's Anxiety at the Penalty Kick*), *Alice in den Städten* (*Alice in the Cities*), *Falsche Bewegung* (*Wrong Move*), *Im Lauf der Zeit* (*Kings of the Road*), *Nick's Film* (*Lightning over Water*), and *Chambre 666* are copyrighted by Wim Wenders Produktion, Berlin.

The still from Nicholas Ray's *Lusty Men* is from the clip in *Nick's Film* (*Lightning over Water*), and the still from F. W. Murnau's *Nosferatu* is by courtesy of Filmmuseum München.

Peter Beicken is indebted to Leo Bartel and Gertrude Bartel, whose financial gift supported, in part, the production of the stills in this book.

The authors thank Mike Mashon, Thierry Jutel, Simon Richter, and Jeff Dickson for their assistance and ideas.

Rainer Werner Fassbinder, Werner Herzog, and Wim Wenders in *Chambre 666*, Cannes, May 1982.

I

The Boy with the Movie Camera

Biography, Historical Background, Student Films

Fathers and Children

"The art of things, as well as persons, becoming identical with themselves" is how Wim Wenders has defined cinema, his chosen art.[1] For Wenders as film-maker the mission of the cinema is to create a self and discover an identity. Asked once to present his raison d'être of filmmaking, Wenders gave a genealogy of his artistic career beginning with his initiation into cinema as a young boy. At age six, his parents gave him an old hand-cranked projector. The desire for the imaginary, for a comfortable, internal world of images, made him seek the pleasures of Chaplin, Keaton, Mack Sennett, and their likes, greats of the movies that his father had favored before him. At Christmastime, the only thing young Wenders asked for was a new Walt Disney or Laurel and Hardy film.[2] When he was about eight, he went to a movie house for the first time, accompanied by his grandmother, to see a Laurel and Hardy film. Instead of the hoped-for pleasure, the visit turned into a nightmare. No Laurel and Hardy, but rather a cheap horror film, *Die Nacht der Reitenden Leichen (The Night of the Riding Corpses)*, which shocked the young boy and traumatized his relationship with the cinema for years.[3]

At age twelve, Wenders was given an 8mm film camera by his father to complement the projector. Seizing the opportunity to renew his relationship with the cinema, young Wenders positioned himself at the window of the family's home, fixing the camera on the street below. Filming the goings-on at an intersection, he was questioned by his father: "What are you doing there with your camera?" The original German words, "Was machst du denn da mit deiner Kamera?" sound inquisitive, and rather than expressing

I

interest or curiosity, they seemed to express a sense of impatience and lack of understanding on the part of the father. They marked a certain parental disapproval, and Wenders answered promptly: "I'm filming the street, can't you see." ("Ich filme die Straße, das siehst du doch.")[4] Wim's answer revealed some annoyance at the paternal impatience, and the response he received in turn – "And what for?" ("Und wozu?") – was met only by silence. Wenders did not have an easy answer, nor could he give any reason for what he was doing. Unable or unwilling to justify his filming, the boy with the movie camera continued to do what seemed to him most natural and beyond questioning: fulfilling a desire to film.

This episode seems insignificant at first sight; but it is revealing that Wenders, thinking about his childhood, needs to locate his aesthetic origins in conflict with the father, whom he recalls both as a nurturing parent (he gives his son the initial filmmaking apparatus) and an inquisitive but disinterested authority who needs appeasing. When he was first asked, "Pourquoi filmez-vous?" by *Libération* in 1987, his initial response was to request a "less stupid question" and not have to respond again to the voice of the past.[5] But then he goes on to make a confession and elaborate rather extensively on this crucial childhood episode. Recalling his childhood experiences, Wenders eschews any theoretical or political response to a very broad and open inquiry. He simply maintains that his present occupation had originated in childhood, as if it were the result of uncontrolled inspiration rather than a chosen act. Filming, then, was a mission beyond explanation and justification, a natural desire, an existential imperative, a gift and challenge from the patriarch.

In this same 1987 interview, Wenders goes a bit further with his memories of cinema making. He talks of his attraction to film as a mixture of instinct and desire, but also associates his childhood fancy with the camera with his later work. This becomes clear when he refers to his actual start as a filmmaker. He recalls somewhat self-consciously that "ten or twelve years later," when he made his first short film (*Schauplätze*, 1966–7) in 16mm, he repeated exactly the exercise he had done as a boy. He trained the camera from the sixth-floor window of a building onto the street below, filming an "intersection without moving the camera until the reel was empty." Wenders recounts: "The idea to stop the running camera before that did not occur to me. From hindsight, I can imagine that [stopping the camera] must have appeared to me to be sacrilegious."[6]

By linking the childhood experience to his professional beginnings, Wenders establishes a continuity of desire and vision that reveals a propensity to mythologize or mystify the origins of his craft. He finds and wants no

The quintessential Wenders view: filming the street, from *Silver City* (1968–9).

explanations for his childhood love of movies and refuses to analyze his art as an adult. "I do not have a mind for theories," he maintains.[7] The little theorizing that he does indulge in grounds his cinematographic inclination in a tradition that legitimizes and ennobles his desire with a metaphysical aura, putting forth basic ideas about filmmaking as a passive act that records the ongoing reality of the world, while refusing to elaborate those theories with analytic insight. A quasi-mystical bent is noticeable when he refers to the Hungarian film critic and theorist Béla Balázs, who, he says, extols the "possibility (and the responsibility) of the cinema 'to show things as they are.'" In fact, what he ascribes to Balázs is essentially the position Siegfried Kracauer, a member of the Frankfurt School, whose writings on film and culture are becoming increasingly more influential. Wenders invokes the cinema's duty to "preserve the existence of things" (*"die Existenz der Dinge retten"*), a statement that recalls the subtitle of Kracauer's *Theory of Film: The Redemption of Physical Reality*. Wenders was familiar with this book at the time he began to film in earnest during his student years.[8] Kracauer, along with the French critic André Bazin, held that cinema's task was to reveal the "thereness," the ongoingness of the world, to act as an instrument that clarified perception, placing the filmmaker and film viewer in direct touch with reality, with space and duration, in ways no other art could manage.

Concern for the redemptive mission of cinema – which Wenders found confirmed in Kracauer – had obviously been present when, as a boy, he intuitively attempted to preserve the constant flux of appearances and phenomena outside his window. He confirms this desire to redeem the transient state of things later, when he refers to a statement by the painter Paul Cézanne, who lamented the "disappearance of things. One needs to be alert if one wants to see anything."[9] Desiring the camera to engage in a great rescue mission, arresting, recording, and memorializing what otherwise continually vanishes in the visible realm, Wenders understands that filming is a "heroic act" directed at the preservation of a phenomenon and its underlying reality. The camera records what can be viewed later, time and again. In fact, it is a "weapon," he says (recalling a phrase from left-wing manifestos of the twenties) "against the misery of things, namely against their disappearance."[10] The boy with the camera intuitively pursued this desire to perceive, contemplate, and record a world that is in a state of constant permutation. Following a basic need to understand the act of perception and to orient himself in the visible, the child indulged in an activity both natural and necessary. Absent from this sensory pleasure principle were the processes and conditions of adult perception and reasoning: intentionality, explanation, and interpretation. Only rarely, out of intellectual need or the pressure of an interviewer, does Wenders attempt to articulate and legitimize his aesthetic premises. But when he does, his explanations take something of a romantic turn, employing the myth of the artist as redeemer of the transient world, despite his oblique reference to an old twenties left-wing slogan about art as weapon in the class struggle.

The filmmaker as redeemer: this was, in 1987, a form of self-legitimation by a star of international cinema. At work on his film about angels, *Wings of Desire*, Wenders attempted to find a hallowed niche for his filmic mission by transforming the politics of personal desire into the metaphysics of art. From his earliest work on, Wenders has presented himself as the unquestionable *vates*, as the seer beyond reason and reproach. At once self-effacing and self-promoting, this attitude has a tendency to imbue his ideas about cinema – and occasionally his films themselves – with stylish prophesies, with an aura of precarious purity and vulnerable ethics. His aesthetic is an intriguing mix of melancholy and imagination, of intuitive vision and self-conscious mission. Ultimately, he appears to be on an endless, quasi-mystical search for the appeasing and accepting father – his real father, who nurtured his desire to film while putting his son's filmmaking practice into question (his father, whom he declared a fascist even while affirming his love for him) – and a search, finally, for the accepting and guiding fathers of world cinema.[11] The wish to please the father imago, this obsessive hold on an uncompleted, perhaps uncompletable oedipal process, seems to foster in Wenders' work a reluctance or inhibition to get involved with reality, no matter how much he claims reality and truth to be his goal. In a way, Wenders is still the boy with the camera fixed on the street scene, where, only far away, at a safe distance, life goes on, social and sexual intercourse take place, and the seer remains a child voyeur in a state of oedipal suspension, hoping for redemption through the passive act of looking.

The films of Wim Wenders reveal a special link between the biographical and the cinematic. Time and again, he manifests a desire for authorship beyond the established notions of auteurism. His work goes beyond the subjectivity, the stylistic and thematic coherence, that one usually looks for in the work of a strong auteur. These are all present, but so is something else. His subjectivity tends to reveal itself in a continual quest for cinematic identity. This search is implanted in his works in a variety of ways. The quest for cinematic patrimony is one. "Personal appearance" – his stepping into the frame at strategic moments in the narrative – is another. There is also his insistence on intuitiveness and the self-evident, that what appears or happens in his films is right because he understood it as right at the moment of creation. One indication of this is given in Wenders' statement to Jan Dawson about one of his earliest films, the short *Alabama:*

> When I was asked by some critics at a festival press conference what the film was all about, I said, "It's about the song 'All Along the Watchtower,' and the film is about what happens and what changes depending on whether the song is sung by Bob Dylan or by Jimi Hendrix." Well, both versions of the song appear in the film, and everybody thought I was pretty arrogant to explain the story this way. But the film really is about the difference between the Dylan version of "All Along the Watchtower," and the Jimi Hendrix version. One is at the beginning and one is at the end.[12]

Asked to explain what the press wanted to understand as the "story" of the film, Wenders retreated to his "unquestionable" personal position, knowing very well that *Alabama* was not an ordinary narrative: "It's a story and it's not a story."[13] His remarks provoked indignation, they introduced a common theme of many of his films – the struggle to tell stories and understand what telling a story entails – and they confirmed Wenders' insistence that his films were personal beyond the realm of analytic discourse. This insistence is not uncommon; many artists claim that they cannot provide intellectual analysis of their own work. However, Wenders apparently wanted to make it even more difficult for the critics to approach his early work (such as *Alabama*), by insisting upon an artistic self-expression that denies translation into ordinary understanding. As his work matured and received greater recognition, he relaxed and became more interested in reaching a larger, responsive audience. This required a somewhat less confrontational stance; yet Wenders maintained his pose of romantic seer (perhaps in a less preposterous way than his colleague, Werner Herzog) and still attempts to authenticate his work with an authorship that seeks a uniquely personal expression, while remaining highly communicative and intuitive.

Cinematic identity and personal identity are inseparable for Wenders. (Frederic Jameson states that "personal identity is itself the effect of a certain temporal unification of past and future with one's present; and, second, that such active temporal unification is itself a function of language," in this instance the language of cinema.)[14] Much of what Wenders has revealed about his childhood, his years of growing up, and his search for a personally satisfying vocation indicates the extent to which his development as a filmmaker is entwined with his search for self. In order to understand this more completely, we must backtrack and look at the major developments of this biography in order to understand what led to Wenders' desire to pursue filmmaking as a personal quest. At first, little in his upbringing pointed to this career, although we recall that his father, Heinrich, a physician and movie lover, initiated his son into the use of both the movie projector and film camera. Heinrich Wenders was a fairly successful and well-to-do physician, and his career led him to assume the directorship of the St. Joseph Clinic in Oberhausen, the industrial town in the Ruhr district known for its festival of short films and – later, in 1962 – the Oberhausen Manifesto, the signal document that ushered in the Junger Deutscher Film (Young German Film) movement and, subsequently, the New German Cinema.

On August 14, 1945, Wenders was born in Düsseldorf (an old, culturally sophisticated town, the birthplace of the poet Heinrich Heine), but his parents soon moved to nearby Benrath. Then, in 1949, they moved again, to the small provincial town of Koblenz. Wenders is aware of the places of his childhood and observes that he spent most of his life away from real urban life, living on the outskirts of the dark cities. He explores these places in *Alice in the Cities* (1974) and remarks that the distance from urban culture had a profound impact on him as a young boy, when at the age of ten or twelve (approximately at the time he got involved in his 8mm filmmaking and home movie projection) he sought out the "only cultural institutions" the outskirts

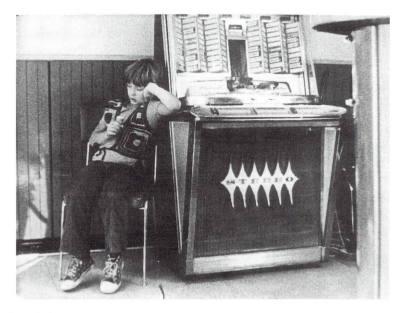

The jukebox: Wenders' homage to rock and roll, from *Alice in the Cities* (1974).

had to offer: ice cafés and jukeboxes.[15] His pleasures were not unlike those of an American teenager, listening – against parental wishes – to Chuck Berry, Elvis Presley, Little Richard, Roy Orbison, and Gene Vincent on broadcasts of the American Forces Network. At the age of fifteen, he became interested in the detective novels of Raymond Chandler (which climaxed two decades later when he made his own American detective film, *Hammett*). Growing up in a society that maintained itself in a state of cultural and historical amnesia, obsessively ignoring its terrifying past, Wenders went about creating a culture for himself out of the bits and pieces of Americana that came his way. Later, he recognized that this re-creation of America in the suburbs of German cities altered his sense of being forever, for these elements make up the very fabric of sounds, images, and themes that will come to constitute his own coherent semiotics, the resonant images that recur throughout his films.

While Wenders pursued his filmmaking hobby and even attended the Oberhausen short film festival a few years after its inception, he did not immediately consider the pleasures of his pastime as the beginning of a professional career. His family were practicing Catholics and attended church services regularly, forcing Wim to attend mass often. However, he would skip services in favor of playing pinball machines in the Casino next to the church whenever possible. Despite his reluctance to attend Mass, one of his early vocational considerations focused on the priesthood. His interest waned, however, and had vanished by the time he was sixteen. Later, he described in blunt terms what he found so disaffecting about church religion: "Catholicism is much more a way of thinking than a question of believing in something. And as a way of thinking, it has a lot to do with capitalism and oppression."[16] His recollection and critique of Catholicism is redolent of the late sixties, when Wenders came of intellectual age within the student movement and its radical politics. He rarely shows interest in such openly political discourse, but his opposition to the church clearly indicates that his contemplation of cinema as a redemptive act was arrived at by means other than institutional religion.

Wenders worked through other interests before settling upon his true calling. Influenced by his family, who for centuries had produced doctors and pharmacists, he now followed the family tradition and decided to study medicine at the universities of Munich and Freiburg after completing his secondary school education in Oberhausen in 1963. He did this for two years, while also pursuing an interest in philosophy. However, finding the university too authoritarian, he became disaffected. He found working in a hospital, where he took a job as an orderly for a year, a depressing ordeal. His experiences did not coincide with his ideas of "what medicine was all about."[17] The prospect of many more years in an oppressive environment took him away from the hospital and to Düsseldorf for a fourth and final semester. His adolescent years seem to have been a process of first moving toward and then reacting against his family's tradition; they also seem to be a period in which the choice between vocational fantasies and the discovery of their unpleasant realities led to his fleeing from both.

Once he gave up medicine, Wenders pursued an interest that was closer to his heart. Enjoying landscapes and having tried his hand at painting, he decided to go to Paris and enroll at the Ecole des Beaux-Arts. Ever the naïf, he discovered that life drawing was a prerequisite for study and that he didn't like it. Without any previous experience in this "ridiculous" exercise that made no sense to him, Wenders followed the advice of an acquaintance and studied with Johnny Friedländer, a printmaker who appeared more congenial because of his orientation to abstract art and liberal attitude toward instruction. For six enjoyable months Wenders spent the mornings in the studio. This left him free afternoons to visit the Paris Cinémathèque, where he – like the filmmakers of the French New Wave before him – indulged himself in viewing as many films as possible, as many as four a day.[18] It was here that he absorbed the vast repertoire of world cinema. A decade later, in gratitude for this wealth of cinema that quite literally transformed his personality, Wenders dedicated his film *The American Friend* (1977) to Henri Langlois, founder and director of the Cinémathèque.

At the Cinémathèque, Wenders finally overcame the childhood trauma that had marred his first encounter with the movies when the horror film was shown instead of Laurel and Hardy. Now he came back to the cinema and rediscovered not only his old pleasure, but its transforming and redeeming power. He was infatuated, carried away. The aspiration to find self-expression in painting gave way to the desire to study at the Parisian film school IDHEC (L'Institute des hautes études cinématographiques). However, as no place was available to him, he applied to the newly founded Munich Hochschule für Fernsehen und Film, which had been inaugurated with funds from the Film Subsidies Bill of 1967. Whereas Rainer Werner Fassbinder, later one of the leading figures of New German Cinema, did not pass the entry examination, Wenders became a member of the institution's first class and, subsequently, its most famous graduate. From the start, because of the newness of the organization and an unstructured curriculum, Wenders, with his dislike for restrictive educational systems, enjoyed plenty of leeway to do things the way he saw fit and at his own speed. Being ambitious and prolific, he engaged in making more films than were required for the diploma, using his own financial means in the process.

A love of cinema had merged with the obsessions with American popular culture, especially rock and roll. Two of the most powerful cultural forces of the sixties revealed to the young German a means of expression and a release of the imagination. He listened to music incessantly and viewed as many films as possible at Langlois' Cinémathèque. He idolized American rock and American film. He wrote about both and, when he began filming, included the music in the films.

The Desiring Gaze

The concept of seeing is central to the understanding of Wenders' dynamics as an apprentice filmmaker. His childhood openness to sensory stimuli was driven by a desire to take in the world visually. He exuberantly exercised this sense of perception in his contemplation of landscapes and cityscapes. And because he was intuitively attracted to the visual, Wenders found in film a medium whose very structure was perceptual and that allowed him to capture and preserve the fleeting and momentary appearance of things. He

The desiring gaze: Wilhelm confesses a "kind of erotic insight" to Thérèse, from *Wrong Move* (1975).

responded powerfully to the psychology of cinematic poetics, which seemed to fulfill his desire to impress his subjectivity upon the fluctuating world of physical reality. The desiring gaze quietly views and contemplates things as they appear and disappear; it constitutes in the eye of the beholder a world fleetingly present to the amazed senses; it moves outward to inscribe its amazement upon that world. The persistence with which Wenders pleads for a truly contemplative perception is remarkable in its intensity. When Wenders, as the boy with the movie camera, directed the motionless camera at the street, he trained his desiring gaze on the appealing motion and traffic that carried him away and focused his adolescent anxieties. The gaze did not merely give him sight and insight, it grounded his emotions and made them authentic.

The eros of seeing is alluded to in *Wrong Move* (1975). Wilhelm, the central character, moves up the winding serpentine road on the mountain over the Rhine and discusses with Thérèse his vision of the world and his concept of writing. Challenged by her to become more observant of his surroundings, he acknowledges that he does not always take notice of things. However, he believes that in counterdistinction to the normal powers of observation, he is specially gifted with an "erotic insight" ("eine Art erotischer Blick"), which makes him "notice something and get a feeling for it" ("Ich seh dann aber nicht nur, sondern krieg gleichzeitig auch ein Gefühl dafür"). As the sequence continues with Wilhelm proclaiming that the writer's subjectivity (his desire) must embrace the world, Wenders tracks along with his characters as they proceed up the mountain, looking at them, embracing them, capturing their subjectivity with his own desire to see it and extend himself into it. Here, as in all his works, he *desires* to see his characters and visualize emotion. Desire gives perception feeling, saturating seeing with emotion. Rather than apprehending the characters, the camera's desiring gaze proceeds to "touch" them. Standing still or moving in gentle, slow rhythms, Wenders' camera caresses the things it perceives with its gaze. Objects are given prominence in their space. Like many of the filmmakers he admires – Yasujiro Ozu, Michelangelo Antonioni, and Andrei Tarkovsky – Wenders creates an articulate space, which embellishes and defines his characters' states of being. When the viewer's eye perceives the characters, they have taken up location and turned it into consciousness. Wenders' camera is an instrument of affection. The feeling eye discovers and expresses the relationships between things and human figures, space and self, establishing the bond of emotion through the act of seeing. The filmmaker's desire is to redeem figure and object, to preserve them from the onrush of time and death, to render them ready for union and permanence. Filming is intimacy, without the threat of the physical. By overcoming the physical, the filmmaker redeems himself.

The eros of seeing is complemented by the ear as an equally important organ of perception. For Wenders, from an early age on, music – rock and roll in particular – was a source of energy and pleasure. Not only does he credit rock and roll with saving his life when he was twelve or fourteen years old, he later realized how much the music inspired his search for self: "It was the first thing I appreciated, like everybody else, that wasn't inherited. There was nobody to teach me to like it. On the contrary, there were plenty of people teaching me to dislike it, to tell me how useless and tasteless it was. . . . But in a way, rock'n'roll led me to everything: it led me to filmmaking. Without rock'n'roll, maybe I would be a lawyer now. And a lot of people would be somebody else."[19] Wenders attributes a power to rock and roll that gives its musical impact a radical, social, and existential significance. It was the most important element in the "Americanization" of Wim Wenders, soon to be followed by American cinema.

By focusing on its cultural relevance for German society of the late fifties, Wenders rightly observes the transforming force that rock and other elements of American popular culture assumed at a time when life in the Federal Republic had come under the dominating influence of American politics, economics, and culture. The postwar democratization of West Germany was accompanied by the materialism of the economic miracle (*Wirtschaftswunder*) and the self-induced, culturally supported amnesia concerning the recent fascist past. This period of resurgent economy and cold war politics fostered conservative attitudes with an attendant desire to maintain the status quo. Americanization played a double role in the process. It was part of the conservative practice of the time, because it substituted the energies of an external culture for the necessary introspections and progress of the native one. But it was liberating as well, freeing intellectuals and ordinary people alike, who embraced it from the burdening legacies of the German past. Wenders became aware of this double edge and the price that had to be paid. "The Yanks have even colonized our subconsciousness," says a character near the end of *Kings of the Road* (1976), in perhaps the best-known phrase from a Wenders film. The character and his creator acknowledge the threat of cultural domination while yielding to the imperial seduction; the comment is made with neither rancor or anger. Wenders allowed the colonization to go on quite consciously and in the late seventies succumbed to the greatest seduction of a European filmmaker in love with American movies and culture: he went to America to make a film under the Hollywood system.

As a teenager, Wenders embraced American rock and roll with abandon. He used it to define his being in the world and inspire an awareness that he found pervasive beyond his own existence: "I think that rock'n'roll gave a lot of people a sense of identity for the first time. In a way, because it has more to do with joy than with anything else. So it was with rock'n'roll that I started to think of fantasy, or creativity, as having something to do with joy: the idea of having a *right* to enjoy something."[20] By the midsixties, American rock groups and their British counterparts, who added a particular working-class attitude and radical self-confidence to rock music, created an invigorating and irresistible force used by their German fans to fill the gaps left in their culture by the legacies of fascism. For Wenders, much of the cultural inheritance appeared to be contaminated. Even classical music seemed to have been compromised by the fact that the Nazis used the German musical tradition for ideological aggrandizement. Wenders confessed that he saw rock and roll to be "the only alternative to Beethoven (and I'm really exaggerating here) – because I was very insecure then about all culture that was offered to me, because I thought it was all fascism, pure fascism; and the only thing I was secure with from the beginning and felt had nothing to do with fascism was rock music."[21] The reaction to classical music and its cultural status reveals a sense of guilt and shame by association that Wenders shared with much of his generation.

Learning about the horrors of the holocaust and the crimes committed during the Nazi period caused many of Wenders' peers to question all value systems, political, social, and cultural. The so-named skeptical generation could not immediately accept the German cultural tradition that had been coopted by fascism.[22] By rejecting Beethoven, Wenders joined many others who aired their cultural and political opposition during the 1968 student movement. The void created by the contradictions and hypocrisies of German culture was filled with the ready-made products of American pop culture. Rock music in particular not only was a mark of rebellion against the generation of their fathers, but offered the sons a sense of spontaneity and creativity in their search for identity and expression of self.

Freeing repressed emotions and finding adequate feelings to express the self were among the attractions of rock music for Wenders. What he experienced as the joy of a life-giving force stirred his imagination, and it was part of his new and inalienable birthright as a sensitive, postwar intellectual.* It was also part of a fascination with form, and this provided another bridge between rock and film: "When I started making films, it was very similar. It was so much the same thing that when I'd shoot – which meant that I had some film stock – the only thing to do was to take a song and put it together. That was the way I started making films. Shooting something, without cutting it – just having a three-minute shot – and then looking for a song to go with it."[23] Music authenticates the visual experience; the eros of seeing and the eros of hearing merge and create an infatuated union of perception and being.

Originally, Wenders listened to rock music without being able or willing to understand the text: "For me, rock'n'roll always used to be pure form."[24] The music, its rhythm, dynamics, and sound, became the message, or what Wenders calls the "means of communication, but on a nonsense level."[25] This is critical, for Wenders seems to have taken to rock music because it was apparently uncorrupted by the cultural discourse damaged by the legacy of fascism. A language before language, a communication before words, and an intimacy before actual contact, unmediated, and all-encompassing – Wenders found his roots in the music that was quite different from everything that surrounded him at his conservative middle-class home. If we are to

---

* A historical precedent for this existential "craze" for music can be found in early German Romanticism. In his *Outpourings from the Heart of an Art-Loving Monk* (*Herzensergießungen eines kunstliebenden Klosterbruders*, 1797), the early Romanticist Wilhelm Heinrich Wackenroder (1773–98) espoused the concept of music as an existential, spiritual force capable of moving those in tune with its universal and religious appeal. Wenders, in his own way, attributes to rock and roll a similar inspirational and transcendental status.

13

believe him, he desired rock and roll as his true vocation, but the desire apparently frightened him so much that he turned to cinema: "Filmmaking, in the beginning, was a substitute, a compensation for not being able to play saxophone and drums and guitar all at once. And I'm sure if I'd had the guts, I'd be a rock musician."[26]

But filmmaking for the auteur is more than just a substitute for playing in a rock band. It must be a consummate activity and experience, a complex act of mediation and discovery. Where rock music fills the adolescent with rhythm and energy, filmmaking enhances the awareness of the self and how it is seen and placed in the world. Seeing is both intuitive and self-conscious. "Cinema is in a way the art of things, as well as persons, becoming identical with themselves."[27] Wenders claims that the cinema issues an identity-creating power insofar as it initiates a differentiation of self from other: "Foreign-ness for me is just a throughway to a notion of identity. In other words, identity is not something you just have, you have to go through things in order to become secure in a different way. That's what I meant about foreign-ness; it's a way of losing the old notion of self-evidence."[28] Rock music filled and ordered the soul. Filmmaking offered a way to impress the soul outward, clarify and redeem it.

Consequently, filmmaking for Wenders induced the merger of the lifesaving power of music and the identity-giving force of filming. The cinema becomes a locus for the realization of self and the reordering of the external world by the subject. By uniting the emotional with the visual, film images serve to rescue the vanishing images of a world threatened by oblivion and to inform those images with desire. For Wenders, cinema as motion and emotion initiates and consummates the creative process and turns it into an act of salvation, freeing the self from the tortuous legacies that had compromised intellectual, artistic, and everyday life in postwar Germany. Searching for uncontaminated forms of self-expression, Wenders reaches beyond the traditional discourses of a traumatized and repressed society – as did most of his intellectual contemporaries. Though unlike some of his peers – Kluge and Straub, for example – Wenders' search was intuitive rather than theoretical. For him, the desiring gaze of filmmaking constructs a visionary union in which the intuition of the filmmaker entices the viewer into a desire for perception.

Wenders' emphasis on intuition becomes clearer still when we examine the ways in which he responded to both his early training and the political atmosphere of Germany in the late sixties. His admission to the Hochschule für Fernsehen und Film was a significant step in his career, although he was not, at that point, committed to a specific vocational goal. But his concentrated exposure to American films increased his attraction to American culture and, perhaps, diverted his attention from the political activism of the late sixties. Things American appealed to him, and his need for individual transformation and redemption made him the odd person out in a politically active commune of students. The intense theoretical bent and uncompromising commitment by his fellow students to a radical change of society was not to his liking; American cinema, with its intriguingly wholesome conventions and expressive-realist form, was: "I was in film school, and I went to see westerns every night, and they [his student colleagues] were talking about imperialism and fighting this and fighting that. . . . I had a hard time with them."[29] Wenders' desire for cinema seemed frivolous to his colleagues; he sensed pitfalls in the doctrinal aspect of their political theories. Most important, he felt uncomfortable with what appeared to him to be the manipulative and alienating impact of abstractions and systematic approaches.

Already in Paris, Wenders had started to take notes in order to keep track of the many films he absorbed day after day. These notes also expressed his immediate intuitions about the films he viewed — records of emotional responses and unpremeditated ideas. His revolt against theory lasted throughout the years of his professional training. He says that he did not learn much from film school, but found his creative sustenance in watching movies, listening to rock and roll, and writing spontaneously about film. Having "no critical method and no other criterion than 'the truth,' " Wenders turned his obsessional film viewing into a double-edged response:

> I was watching movies, but as much as I was looking at the screen, I was also aware of myself as the observer. Writing was as much self-observation as film observation: I was not reflecting *upon* movies, I was reflecting them, period. I felt films were extraordinary, necessary; they were about life, they gave me life and life had given them to me, I gave them life, too, I passed them on. Writing "about a film" was passing on the experience with it.[30]

These comments were written in 1989, and Wenders had already demonstrated what he meant in 1974, when he appears in a cinema watching his own 1973 film, *The Scarlet Letter,* as part of a sequence in his television film *Die Insel* (1974). There is a certain pathos, and perhaps a suggestion of the disingenuous, in his infatuation and willingness to yield himself so thoroughly to the object of his desire.

However, despite his professed and willful ignorance of film theory, and the bliss with which he accepts the film-viewing experience, Wenders is able to express his dissatisfaction with certain films. His remarks indicate an awareness of theoretical tenets as well as a personal predilection for Hollywood conventions. For example, he refers to Sergio Leone's *Once Upon a Time in the West* (1969) as a "terrifying Western." He condemns the exaggerated self-consciousness of form in this film, which he construes as an attack upon the classical codes of an essentially American genre. Leone's operatic celebration of the Fordian narrative and overt politicization of the Western mythos disturbed Wenders' sense of generic purity:

> Kracauer spoke of film as the "redemption of physical reality," meaning the tenderness that cinema can show toward reality ["tenderness" is not a term that Kracauer would ordinarily use; "faithfulness" is perhaps more appropriate, though this would be more typical of Bazin]. Westerns have often brought out this tenderness in a dreamily beautiful and quiet way. They respected themselves: their characters, their plots, their landscapes, their rules, their freedoms, their desires. In their images they spread out a surface that was nothing else but what you could see.[31]

To Wenders' eyes, Leone substitutes a ferocity of vision for the tender erotic gaze, attacking the authenticity of the genre and refusing the conventions of a "gentle cinema." The Western may indeed be a violent genre — as is the fifties gangster melodrama to which Wenders is also attracted — but the persistence and clarity of form he discovers in American genres signal a kind of purity, an honesty even, that he finds a key virtue superseding all else.* Generic conventions are *stable,* seemingly without political taint, and like rock and roll music, they form an emotional ground. These values figure as a point of certainty. They deliver Wenders from the constraints imposed by his family, his culture, and its history.

Wenders' posture toward the cinema is informed by a strong ethical stance. (Ethos is added to eros, producing a strong ground for sincere self-authentication.) When he laments the decline of cinematic purity by lambasting Leone's perceived corruption of the Western genre, he expresses a sense of horror clearly set forth in the title of the essay that contains his criticism: "From Dream to Nightmare."[32] For Wenders the endearing and ethical quality of American films used to lie in their "*stance,*" a way "of quietly and unobtrusively spreading out the surface of their world for ninety minutes and nothing else."[33] They provide certainty and offer security to the viewer.

---

* The gangster genre, as we will see, was particularly attractive to Wenders in his early school films. With its inherent rebelliousness and subversive moral ambiguities, its ability to telegraph sharply defined codes in rapid narrative strokes, the gangster film has always been attractive to Europeans.

This perception of a simple and unmediated American cinema is as naive as the quality Wenders seems to approve of. He *wants* American film to be innocent, intuitive, with a dreamlike simplicity, no matter how much he must supply those qualities through his perception and no matter how much he may deny those qualities in his later work. At the same time, however, he approves a simple, "natural" plenitude, a rich and unvarying cinematic world that promises no surprises. He approves of it in American film and in the work of his own colleagues when they attain this "stance." He describes Rudolf Thome's film *Rote Sonne* (*Red Sun*, 1969) as "one of these rare European films that don't simply try to imitate American cinema . . . but have rather taken their *stance* from American film." Thome makes "naturalness . . . visible in every frame," and Wenders praises "the constant flatness of the shots . . . the monotony of the camerawork . . . the banality of the camera movements," and "the remarkable colourlessness of the colours, which is exactly that of Mickey Mouse books." It is the lack of pretense and the singularity of vision that gives this film the quiet and unobtrusive "stance" of American cinema.[34] This is a remarkable statement, for cinematic banality is not a quality one would expect a young film student to admire. Perhaps Wenders is reacting to the self-conscious complexity of European cinema at the time. Perhaps secure, apparently simple images and the uncomplicated emotions offered by American cinema were what Wenders needed at the moment he was gathering up his own imaginative forces. Perhaps he was responding to the simple artifice of American film, which is "natural" insofar as it perpetuates a number of sophisticated conventions that establish an unpretentious sense of visual and narrative presence that is dependable in film after film. Perhaps, too, he needed to maintain the myth of America as a stable nourishing culture.

America continues to be mythologized by Wenders until it has become a grandiose cinema, a cinema of totality. In his 1984 poem "The American Dream," he encapsulated his "imagined America":

> a country of excess,
> of great illuminated signs
> to give you wings and enlighten you.
> I saw America as the country where vision was set free.[35]

America and its cinema – America *as* cinema – is liberating and all-encompassing at the same time. It liberates the senses, authorizes the identity of the artist, and to one willing passively to observe and record, offers up the truthfulness of its vision. To the accepting, loving gaze, America reveals its naturalness. Physical reality and human events are shown with "utmost precision and as thoroughly as possible."[36] An equality of perception and a subtle, but palpable link between the human figure and the landscape is suggested. Visible phenomena are not merely transparent signs to be deciphered within a given hierarchy of codes and symbolic meanings; they are there, ongoing, redeeming. America's Westerns, for example, depict a world that unfolds predictably in film after film; violent action in defense of the domestic community occurs as part of a larger movement toward democratic harmony – as John Ford indicates repeatedly. And not only Ford. Wenders discovers this calm and harmony across the genre. Discussing Raoul Walsh's *The Tall Men* (1955), Wenders notes an aesthetics of equality and tranquility:

> Slowness in this Western by Walsh means no action is worth so little that you could speed it up, shorten it or even leave it out to make way for another, more exciting or more important one. And because all the images are of equal value there is no suspense to suggest peaks and pauses, but only a constant feeling of tension, to present all the physical and psychological events as clearly and as comprehensively as possible, and in the right order, too, so they can be "experienced."[37]

"Experience" for Wenders is always related to the totality of an event, situation, or being, to a tension-filled calm that permits all elements to be revealed and given weight. The psychological corresponds to the physical, and film sets emotion into motion and vice versa. Rather than merely visualizing an inner state, film frees the emotional on screen and in the viewer who partakes in the act of seeing. The "tenderness" of the camera, the loving stance of the cinema that foregrounds all details of the mise-en-scène, offers the viewer the opportunity to be as engaged as the filmmaker.

This union of filmmaker, landscape, figure, and viewer, by its very nature a slow and peaceful interaction, is the antithesis to the "hectic" cinema that rushes the eyes of the viewer with violent action and invades the senses with aggressive imagery. At various junctures in his writings, Wenders extolls the loving camera, the longing desire for the infinite ("*Unendlichkeitsverlangen*"), and privileges the qualities of the "contemplative cinema," which allow for the ultimate cinematic experience, the realization of a moment of truth.[38] That he should discern this contemplative stance in the often violent, rarely subtle structures of American film is either an act of naive misprision or strong appropriation. He needed a certain kind of cinema. He loved American movies. He therefore allowed himself to see what he needed in what he loved. He escaped into the fantasies of his desire.

A typical early Wenders image: the street scene below, from *Summer in the City* (1971).

The School Films

Wenders' love of the American Western was not at the expense of other kinds of films that are quite different in their tradition and purpose. His very first published essay, "no 'exprmnts': Filming in one shot only – thoughts on 'Exprmntl 4,'" is quick to identify two examples that embody the "contemplative style" in two unconventional, "avant-garde" films, Lutz Mommartz' *Railway* (*Eisenbahn*) and Michael Snow's *Wavelength*.[39] The latter film has become something of a hallmark of the contemporary avant-garde, a "minimalist" film made up of a "forty-five-minute zoom from the depths of a room to a photograph on the opposite wall, whose windows look out on a lively street." Through the duration of the zoom only "four brief actions in the room interrupt the otherwise continuously advancing tracking-shot."[40]

Snow's approach, which reduces narrative content to the inexorable logic of cinematic form, appealed directly to Wenders' aesthetic sensibilities at the time. Recall that in his very first attempt at filmmaking, Wenders settled into the stance of patient observer, intuitively using a fixed position to record the field of vision without any apparent stylistic intrusion or manipulation. When Wenders began his first film school exercise in 1966, *Schauplätze,* he continued where he had left off as a boy. Only two shots from *Schauplätze* are still extant and were incorporated into his second short of the Munich period, *Same Player Shoots Again* (1967). These fragments reveal the method that Wenders employed at the time: his preference for a single focus, his deemphasizing of the story, his undercutting of representational aesthetics, his strategy of allusion, and his desire to allow the image to suggest emotion without the direct imposition of narrative. These traits are not common to commercial American film; they are qualities Wenders perceived nascent in that cinema, however, and they are foregrounded in his early work.

The German word *Schauplätze* means "locations," referring to the generic place where events occur and can be observed. The more technical term for cinematic location — the pro-filmic space where events take place for the camera — is *Drehort*. From the start, then, Wenders looks at all the world as a *theatrum mundi*, as a location for the camera's gaze. There is no notion of a special place marked off for cinema, but rather the desire to make cinema out of the world as it is, to reveal cinema in the world, as both Kracauer and André Bazin had suggested. Conceptually, the "banality" and consistency, the "naturalness . . . visible in every frame," that Wenders admires in commercial American cinema and in the avant-garde informs his earliest attempts at image making.

Same Player Shoots Again begins with a shot from *Schauplätze* in which a television screen to the side of a room shows a pair of hands mixing cards at a table. While the player on the television screen gets ready to deal the hand, the camera moves to the front and side of the television set where an array of empty bottles on an otherwise empty table suggests, in the manner of an "after-action," an earlier drinking scene. In the next shot, the camera is fixed on an empty telephone booth; the telephone receiver hangs dangling above the ground, the door to the booth closing by itself, suggesting someone has just left. The music on the sound track appears to have been lifted from some Hollywood film noir (it was in fact lifted from an old LP) and indeed the two shots are heavily, if obliquely coded with conventional gangster film lore: the montage of card play (on the television set), drinking scene, and interrupted telephone call hint at a narrative of male camaraderie and violence.[41] The rest of the film abjures further narrative development. In one two-minute shot, repeated five times, a man, wearing a long coat and holding a machine gun, is photographed in midtorso (his face never revealed), wounded, stumbling, running. In the final shot, a man with blood running from the corner of his mouth is seen seated in the back of a car that is driven away, while the camera moves from his face parallel to the rear side window observing the passing landscape.

Deemphasizing coherent narrative and the figure, from *Same Player Shoots Again* (1967).

Schauplätze, as incorporated into *Same Player Shoots Again,* begins by suggesting a standard narrative (even as it displaces its own suggestion by showing a major element of action on a television screen). But it quickly denies narrative, and in its somewhat standard avant-garde repetition of an unexplained image, deemphasizes the importance of the story, leaving a void behind the image.[42] What is important here is Wenders' desire to downplay action and narrative direction in order to make room for images that present the visual field as a staging place for the imagination of the viewer, a modernist technique with which Wenders was much taken at this early part of his filmmaking career (and which indicates that his responses to American film were, in fact, a bit disingenuous). On the basis of his familiarity with the given fragments of action, the viewer is requested to piece together a story line that links typical, rather than unique, elements. The viewer is, in short, put to work, made an active part of the reception process.*

---

* Many elements are at play here. The request for the viewer or reader to complete the text is fundamental to modernist aesthetics and an important part of Brechtian theory. Roland Barthes discusses it in his concept of the "readerly" versus the "writerly" text. Wenders was probably aware that the concept of the viewer and reader who constitute and complete a given text made up an important part of the influential late sixties "reception theory" (*Rezeptionsästhetik*) movement of the Konstanz School led by Hans Robert Jauss and Wolfgang Iser.

That Wenders, in fact, intended to rely on viewer familiarity with given cultural and generic codes is evident from his use of the pinball game: the five shots in the film correspond to five balls, and the title is derived from the message "Shoot Again" that lights up during play.[43] While the gangster film clues do not add up to a full gangster story, they evoke a milieu, recall generic expectations, sometimes in a most circuitous way – a Coca-Cola logo is inserted above the word "TILT" before the final sequence – in the manner of Jean-Luc Godard. The most influential filmmaker of the sixties, Godard evoked America via the signs of its popular culture. For a moment, Wenders evokes American culture via Jean-Luc Godard. But it is for a moment only. While he will often allude to Godard (as he will to many, many other filmmakers), his sympathies are finally not with him. Everything Godard does is critique as well as homage, an investigation of the image as well as an embrace. Wenders, however, is more taken with America than he is critical of it. Culturally and aesthetically, he is more comfortable with a passive stance, a tender and receptive openness, a willingness to perceive and accept rather than confront and criticize. The Godardian artifice of interrupting narrative with images of semiotically rich graphics was not to be a favored device.

Same Player Shoots Again is followed by another exercise in contemplative passivity, *Silver City* (1968–9). A twenty-five minute exploration of the urban landscape, it consists of a series of three-minute-long shots, composed mostly from high angles from the third, fourth, and fifth floors of the apartments in Munich where Wenders lived at that time:

> They all showed streets or crossings, first very early in the morning, at three or half past three when they were completely empty, and the lights were turning from green to red to green again. . . . The film was extremely contemplative. It was really like standing at a window and looking down on the streets, either completely empty or, on the contrary, completely "stocked." Only in the very first shot was there anything like a hint of a story. The very first shot was of a railway line – just an empty landscape, very early in the morning, too, and after two minutes of a completely empty shot, someone crosses the rails from one side of the frame, and leaves the frame on the other. Immediately after he has crossed the rails, the train appears: that is to say – the camera is very close to the rails and – bang – the train is in the shot, and it passes, and slowly disappears in the distance. You get the impression that maybe it's the start of some kind of story, but nothing

happens until the end. Just the empty streets, and the views out of the windows. I'm not sure why I called it *Silver City*. I still think it expresses the mood of the film very well — just the sound of the two words. Maybe it's the alliteration that makes it. I don't know.[44]

This description and interpretation reveal another substantial insight into the filmmaker's frame of mind: His film aesthetic, like his attitude toward life, is understated, if not inhibited and timid. Wenders takes refuge in the distancing and "safe" posture of visual contemplation in which the linkage between self and life relies on a vaguely poetic exercise of creating a subjective mood. But, so far, his image-making powers are simply not up to the task of effectively generating that mood. *Silver City*, like the other school films, demonstrates the abstractness of the young, experimental filmmaker, whose object, the street, the concrete passage of urban life, can only be gazed upon from a safe distance.

The street as a conduit for life — a prime image for Kracauer in his *Theory of Film* and an important metaphor in the street films of Weimar cinema — appears again in Wenders' fourth short film, *Alabama: 2000 Light Years* (1969). Produced at the Hochschule as a required part of the study program, it was Wenders' first film shot in 35mm and the first collaboration with Robby Müller, who would be his cameraman for all but two of his feature films. The story — and this time there is a story with a beginning, middle, and an end (though not quite in a conventional and conclusive form) — again refers to gangster conventions. The focus is on a gang and its leader, though perhaps in a quasi-Brechtian attempt to distance the viewer from immediate identification with the character, Wenders never shows the man's face. When he dies at the end, the camera observes only the outside of the car he travels in, and the shot fades to black signaling the death of the "hero," the end of the gaze. It is as if the gangster's vehicle, the central sign of the genre and here rapidly developing into a central image for Wenders, takes the place of the character's own personality. The car, for Wenders, is life and death, a place of mobility and identity, and a place to listen to music. The primacy of the music — John Coltrane's "Alabama" supplies the film's title; the Rolling Stones' "2000 Light Years" and Jimi Hendrix' and Bob Dylan's versions of the harrowing song "All Along the Watchtower" accompany the rest of the film — carries the action, supplying emotion and suggesting narrative action beyond dialogue and visuals.[45]

Alabama, like all of Wenders' school films and most of the early features, is an étude in alienation and a movement along the borderline of cultures. It

A scene from the cinematic underworld: *Alabama* (1968–9).

expresses the estrangement and disillusion of an entire generation shyly imaged in an idiom that plays out a fascination with the American underworld (as portrayed in movies), driven by the dissonant rhythms and rhymes of a music that belabors the quest of heroes in their loneliness. For Wenders, the act of quest is contained in its most basic contemporary, cinematic signifier: a man alone in a car, driving through the city or on a superhighway (which, in modern culture, is the extension of the city, a way to negate rural space), listening to rock and roll. Often, as in American film noir, there is a source of violence or the threat of continued harassment that forces a dislocation of self. But in the early works, that dislocation is only suggested by the mise-en-scène and the music; it has not yet become narrative material.

Wenders was a great admirer of *Easy Rider* (1969), a film in which the songs "don't simply illustrate the film's images, the images illustrate the songs."[46] In his fifth short film, Wenders attempts to achieve that same reversal of sound and image. *3 American LPs* (1969) is his first collaboration with his friend, the Austrian-born playwright and novelist Peter Handke. On the sound track they discuss music and America. They play one song each by Van Morrison, Creedence Clearwater Revival, and Harvey Mandel. They make images from cars riding through the Munich suburbs – drive-ins, used-car lots, American simulacra. Unable yet to go to the United States,

Wenders imagines it, without gangsters, this time, and full of a yearning not only to think about America, but to think American, to conjure up sound and image that might replace the current void.

This initial collaboration with Handke started a profound relationship. Wenders discovered in Handke a kindred spirit, a writer – already very well known both for his controversial plays and his strategic acts of self-promotion – who shared a love of things American and, even more, a sense of the artist at odds with the world. In 1969, at the peak of the student movement, when collective, theoretical discussion dominated intellectual and political activity, Handke and Wenders both felt the need for separation, for subjective, individual statement. The feature films that Handke authors – *The Goalie's Anxiety at the Penalty Kick* (1972), *Wrong Move* (1975), and *Wings of Desire* (1987) – are markedly different from those Wenders writes on his own or with other collaborators. They differ in the use of verbal language, as might be expected with a novelist collaborator, but they differ as well in textual and thematic intensity, and in sense of mission. The collaborations with Handke are more introspective, less fluid, less generous toward both their characters and the viewer than the other films. But this difference is not yet visible in *3 American LPs,* which is *more* fluid and *less* introspective than the other student exercises. Handke is able to add some depth to Wenders' images. Their discussions on the sound track about American music elevates it to a position that Wenders felt, but could not, until now, fully articulate. The film represents a greater self-confidence on Wenders' part, a further working through of his preoccupations and fancies. But no matter how far he has come to this point, the student films remain obsessive in their images of cars and the sounds of rock and roll. They are exercises in which motion is contained and entertainment is solitary, in which narratives suggest the dynamic lives of gangsters constrained within the timid imagination of a student filmmaker seeking out comfortable, unthreatening, safely cinematic signs of escape and fulfillment.

The first period of experimentation comes to a productive end with *Summer in the City* (1971), a two-hour film in which Wenders attempts to synthesize the elements central to his filmmaking studies so far: his obsession with rock and roll, the road, and a sense of tenuous identity with his culture that is expressed in his vicarious homesteading in the American gangster film. There is more narrative in this film and, especially, more definition of the uprooted, disenfranchised male that will be the center of all of Wenders' work to come. There is yet more cinematic allusion – almost of a self-congratulatory nature – and a further consideration of the movement

The law as masked militarism and gangsterism: cinematic critique through irony, from *Polizeifilm* (1969).

away from political commitment.* The central character, Hans, is another figure on the run, in this instance from his associates who pursue him to get the money from a holdup that put him in jail in the first place. The character's attempts to extricate himself from a suffocating past echo the larger issue of Germans dealing with their history that insinuates itself through Wenders' films. But unlike many of his colleagues, Wenders never looked beyond the personal aspects of this problem, and we can speculate that, in this student film in particular, he may be attempting to defend himself against the attacks of his more radical friends in the student movement by trying to authenticate individual over collective action, the subjective over the political. (In 1969, Wenders made a short work, *Polizeifilm,* about police and demonstrators. Perhaps this was a sop to his colleagues, or a working out of his own feeling about political noncommitment. Whatever the reasons for its making, he never moved this close to the world of violent politics again.)

Moving through Munich and Berlin, from friend to friend, appearing isolated and uncommunicative, Hans summarizes the existential impasse of the previous student films and epitomizes Wenders' growing concern with

* The film is full of cinematic and literary references. For example, in one central episode, someone relates the plot of Ford's *Three Godfathers* to illustrate to Hans, the central character, the precariousness of his own life. Subsequently, the two go to see Godard's *Alphaville,* a film in which characters drive around a desolate city of the future. At one point, Hans refers to the story "Der Kulterer" (1962) by Thomas Bernhard (1931–89), whose tale of a man who becomes a self-sufficient thinker and writer in prison reflects Hans' state of mind and being at this time.

the phenomenon of existential, spiritual, and cultural exile. But he also points to a possible solution to the dilemma that will be investigated in the later films – the growth of self-possession, the ability to thrive in solitude, to be quieted and even energized by the environment.

Also crucial to Wenders' aesthetic maturation here is the growing sureness of his craft and style. The film is dominated by extended shots that provide long sequences of uninterrupted observation. The rhythm of Hans' search for a safe place becomes the rhythm of his perception of the world around him. Long drives or walks through the city streets depict a wanderer unable to find haven; yet they ground him in his search. They also display the city as a space transformed in the eyes of the beholder. The buildings of Berlin – the Metropol cinema at Nollendorfplatz with its sweeping expressionist lines; the functional and elegant Bauhaus facade of Emil Fahrenkamp's Shell-Haus near the Tiergarten; the monumentalism of Tempelhof Airport – are made part of an urban wasteland and part of the character's sensibility. As in *Alphaville* (the film Hans and his friend go to see), the city becomes an uninhabited and perhaps uninhabitable space that defines the character.[47] Wenders is attracted to this space and needs, here and in his future films, to look at it closely, even as his characters pass through. Combining Kracauer's notions of cinema as a means to redeem the physical world, Bazin's desire to allow the camera to be faithful to temporal and spatial duration, and his own faith in the desiring gaze, Wenders allows the image to tell his character's history: the character in motion, the places he visits, the gestures of escape and desire, the notion of permanent exile set up a visual and narrative pattern for all the films to come.

2

On the Road

Exile and Innocence

The urban street or the highway, seen from the window of a moving car, dominates the image pattern of Wenders' films. But there are other images that determine that pattern, images from films and filmmakers that Wenders admires and refers to continuously, almost obsessively. John Ford looms like a specter. Two Fordian images in particular – the opening and closing shots of *The Searchers* (1956), in which a woman, looking out at the Texas desert from the door of a homestead, sees the figure of Ethan Edwards, the film's enigmatic hero, come toward her at the beginning of the film and then, at the end, leave again for the desert, forsaking the dark, comforting warmth of the house – provoke and infiltrate every film he makes. The lone figure in the desert appears at the beginning of *Paris, Texas*. Other shots from *The Searchers* are alluded to in the science fiction film-within-a-film at the beginning of *The State of Things* (1982) and on the rocky Spanish coast, made to stand for the early New England coastline, in *The Scarlet Letter* (1973). But even if not directly copied or alluded to, these images and the narratives they construct, along with those of Nicholas Ray and Samuel Fuller, are always lurking in the films. They seem for Wenders, whose imagination is nourished and driven by them, to circumscribe the modern male hero as lone migrant and wanderer, always displaced and only temporarily able to enter the realm of domesticity. They help authorize exile as a permanent condition, to give an American cinematic stamp of approval to the angst of the modern German troubled by history and without cultural shelter.

There is nothing novel about a young European filmmaker falling under the sway of American images, and Ford, Ray, and Fuller are not the only directors who gain Wenders' attention and then his emotional and intellectual allegiance. From the French New Wave on, cinéastes have discovered inspiration in the American cinema and fallen into a kind of trance before the images of John Ford. Part of this phenomenon is the result of a celebratory joy in the discovery of a cinematic community that offers the imagination a place to dwell in an American home. Another part grows from the paradox of aesthetic innovation that is modernism, a movement in which (among other things) a new generation of artists consciously seeks legitimacy by developing new expressive forms both *against* and *from* the past. There is a continual process of selecting and adapting, determining what is usable from that which must be discarded, sometimes violently. But young German filmmakers in the sixties and early seventies constitute a special case. While the French used American film to do battle against the deadened images and petrified narratives of the postwar Cinema of Quality, the Germans had no body of images and narratives to struggle against. More accurately, the images they had were so inextricably tied to the past as to be useless to the imagination. As we pointed out in the previous chapter, Wenders comes from a generation who willfully, perhaps inescapably, were born into a state of historical amnesia. With a past too frightful to remember and a present eagerly offering the means to forget, the young German intellectuals of the sixties had to re-create themselves and their history; they had to invent images, to develop representations for a past and a present that resisted the very work they were undertaking.[1]

By the early sixties, they were searching for new images. The Oberhausen Manifesto of 1962, a document that recognized the need for different images and a different means to fund and distribute them, articulated their dissatisfaction with the status quo:

> The collapse of the commercial German film industry finally removes the economic basis for a mode of filmmaking whose attitude and practice we reject. With it, the new film has a chance to come to life. The success of German shorts at international festivals demonstrates that the future of the German cinema lies with those who have shown that they speak the international language of the cinema. This new cinema needs new forms of freedom: from the conventions and habits of the established industry, from intervention by commercial partners, and finally freedom from the tutelage of other vested interests. We have specific plans for the artistic, formal and economic realization of the new German cinema. We are collectively prepared to take the economic risks. The old cinema is dead. We believe in the new.[2]

Positioning the "new" against the established industry, its economic power, and cultural amnesia proved a long and complicated task. But by establishing a voice, and seeking to model themselves after the French New Wave by

Cinematic fathers I: Robert Lander in *Kings of the Road* (*above*) modeled after
Ethan Edwards in John Ford's *The Searchers* (*facing page*).

creating a cinema of subjectivity, an *Autorenkino,* the Oberhausen group,
and those who came after, were able to begin the process of re-creating a
usable tradition through renewed cinematic representations. Each of the
young filmmakers developed their own vision of the past and selected from
the tradition those formal and contextual elements that legitimized their
aesthetic mission. It will be useful, in this context, to examine some of
Wenders' predecessors and contemporaries in order to understand the new
cinema aesthetic that surrounded him and led him to embrace American
film.

Alexander Kluge was one of the prime movers of Oberhausen. An image
maker in the modernist tradition who sought to evoke the forgotten past
through a new, documentary-inspired cinema and literature (he is a writer as
well as a filmmaker), Kluge sought ways of countering the conventions and
representations of the dominant ideology. His films are openly didactic and
seek to engage intellectual rather than emotional response. *Abschied von
Gestern* (*Yesterday Girl*) (1966), for example, presents the life story of a girl
who, traumatized by the war, becomes a wanderer between two worlds, East
and West, and fails to be integrated into the postwar society, which has not
overcome its fascist legacies. Kluge makes historical situations manifest in
small life stories. (The film is derived from a short prose sketch in his 1962
Lebensläufe, or *Curricula Vitae.*) Kluge's films are, in a sense, impersonal.
They seek images for a culture in fragments, authored by a coherent, as-

sured, and somewhat detached intellect. Unlike Wenders, Kluge does not seek to affirm himself in his films, but rather to offer his culture ways of perceiving a past and reconciling the present.

Jean-Marie Straub – a filmmaker Wenders knew in Munich and admired for his radically modernist approach – goes even further than Kluge in creating distanced, intellectually demanding work. His and Danièlle Huillet's *Nicht Versöhnt* (*Not Reconciled*, 1965), adapted from Heinrich Böll's novel *Billard um halbzehn* (*Billiards at Half Past Nine*), is as severe and challenging a film as any made by the new German filmmakers. Taking a decidedly antiestablishment stance in both form and content, it demands that the viewer seek information in stark and oblique images that suggest rather than reveal narrative continuity. Meanings must be constructed by the viewer, who is asked to analyze images, lay them over the narrative of the novel, and re-create a discourse that, when understood, indicts modern German politics for not making a clear break with the past and urges the activation of a radical political consciousness.

The power of Kluge and Straub and Huillet was not lost on Wenders in his formative years. Indeed, the school films bear something of their mark. But with his entrance into the world of commercial filmmaking, he took a different tack and chose to challenge the viewer by other means, without direct, politically motivated confrontation or a structure of expression that seeks to alienate or disengage the viewer's emotions from the film text. Like Kluge and Straub and Huillet, Wenders sought a new methodology of the image and a new manner of addressing the film audience. But his image making and narrative strategy would be more personal and accessible, more immediately emotional, and would be driven – directly or indirectly – by the American filmmakers (and, later, by the Japanese director Yasujiro Ozu) whose authority gave him imaginative strength. That authority was multifaceted: It confirmed Wenders' own cinematic subjectivity and provided one means for him to drive through the gap in Germany's history, to discover continuity and meaning beyond fascism through cinema. It was also a way to make certain he retained contact with his audience. Awareness and need of the audience is an important component of the work of the New German Cinema. Choosing a mass art to express a new vision, they were impressed by the fact that a reasonably sized viewership was an important way to authenticate that work. Each of the major figures of the movement sought various methods either to achieve an audience or, in some cases, to force it into a new perceptive stance.[3] Their differing strategies explain a great deal about the contradictions, the successes and failures of the movement.

Attempting to adopt a cinematic version of the Brechtian alienation effect (*Verfremdungseffekt*), Kluge and Straub and Huillet so demanded active audience engagement in the meaning-making process that they were never able to achieve a large viewership. In their struggle to give German cinema the integrity it had lost after 1933, they achieved an extraordinary aesthetic, but not commercial success. The latter was never their particular goal, and this stood as a negative example to the filmmakers who followed them. Rainer Werner Fassbinder, like Wenders, experimented with unconventional forms in his early work and, again like Wenders, went on to synthesize other, notably American, elements in his films. He had this to say about Straub and Huillet's work: "Films from the brain are all right, but if they don't reach the audience, it's no good."[4] Fassbinder turned to the work of Douglas Sirk, finding in the excesses of American melodrama of the fifties a way to reintegrate emotional vitality into the intellectual detachment of Brechtian inquiry. Wenders gave up Brechtian methods of alienation almost completely and very early in his career. In seeking out Ford, Nicholas Ray, Yasujiro Ozu, and Fritz Lang – the native German filmmaker who moved to America in the early thirties – he looked for models of emotional continuity and pervasive cultural grounding. He sought in these filmmakers a patrimony of affect, discourses of desire, and guides to a cinema of homecoming and redemption.

Other of his peers went in different directions. Some filmmakers of the movement avoided modernism completely. Early in his career, Volker

Schlöndorff readily adopted the classical Hollywood style, with its conventional cutting patterns, psychologically motivated characters, and linear chronology. From *Der junge Törleß* (*Young Törless*, 1966) to *The Tin Drum* (1979, the film that marked the apogee of popularity of the New German Cinema by winning an Academy Award), he used the conventions of Hollywood to present character studies that allowed for identification and insight into the dark abodes of minds and souls confronted with the temptations of fascism. Schlöndorff ultimately made the transition to Hollywood filmmaking, working in America, making, among other things, a television film of *Death of a Salesman* (1985) and the commercial feature *The Handmaid's Tale* (1989).

Werner Herzog worked more eclectically, skirting the edges of modernism in an attempt to visualize historical struggle through the signifiers of romantic mysticism and expressionist ecstasy. In some of his work, his goal was to re-create images of the recent past through the evocation of an even more distant past. He allegorized the development of fascist behavior through a narrative of sixteenth-century colonialism in *Aguirre: Wrath of God* (1972), a film that gave the audience action, character, and a bizarre variation of the Hollywood costume drama. Unlike Schlöndorff, however, Herzog undermined the comforts of psychological identification. He reawakens the mad spirit of German Expressionism and uses the power of parable and historical allegory to indict white colonialism and more recent fascist terror at the same time. In *Aguirre* and his other films, figure and landscape merge into dreamscape where romantic longing and a dementia, harking back to Dr. Caligari, produce a sense of estrangement that is destructive of the individual and the body politic as well. But this destruction is attractive at the same time as it is horrifying and distancing. To borrow Joseph Conrad's phrase, Herzog immerses himself and his viewers in the destructive element. His romantic fascination with the irrational weakens his ability to provide a measure of clarity and distance. Aguirre's will to power and sense of racial superiority make him a protofascist in historical disguise; yet his madness has grandeur and exerts an uncanny and irresistible attraction that invites identification with his character at the expense of enlightened detachment.

Herzog's blending of styles led to an expressive and imaginative impasse. He tackled contemporary subjects in his fiction films only rarely, and finally took to a repetition of content in a style that no longer cohered. Fassbinder was a risk taker of another order than Herzog. Where the latter gloried in heroic exploits and dangerous locations, Fassbinder remained in Frankfurt or Munich, examining pre- and postwar Germany through a supple and creative synthesis of the melodramatic and the modernist. By combining

Brecht and Sirk, he created images and narratives that both explained the existence of fascism in contemporary memory and were emotionally accessible and strikingly analytical. Fassbinder concentrated on the fifties and seventies (only one film, *Lili Marleen*, 1980, is set in the Nazi era; his greatest work, *Berlin Alexanderplatz*, made in the same year, is set in the immediate prefascist period of Weimar's collapse). His work develops ironic, contemplative, sometimes hysteria-laden images of trapped and oppressed working people and members of the petit bourgeoisie whose lives are perceived as melodramas of despair, a suffering that bears the weight of Nazi history.

Because of the controlled emotionality of his films, the ironic distance from the characters, and the clear political thrust of the narratives, Fassbinder's work leaves the viewer with a sense of unease and disturbance. Fassbinder demanded his audience respond not only to the internal debates of the characters, but to the external debates his narratives held with the culture at large. Perhaps for this reason his theatrical films (as opposed to his work for television) were never as popular in Germany as they were abroad. Fassbinder's films are often rude and violent; they almost all concern working people or the disenfranchised; their aim is to create perceptual disruption.

Wenders, in marked contrast, is a quiet, reticent filmmaker. Like Fassbinder, he sets his work in a contemporary setting (only his "assigned" projects – *The Scarlet Letter* and *Hammett* (1978–82) – take place in the past), but his is a calmer world where even travel on the road is quiet, filled with melancholy, and usually without threat. Unlike Fassbinder, Wenders rarely attempts to disturb, but rather to coax, his viewer into a position of understanding and, if not sympathy, compassion with the characters he creates – mostly lower-middle-class men in a state of self-exile without secure emotional footing.

Like Fassbinder, but in more studied, oblique, and subjective ways, Wenders contemplates postwar Germany and the legacies of the fascist past. His specific allusions to the Nazi period are few: the confrontation of Wilhelm and the former Nazi Laertes in *Wrong Move;* the brief reference to National Socialism by the confused cinema owner and the candle carved in the shape of Hitler's head in *Kings of the Road;* the film-within-a-film of a prison camp in *Wings of Desire.* He is not interested in the particular manifestations of fascism from 1933 to 1945, or in its legacy of oppression upon the disenfranchised. In fact, like most intellectuals of his generation, Wenders is concerned with fascism's absence – not merely the absence of concrete references, but of cultural and historical memory embodied in the central figure who inhabits most of his films, the young man or male couple unanchored in history, place, or a knowable, stable milieu. He is concerned as well with the cultural corruption that occurs when the past is ignored or dealt with uncritically. Depicting his characters as uprooted and searching, Wenders addresses the loss they have suffered, a loss of home and identity that, for the most part, remains hidden from the figures who suffer it. The wandering amounts to a state of exile forced upon them by the legacies of the past. While they respond to the compulsion to move, they rarely gain insight into the traumatizing conditions and the hidden forces that drive them. They live on the road, in narratives that drive them, usually with gentle persistence, though occasionally with violent starts, from place to place, country to country, seeking – until *Wings of Desire* and the rest of angels – only more movement.

The obsession to wander is linked to, indeed overdetermined by, that obsession with the images of American cinema we have been discussing. Wenders finds in them not only continuity, but a spatial certainty. The wanderer of American cinema is peculiarly bounded, usually moving toward or from (and never very far from) a domestic place of rest. Ethan Edwards rides the desert, but the domestic space remains the point of reference, security, and the place of longing. Indeed, it is from its vantage point that the viewer regards the action. As much as they wander, the figures in American Westerns and road movies want a place of rest and containment. Wenders' central figures are all children of Ethan Edwards, all questers, men on the road seeking out domestic landscapes, hoping to root themselves and to be free of roots at the same time. Their movement is conditioned by the exiling impact of their peculiar historical and cinematic inheritance, and it is also a reflex motion, a reaction to an inner urge and an attempt to escape the urgency that charges them to go forth. Like the culture they come from, Wenders' figures turn a blind eye to a past too hideous to recall. Like their culture, they often operate in bad faith and suffer from a desire that feeds upon its own inability to be satisfied.

But the image of Ethan Edwards, emerging from and returning to the desert, refusing the comforts of home and the fantasies of domestic peace, is unattainable for Wenders (at least until his most recent and thematically most problematic films). Ethan's wandering is safely confined within the American landscape and, even more important, the cinematic landscape of the American Western. No matter how Ford questions the Western genre in his later films – no matter how much Ethan himself stands as Ford's own interrogation of the psychotic aspects of the hero – he is still rooted in knowable cinematic boundaries. It is because of this that Wenders looks to

cinema as an alternative memory, hoping there to find haven. If his characters are unable to understand where they are, or know where they want to be, at least their creator can rest secure in a cinematic universe that assures imaginative and intellectual nourishment, that perhaps offers respite and ways to find himself by means of the shared culture of cinema.

Wenders and his characters become double wanderers, seeking a response to and a place in (or out of) a culture that has disinherited itself – seeking a place in the cinematic landscape that provides images, narratives, and above all, community and security. Both places are imaginary. But the attempt to constitute the self and give it ontological locus and cultural identity is real, laborious, and a journey in itself. Wenders searches for memory, or at least a representation for memory that more adequately expresses the *longing* for memory, the desire for place, history and ways to see it – for forms of expression that would themselves create a desire in his audience to see and understand.

His cinematic imaginary is in a state of tension, filled with a desire to resolve contradictions. As a result, his films attempt to establish a transnational space, unstable and full of longing for someplace else, for someone else – a figure to authorize his images. "I don't think that any other country has had such a loss of faith in its own images, stories, and myths as we have." Wenders has written, "We, the directors of the New Cinema, have felt this

Cinematic fathers II: a street in Murnau's *Nosferatu* (1922) *(facing page)* and its reappearance in Wenders' *Kings of the Road* *(above)* — the imitative mode.

loss most keenly: in ourselves as the absence of a tradition of our own, as a generation without fathers."[5] *Opas Kino ist tot!* (Grandpa's cinema is dead!) German cinema is left without patrimony, without the guide into adulthood — memory, responsibility, language, order, knowledge of self, and the law — that is part of the oedipal process that places the inquisitive imagination in an ordered structure of expression. Without such guidance, Wenders finds himself without imaginative footing; his films and his life are a continuous quest for a reliable male figure to show the way. This preoccupation pushes women to the periphery of his films, effectively keeping them in a marginal space, while the characters and their creator worry about finding a center for their male identity.

In the history of German film, Wenders could find only one patronymic figure to look to: Fritz Lang.* But Lang — who left Germany for an American career when the Nazis took power and was largely ignored by his countrymen after the war — provided only a reinforcement to Wenders' anxiety about the way German history had destroyed its dominant figures and how postwar filmmaking ignored them.[6] While he admired and

---

* There are a few visual and verbal references to another major figure of early German film, F. W. Murnau. The director in *The State of Things* is named Friedrich Munro and called "Fritz," combining the two filmmakers into one. A composition in *Kings of the Road*, a shot of a street symmetrically flanked by rows of houses, resembles the mise-en-scène of Murnau's *Nosferatu*.

honored Lang, whose work and personality stand something like guardian angels over Wenders' films, no other German filmmaker was able to perform the appropriate patriarchal function. Wenders left the disinherited cinematic minds of his culture behind and allowed American filmmakers to form the root of his search for a cinematic patriarch. Ford's images were simultaneously foreign and assimilable, but apparently still insufficient. So Wenders supplemented them by the work of another director, whose life, characters, and the landscapes they inhabit, while essentially American, more closely corresponded to his own imaginative needs. That filmmaker is Nicholas Ray, who exerted so strong a force that Wenders copied a sequence from one of his films in *Kings of the Road,* gave the filmmaker himself a prominent role in *The American Friend* (1977), and at the time of Ray's death, placed him at the center of a full-scale oedipal struggle in the film *Lightning over Water* (1980).

The Ray–Ford axis offers another doubling structure, another set of images that further set out the contradictions in Wenders' work: the pull toward stability, the need for paternal security, the controlled patterns of human relationships that Ford seeks to express, the restlessness, the dissatisfaction with place, the feeling of anomie and despair in all places endemic to the characters of Ray's best films. Ford made Westerns, which are among the most solidly structured of Hollywood genres, and he was himself secure within the studio system – safe and free within its bounds to do the films he wanted, as long as they continued to be commercially viable. Ray was an independent, rootless figure. He started in Hollywood in the late forties under the aegis of John Houseman, worked in a number of genres – most successfully in the Western, film noir, and domestic melodrama. In films like *They Live by Night* (1949), *In a Lonely Place* (1950), *On Dangerous Ground* (1951), *The Lusty Men* (1952), *Johnny Guitar* (1954), *Rebel Without a Cause* (1955), and *Bigger Than Life* (1956), Ray was able to explore the disappointments and dangers of domesticity and a longing for romantic security with a delicacy and emotional strength unusual in early fifties Hollywood films. Never very consistent in the quality of his output, and subject to the whims and demands of the studio system, he finally fled Hollywood in the early sixties, after directing some of the bloated "epics" that marked the end of the first major phase of the studio system. He took up teaching and worked continuously on the personal documentary, "We Can't Go Home Again," which he began with his students at Harpur College in the seventies and which he still speaks of completing in *Lightning over Water.*

Ford's films offer Wenders a haven of rest and security. Their aesthetic legacy is strong, their expression – even when they question their generic

38

boundaries – is safely delimited by a landscape and characters whose familiarity belies the insecurity found in the late work (in films like *The Searchers* and *The Man Who Shot Liberty Valance* [1962]). The conflict between disintegration and restoration, between disturbed peace and rebuilt community, is always in Ford played out as a mythical, conservative affirmation of culture. The films of Nicholas Ray, however, offer the opposite of affirmation. Ray is an archetype of the unsettled filmmaker, saddled by the Hollywood system, finally unable to do anything but escape its oppression. His characters, from Bowie in *They Live by Night* onward, are the models of the uprooted, wandering figure. They obsessively seek domesticity and more often than not are destroyed when they find it. They are never heroes. Johnny Guitar, the central male figure in Ray's great Western, is the obverse of Ethan Edwards: quiet, self-effacing, melancholy, and passive, a stranger wherever he goes. Ray's characters and their narratives are deeply embedded within Wenders' films.

Where *The Searchers* offers a crucial reference point and an occasional source of visual citation in Wenders, Ray's films infiltrate his work to the point where, as we said, a whole sequence from a Nicholas Ray film is reconstructed in *Kings of the Road*. Bruno and Robert, the film's main figures, take off on what at first appears to be a liberating motorcycle trip to the Rhine River. The shots of their bike and the energetic score that accompanies the images are in full homage to Fonda and Hopper's *Easy Rider*. (He calls *Easy Rider* a political film, which it certainly was in 1969 America, and at the same time, a science fiction film, which it must have seemed to a young German intellectual in search of American images).[7] The destination of the motorcycle trip is Bruno's childhood home, on an island in the middle of the Rhine. Bruno arrives at his house and looks under the front steps to find an old comic book in a movie can. The sequence duplicates a passage that occurs early in Nicholas Ray's *The Lusty Men*. There, the rodeo rider Jeff, near the end of his career and hurt in a fall in the arena, returns to his childhood home. Unable to get in, he crawls under the steps, where he discovers an old gun and a rodeo program. Jeff's recovery of his childhood is cut short when the owner of the house returns and points a rifle at him.

Jeff's return is a quiet, underplayed moment of discovery on the part of a character facing the end of his active life. Even the potential violence threatened by the appearance of the rifle is downplayed and turned aside. The owner of the house invites Jeff in and soon introduces him to the couple who want to buy the house and who will briefly change the direction of his career. Wenders' appropriation of this material charges it with a different sense of homecoming, with grief more than nostalgia. Bruno enters the empty house,

Cinematic fathers III: Jeff in Nicholas Ray's *The Lusty Men* (*top*) returning to his childhood home and Wenders' "imitation" of this scene in *Kings of the Road*, where Bruno returns to his hidden childhood mementos (*bottom*).

and the memories it inflicts upon him force a violent act of smashing windows (an image that appeared earlier in *Wrong Move* and turns up again in *The State of Things* as a sign of emotional upheaval, frustration, and anger). After this moment of disturbance – rare in Wenders' work, and particularly rare for this character – Bruno sits sadly on the steps, crying, diminished, and hurt by his memories. Returning to the place of his childhood, he comes to realize the loss of *Heimat,* the secure place of origin and rest.

The sequences in both films place the characters at turning points. Jeff's return to his home occurs early in the narrative and is an arrival that sets up the departure of the character into a new relationship: that of an older man who teaches a younger one the craft of the rodeo, in the course of which he becomes a threat to the couple's domestic longings. The sequence in *Kings of the Road* occurs in the central part of the film's narrative. The relationships between the two main characters are fairly well established – though "established" is not quite appropriate to a film whose purpose is to question and disrupt established emotional states. Bruno is perceived throughout as too calm and controlled, even too adjusted in his solitary, itinerant life, and the visit to his boyhood home begins, forcefully, to break that control down, to reveal to him emotions and desires he had suppressed. His response is presented as a sign of internal change, of a shift of perception of self, not quite visible on the level of plot, that will finally alter the character. By turning to Ray, Wenders obviously found an appropriate model, in image and movement, of the moment when the adult reclaims childhood and discovers personal history. Though *Kings of the Road* depends less upon narrative coincidence, less on plot turns that affect the characters, than Ray's film (or most Hollywood cinema, for that matter), it still claims its heritage.

The American cinematic patrimony serves Wenders well in its offering of emotion-laden images, its sense of loss and despair, and its narratives of recuperation. Wenders' appropriation of these models goes beyond imitation. To an extent greater than Ford or Ray, he creates characters who are caught in a double despair that emerges from a past too painful to recall and a future too unarticulated to desire. They mourn their inability to remember the past, have no direction with which to leave it, and remain trapped in a present that is, at the same time, energizing, depressing, and incomplete.

Allusion and intertextuality are methods Wenders employs to stave off the pain of mourning and the loss of history and to provide himself with cinematic security. Within his films, his characters repeat their own rituals of protection against an absent past. They inundate themselves with sounds and images of the present. They listen to rock music (or it is provided for them and the viewer on the sound track), and it becomes an emotional if not existential haven for them. Or they attempt to inscribe themselves into the visible realm in order to achieve a measure of permanence. The images made by the Polaroid camera or the five-and-dime photo booth become, for Wenders' characters, signs of their insecurity and a mark of their creator's interest in the problems of representing individual experience. Picture taking is the validation of the visible and a method of orienting the self in the world. With it, Wenders creates a paradigm of affirmation. The self, haunted by the transiency of existence, tries to overcome its vulnerable state by establishing an irrefutable representation of being in the world. Picture taking is, on the one hand, childlike play, innocent in its self-absorption. On the other, it is a means of analysis. Friedrich's wife in *The State of Things* takes photos of the landscape to discover its formal essences and locate her subjectivity; she "reads" the Polaroids taken by her children to understand the ways they perceive gender. Thus, for Wenders' characters, picture taking becomes an essential means to understand and affirm the self.

However, self-photography slides into obsession when the narcissistic desire makes the image the only object of the subject's gaze. Mark, in *The State of Things,* lies in the bath, his camera on a tripod, automatically snapping his picture as he sinks under the water. The apparent harmless narcissism of the act can escalate into a perverse obsession where self-emulation becomes violent. Ripley in *The American Friend* takes Polaroids of himself lying across a pool table; the images tumble over him as they fall from the camera. Ripley keeps a verbal diary on a tape recorder and becomes trapped in an excess of self-portrayal and egocentrism that finally explodes. In Ripley's case, his search for a secure self insulates and finally isolates him so severely that his attempt to keep the world at bay cannot prevent it from crashing in on him. Despite his need for friendship (which allows him to make a killer of an otherwise passive man), he remains entrapped within himself and responds with the violence of a gangster. (Wenders' other quasi-solipsist, Friedrich, the film director in *The State of Things,* becomes so passive in his self-absorption as image maker that he winds up a victim of violence and is murdered. The ultimate narcissism of self-representation occurs in *Until the End of the World* [1991], in which the characters fall victim to interior images of their childhood, made visible for them by the father of one of the film's characters.)

The excess of self-consciousness in both the characters and their creator is striking. Wenders wanders through the imaginary of film history, attempting to find cinematic fathers and re-create images that will validate and make sufficient a narrative about characters who struggle to turn their lives into pictures and stories. Wandering through a physical and psychic landscape, they seek authenticity with images of themselves. An endless cycle of representational validation is created inside and outside each of the films. The cycle is driven by a fear of being unable to find appropriate images, of becoming unable to connect the images into an appropriate story, leading to doubts about the sincerity of the whole attempt. "I don't know where to start," Wenders writes:

> if I want to talk
> about the exploitation OF images
> and the exploitation BY images.[8]

"Everything gets pressured into images," says the director Friedrich to his producer, Gordon, in *The State of Things*. They are riding in the back of a mobile home through the streets of Los Angeles, fleeing the mafia, who are out to kill them because Friedrich is using their money to make an uncommercial film. "Death," he says, "that's all stories can carry. All stories are about death . . . *Todesboten* [messengers of death]." Stories, narratives, and the images that make them up are of necessity time-bound, and in an existential sense, death is the end of all stories. The filmmaker – real and fictional – who would be free to explore life and death in narratives and images of his own device is exploited by the medium and its economics into falsifying himself by giving up his art to the conventions of commercial necessity. The characters he manages to create are themselves obsessed with the images that give them life. Wenders and his characters alike fear the emptiness that precedes stories and the void that follows. They desire to be embodied and fear the results of embodiment.

Paralysis and violence – the outcome of this existential impasse – infiltrate Wenders' films, but do not silence them. Wenders escapes the dilemma by creating works that are forever about movement. Instead of allowing his characters to succumb (only a few of them do), he sets them on the road and hopes that salvation will be found in the controlled motion of an automobile. While images from *The Searchers* may be superimposed over Wenders' films and the narratives of Nicholas Ray support them, while the characters sometimes reach a narcissistic paralysis in front of a Polaroid camera, the essential images that construct Wenders' films are made up of shots of a man driving a car and its reverse angle, what the driver, looking out the window of the car or walking on the highway (or in a train, bus, or plane) sees. From his early school films to the reincarnation of angels in *Wings of Desire,* Wenders replays the myths of male odyssey, the belief that movement will produce experience, that change will satisfy desire. Women

43

are on the periphery, figured as a threat, as the end of the story, the end of wandering. The point of arrival, figured as the discovery of heterosexual love, occurs prominently only in *Wings of Desire*. The female as wanderer makes an appearance only in *Until the End of the World*.

Wenders' male drivers, walkers, travelers offer in their unrelenting movement an expression of loss and depression, but at the same time, they carry with them an image of self-preserving containment and freedom. As a result, in their persistent motion these wanderers become signs of disoriented beings lost in contemporary history, while maintaining a sense of security within themselves. They cousin their despair and sooth their sorrows with the movement and music that make up their life on the road. In the face of their despair and the almost homogeneous landscapes of Europe and America through which they pass, they maintain the secure borders of their own personalities. Unlike their counterparts in American road movies, they are only occasionally outlaws on the run (the police are the usual catalysts of flight for most characters in American films of the road; Wenders' characters travel voluntarily). Bloch in *The Goalie's Anxiety at the Penalty Kick* flees a murder he is only half-aware he committed, though he is never actually pursued by anyone; Philip in *Alice in the Cities* and Wilhelm in *Wrong Move* move to evade their own discomfort and ennui. Robert escapes from a broken marriage and a failed attempt at domesticity in *Kings of the Road*. Damiel flees the boredom of eternal disengagement as an angel in *Wings of Desire*, while Claire, in *Until the End of the World*, flees domestic boredom and a threatened nuclear disaster but gets entangled with various pursuers as she joins with a man seeking images for his blind mother. Bruno in *Kings of the Road* appears to be fleeing nothing. He seems at peace in his wanderings, adjusted and content. He suffers a certain emptiness; he has limited desire; but he is otherwise secure within his travels to cinemas along the East German border. Travis in *Paris, Texas* has fled from a violent and destructive domesticity, withdrawn into muteness, and removed himself from community. He is the character closest to *The Searchers*' Ethan Edwards. But the film's narrative sends him back into community, works him out of madness into a confrontation with the violence that destroyed him. Far from aimless, Travis moves on a trajectory toward reconciliation and an ability to understand the limits of domesticity. Few of these characters are aimless, fewer still express the melodramatics of longing or the ravages of loss. That they *are* lost is the given of their journeys, as is the uncertainty of how their journeys will end. Their redemption is in the movement itself and the adventures they meet in the course of their odysseys.

By redemption we mean an ability on the part of the character to acknowl-

A cinematic icon: the "framed" frame maker, Jonathan Zimmermann, in *The American Friend* (1977).

edge his emotional landscape, traverse it, and perhaps locate a route out – go through a process of recognition, attainment, and change. Most of Wenders' exiles and wanderers realize this to some extent. The viewer, positioned to see the totality of character and landscape and to make connections the character cannot, is given a special opportunity to comprehend the potential redemptive state. This may be made clearer if we examine two films that offer the *least* redemptive potential in the Wenders canon, *The American Friend* and *The Goalie's Anxiety at the Penalty Kick*.

Tom Ripley and Jonathan Zimmermann, characters with little sense of self-possession, do find moments of solace in their wary, intercultural friendship. But both are badly diminished from the start and do not gain much sense of self as their story progresses; the imbalance and play for power between them lead to violence and betrayal. Ripley drifts from country to country in a state of rootlessness and fear. ("There's nothing to fear but fear itself. . . . I know less and less about who I am or who anybody else is," he says into his tape recorder, reducing President Roosevelt's historical imperative to a statement of individual isolation in postwar Europe.) Ripley's German friend Jonathan is a picture framer whose professional ethos is evident in the meticulousness of his craft. He is, however, only a reluctant representative of his class and profession, with its stereotyped qualities of reliable workmanship and uncorruptable standards. He is, in fact, a man oppressed by the details of his life and work, hemmed in by domesticity and the fears of a fatal blood disease. While he recognizes from the start that Ripley is a crook trying to deal in fakes, a fact that makes him refuse to shake Ripley's hand when they first meet, Jonathan suspends and even betrays his moral reservations by slowly getting entangled in the net that Ripley has cast.* When, under Ripley's tutelage, he turns into a petty hit man for the mob, he gains a brief sense of self-possession and pleasure that belies, or perhaps underscores, the fact that his life is being turned inside out.

The ways Ripley and Jonathan work out their despair in *The American Friend* is overdetermined by a specific American film genre, which drives their actions as much by generic necessity as by the psychological motivations in their characters, notwithstanding "personal" interventions on the part of the director. Their contemporary cultural angst is spoken through the fifties American gangster film, in particular the narrative of a lower-middle-class family man of failing means, who permits himself to be seduced into crime by an attractively tough gangster. This seduction typically leads to the near ruin of the domestic scene, and often to the death of both male characters. Like so much of fifties melodrama, the site of uncertainty and stress is the family, that fantasy space of peace and security promoted by the dominant culture. Fifties melodrama often questioned this fantasy; filmmakers like Nicholas Ray expressed the tentative, even threatening, aspects of domesticity. (In fact, *The American Friend* is something of an homage to Ray's 1956 melodrama *Bigger Than Life*.) *The American Friend* is Wenders' most consciously genre-driven film (as opposed to *Hammett,* whose structure was studio-driven) and the one in which the fragilities not only of domesticity, but of male friendship as well are exposed.

The gangster genre brings the issue of male friendship to something of a crisis, suggesting — though of course never dealing with — the homoerotic nature of the relationship between two men. Like its generic antecedents, *The American Friend* deals with the male couple as the site of dominant and passive behavior. Ripley, though less assured and less vicious than the average early fifties movie tough, still moves with an ease that attracts Jonathan.

---

* Ripley, played by Dennis Hopper, sells paintings by an artist, played by Nicholas Ray, who is thought to be dead — Ray once directed Hopper in *Rebel Without a Cause.*

46

Ripley wanders from New York to Munich to Paris to Hamburg, selling his forged paintings. He acts also as middleman for a Parisian gangster. In this role, he uses Jonathan as a not terribly unwilling tool, turning him into a murderer and a wanderer himself. Ripley offers Jonathan a movie-like life of intrigue, assassination, and gangster martyrdom. Indeed, references to cinema abound in the film, from the European and American filmmakers who play minor roles, to the various gadgets of film (including a little viewer that demonstrates lighting techniques with pictures of naked women) that appear throughout.

Ripley exploits Jonathan, but no more than Jonathan exploits Ripley. In fact, in addition to gangster conventions, the film plays on much older literary conventions, particularly those of the American abroad, corrupted by subtle European amorality. While, on the surface, Ripley seems to be the agent of danger – the smooth-talking American taking advantage of an innocent German family man, ready and willing to be corrupted – it is finally Jonathan, thriving on his new criminal life, who turns and betrays his mentor. Here is the point where Wenders alters the structures of male friendship, examining them more carefully than commercial cinema is used to doing. Ripley and Jonathan become, finally, two extremes of the exiled self: the one uprooted, beyond good and evil, the other desiring uprooting and, in the process, succumbing to the betrayal of friendship and domesticity. Like the fifties domestic melodrama and gangster film, *The American Friend* is marked by lost opportunities, failed lives, and a precarious sense of despair that disallows redemption in the social and psychological realm. For Wenders, the gangster genre provides another emotional and moral landscape for his wanderers, one with no exits.

The American Friend explores the wanderer's movements at the borderline of immorality and dissolution. At its end, Jonathan Zimmermann dies after leaving Ripley alone on the beach with an ambulance full of gangsters he's blown up. Though other Wenders films end in death (most notably *The State of Things*), no other suggests the impossibility of self-reconciliation. In the development of the wanderer motif, from the school films on, Wenders attempts to find the small ways his characters can redeem themselves from their state of self-exile and exile from self. The attempts are never completely successful, for often his exiles cannot overcome their alienation, nor can they move from an internalized existential dread to a position of freer observation of the world around them. Their road is either generically predetermined or their obsessions are too constricting to permit a major alteration in their course.

Hans, in *Summer in the City*, can only move toward escape. Alone in the streets, self-consciousness prevents any articulation other than quiet despair and a desire to flee. *The Goalie's Anxiety at the Penalty Kick*, which follows *Summer in the City*, moves still further inward. Tracing the loss of language and identity (rather than searching for it, as in the previous film), *Goalie* marks the movements of its character through successive stages of alienation, from disenfranchised sportsman to disenfranchised murderer to disenfranchised observer of his own past. In the novel upon which the film is based, Peter Handke was able to create a clever sense of disassociation of the character from the things that surround him and, finally, from the very language that he shares with the world. The film manages to create only a kind of mask between the character and his world – both of them impassive, both unable to interact with each other. The mutual impassivity becomes so extreme that, by the end of the film, the camera can only withdraw, pulling up from Josef Bloch as he sits in the stands of a soccer stadium, talking to a stranger, telling him to keep his eyes on the goalie and not the ball.

Wenders, in this film, asks the viewers as well to keep their eye on the goalie, while the various plays occurring around that figure, the rooms and streets and towns through which he wanders, and the people with whom he can barely make contact, drift in and out making no impression on his consciousness. The result is a stalemate between form, the content it generates, and perception. The editing of the film disables the links created by conventional patterns of shot–reaction shot, resulting in a kind of perceptual slippage. But it is finally unrevealing. Eschewing a political or cultural centering, concentrating instead on an intensity of self-absorption and the paralysis of absolute solitude, *Goalie* offers neither its character nor the viewer access to a way of understanding.

The Goalie's Anxiety at the Penalty Kick is an extension of the earlier school films insofar as it withholds emotion while foregrounding an active alienation of character. The spareness of its dramatic and perceptual interactions, however, is not the equivalent of the earlier works. In those films, Wenders was actively engaged in testing out signifiers of aloneness in motion – young men riding in cars through the city – whereas in *Goalie* he examines an alienation that is unyielding to any motion or presence. There is a coldness and distance – of character from environment and viewer from mise-en-scène – that is uncharacteristic of the works that precede or follow. There is no warmth generated from the character and no compassion asked from the viewer. In contrast, even the complex, morally suspect characters of *The American Friend* are portrayed with an interest that approaches infatuation.

Wenders' films are most successful when his contemplative style offers a generosity to his characters by mediating his and the viewer's attraction to

A view of the man with the camera: Philip Winter under the boardwalk in *Alice in the Cities.*

them with a certain distance in both mise-en-scène and narrative. An intricate positioning of character, filmmaker, and viewer balances an attitude of innocence, knowingness, and a certain despair in narratives where characters are offered at least an opportunity to prevail. This dialogic style of multiple address, a "delicate sincerity," in which all parties are engaged and attended to appears first in *Alice in the Cities,* which was made directly after *The Goalie's Anxiety at the Penalty Kick.* Like Josef Bloch, Philip Winter (the film's central male figure) begins in a state of splendid isolation, though it is immediately clear that this is not a psychotic state and threatens little danger. The first shot of the film is of an airplane, gliding through a gray sky, an image that picks up where the last shot of *Summer in the City* ends, with its main character flying into exile.

The camera pans past the plane and, as if in the same shot, picks up a street sign on a boardwalk on the New Jersey shore. The pan continues to the sea and then cuts to the boardwalk itself. Apartment buildings are in the background, and the entire space is without human figures, until the camera, craning down and moving left, picks up Philip, sitting against a pylon under the boardwalk. This long establishing sequence not only locates character and viewer, but, in its grayness and emptiness, implants an awareness of depression and isolation that surrounds the character. When the camera picks up Philip, he is indulging in that major act performed by Wenders' loners that helps fend off their anomie. He is taking Polaroids. He looks at the print that comes from his camera, then looks up, and Wenders cuts to a shot of what Philip sees and is photographing, a deserted lifeguard stand on the beach. Gulls fly around it. There is a cut back to Philip and another point of view shot, this time of the photograph itself. A gray, flat, constricted composition of the lifeguard's stand.

Early in *The Goalie's Anxiety at the Penalty Kick*, Bloch goes to a hotel room after leaving his football team. He plays with a television set at the reception desk, and some time passes before he can get an image. When he does, it's a replay of the goal he missed just before he left his team. Rather than dwell on his reaction to this, there is a cut covering a change in time and space to Bloch in his hotel room. The camera is behind him and drifts past him to the window he looks out of. In this instance, Wenders plays with certain modernist structures of disconnection that deny or prevent coherent comprehension of character. During the opening sequence of *Alice in the Cities*, however, the character is constructed quite coherently through the most conventional of means, the shot–reverse shot, which always has the effect of sealing up the psychological space between the character and the viewer within the narrative space of the film.[9] The result is that even though the opening shots and the image of the lone figure taking Polaroids of a vacant beach express a lurking anguish, they do not allow the viewer to fall into any easy alienation, and they most certainly do not allow the anguish to saturate the mise-en-scène.

Wenders, from the very start of the film, works both mise-en-scène and a cutting pattern that will construct a dialectic of conventional and modernist techniques, of identification and alienation, of a character who is comprehensible and attractive to the viewer (if not to himself), and of change within a world that seems, at first, unchangeable. He constructs a narrative that leads somewhere, that establishes a search that proposes a purposeful end. It does not lead to the closure and equipoise of classical Hollywood cinema (this doesn't happen until *Wings of Desire*), but to a point of alteration, to a moment when, if not resolved or even concluded, narrative events and the characters created within and by them point out that something different might happen. This possibility of change is indicated in the very shot–reverse shot cutting of *Alice's* opening sequence. By noting Philip's reaction to his own photograph – he smiles very slightly and sings, revealing that he is not in total despair – by simply showing that he is reacting, Wenders gestures to the viewer. Modernist practice rarely makes such gestures, forcing distance and requesting that meaning be weaved from a play of signifiers with little assistance from conventional cinematic or cultural codes. Here the viewer is permitted to share not only the character's gaze, but some comprehension of his emotional state. There is no great expression of emotion, and that "state" is not a convention-driven response. Philip looks at his photo and begins singing (in English) the pop tune lyrics "Under the boardwalk / Down by the sea / Sitting with my baby / That's where I wanna be." He raises his head and smiles. There is a wider, higher shot, he picks up his photos, puts his bag over his shoulder, and walks under the boardwalk (into the rear of the composition) to the street.

The invitation to respond to the character made by the film's cutting continuity and the character's own reactions indicate that – unlike Bloch in *Goalie* – the character is able to recognize and accept who he is. His picture taking and his singing act as a doubling mechanism. He is comfortably situated within the narrative and, by an extranarrative gesture of ironic self-reflection, placed outside of the narrative as well. The viewer is asked to share the gesture, or at least to receive it, and this has a softening effect. Identification with the character is replaced by collaboration with the filmmaker and his creation, and modernist irony is assuaged by pleasure at the recognition of the character's own ironic self-awareness.

The character's sense of his own solitude is tempered as well. His self-possession is constructed by acts of mutual recognition, by precise allusive gestures, ironic self-reflections, and a generosity that allows a comfortable space to develop between character, narrative, and viewer – a space of introspection without coldness, hysteria, or self-pity. The narrative continues presenting Philip as a potentially depressive figure, alone in a foreign, empty landscape. His attempts at human interaction seem futile: his New York editor yells at him for not turning in his work (he is a magazine photographer); a woman friend in New York refuses him room and comfort, hopelessly attempting to reveal to him the fruits of his withdrawal and inability to make commitments. As he is ready to leave the country for Germany, he meets another woman who leaves him her daughter to take back to Europe. The film, at this point, threatens to assume quite conventional status, as Philip and Alice attempt to make their way home. But the episodic structure, the ironies of the exiled man turned into maternal figure to a little girl, the persistent movement along the roads of the western part of Germany, diffuse the ordinariness of the narrative, as does the barely stated sexual tension between the young man and the little girl.

Image and reality, ersatz father and child: Philip Winter and Alice in *Alice in the Cities*.

This tension is diffused whenever it threatens. Children's sexuality (indeed any sexuality) is something of a moot and repressed point for Wenders, who sees in childhood a site for his character's salvation. Alice's function in the film is to give Philip a narrative to follow in his search for his own homeland. Assuming the role of a substitute parent, he travels with her through the country, seeking to match the houses they see with the photograph of the house Alice carries with her. Given a story, Philip has direction; given a new role, Philip also has purpose; with direction and purpose, Philip is relieved of his obsessive introspection. He is, in effect, put into a state of grace by the child, who offers him redemption.

For Wenders, children are key elements of retrieval and recognition. They retrieve his adult characters from local despair and, through their presence, permit them to recognize probabilities of change. They are open, rather than simply innocent, and more responsive to the world. They contain the energy as well as the emotional and linguistic freedom the adult characters lack. Their intelligence and self-awareness are qualities they share with the children in Truffaut's films. (*Wings of Desire,* in which the central adult figure is a child by virtue of his angelic nature, is dedicated in part to Truffaut.) Not given to despair, Wenders' children are able to filter out the despair of the adult figures. They provide stories and images that offer respite to fatigue and ennui. Living in an immediacy of perception, with a sense of ownership and ease in their experience of the world, they provide an anchor for the adult characters, who are unmoored or too obsessive to yield their subjectivity. Existing in the fullness of the imaginary realm, in a pre-oedipal state, they offer by their very presence guidance to adults who are on the rim of experience. In an almost Wordsworthian sense, the Wenders child represents the richness and immediacy of being, where connection rather than fragmentation prevails.

In *Kings of the Road*, for example, Robert and Bruno are twice offered by children an opportunity to look beyond their individual sadnesses. In the first instance, they stop to repair a broken loudspeaker in a movie house where some schoolchildren are gathered for a morning's entertainment. The lights behind the screen where they work suddenly go on and cast their shadows on the screen for the audience to see. Realizing their sudden public presence, they begin with childlike abandon to do a slapstick routine, making, in effect, a silent movie for the delight of the children. This moment of spontaneity and pleasure is constrained only by the appearance of a rope tied like a hangman's noose, entering the frame as a reminder of frustrations and despairs shared by the two men. But their ability to entertain and the delighted reception of that entertainment overcome the mark of despair. They make an imaginary cinema, and since cinema is itself an imaginary realm — a realm of images — they are making cinema twice over. For Wenders, this is a kind of paradise, somewhat tainted, but agreeable — all the more so in that it joins the two adults and their audience on the other side of the screen. The oedipal shell is not breached — the adults remain separated from the children — but the connection is made tangible through their reinvention of cinema as mediator of desire and pleasure.

Near the end of the film, Robert encounters a child at a railroad stop. The sequence is one of a series of narrative climaxes in which the two main characters succeed in breaking from each other, regaining some subjective power, enabling themselves and each other to go off slightly changed by their encounters. Robert is a linguist of childhood speech. (Early in the film he pulls out a book entitled *Enfance aliénée* [*Alienated Childhood*], a title that indicates the kind of work he studies and the kind of position he is in and that also refers back to the child in *The Goalie's Anxiety at the Penalty Kick,* a mute murdered in the countryside where Josef Bloch wanders.)[10] He stands in awe of the directness and simplicity of that speech and this particular child's ability to connect signifier and signified in apparent innocence of

Seeing, language, and being: the child philosopher and Robert Lander, the linguist of childhood language in *Kings of the Road*.

the complexities of cultural interference between word and the thing the word is supposed to represent. Many of Wenders' adult characters – most especially Travis in *Paris, Texas* – are struck to the point of dumbness by the treacherous slippages of verbal communication, the uncertainties occurring between the spaces of intent, language, and meaning. But the child, and especially this child at the railroad station, is aware of no treachery or danger. He simply beholds the world and writes a description of it, trusting fully in the authenticity of his perceptions.

In a series of powerful one-shots – Robert and the child, each in close-up, with the spaces of the rural landscape bright and in deep focus behind them (a man rides a bike in the distance, the sound track is punctuated with the barking of a dog) – the child describes the things Robert shows him or points to, referring to him in the third person, solidly recognizing his objective existence. "A man with a suitcase, an empty suitcase, a grin, a black eye, a fist, throwing a stone. . . ." "As easy as that?" Robert asks. "That easy," the child responds. Robert offers his sunglasses and suitcase for the child's notebook. "A good deal," the child says.

The tensions and resolutions offered by the sequence are subtle and moving. Robert, his eye blackened from a fist fight with Bruno the night before, feels ready to leave his brief respite from domesticity and responsibility and return to his life. The train station and the open country around it offer visual expression to his own ambivalent sense of purpose. Like many another of Wenders' wanderers, he remains – no matter how ready to move – stalled in the very place of movement, the railroad station. The child, seated comfortably, secure in his place as he is in his perceptions, cheerfully welcoming the stranger, offering him the security of unquestioned and innocent linguistic power, is a momentary center weight for his ambivalence. Robert, coming out of a state of extreme dissociation, is eager to make a trade for the child's ease and delight. The child is pleased to receive Robert's useless baggage; Robert is happy with the notebook – though with it he gets only the child's written words, not his prelapsarian ability to enjoy unmediated language and the simple relationship of word and thing, of language and being.

Wenders is willing to allow this simplicity to all his child characters, who remain for the while unhurt by the world and able emotionally to support the adults who surround them. Jonathan's son, Daniel, in *The American Friend* and Friedrich's children in *The State of Things* – two films considerably darker than *Alice in the Cities* and *Kings of the Road* – retain their grace even while brought more deeply into the symbolic realm of adulthood (an event that does not hold in *Goalie* or in *Hammett*, whose main characters find no grace and therefore no guiding children). Friedrich's wife notices that her daughters are already seeing the world in patriarchal terms. Looking at snapshots they've taken, she remarks how they have framed out the women and given the male figures centrality in the composition. But even as they become marked by gender, they are still able to exercise an innocently joyful perspective. They remain untouched by the despair of the film crew around them and their father's increasing obsessiveness with completing his work. When last seen, they form an amused audience to their parents' joyless lovemaking. They watch without shock or disapproval at a ritual without feeling. While the film spends no time considering the relationship between the children and their parents, their presence acts as a kind of counterbalance to the depressive scene around them. In "The Survivors" – the postapocalyptic film-within-a-film that the film crew in *The State of Things* is making – the children emerge as figures of hope for the future, playing out the redemptive role Wenders so often assigns them.

Jonathan's son in *The American Friend* has a more passive role, forming the point around which his father turns as he attempts to exit the domestic

55

Hommage à cinéma: Buster Keaton's *The General* as a luminous lampshade in *The American Friend.*

sphere. He has surrounded the child with signifiers of movement and cinematic fantasy: a lamp shade that has a picture of a railroad engine (*The General,* from Buster Keaton's film) and a model tram that runs across the child's bedroom. Jonathan always hits his head on it when he is in the room, as if the objects of childlike escape are a hindrance or even danger to him. His wife and son offer him the security of ordinary life but represent its duties and dangers as well: responsibility, boredom, routine, isolation – like the family in a fifties American gangster melodrama. Jonathan offers himself as a "son" to Ripley, who guides him into a world of murder and adventure. Here the adult male characters perform a less than innocent attempt to become children, to engage in play that turns destructive and immoral.

Hunter, Travis's son in *Paris, Texas,* plays a much more active role than Daniel. But the oedipal trajectory in this film and the child's place in it becomes strangely distorted. Travis is seen first as a child, inarticulate and withdrawn into an almost autistic state. He is a character ruined by the terrors of uncontrolled domestic violence, a modern-day Ethan Edwards who does not have the wilderness to contain his madness. His son takes up the role of father to his father, guiding him on the road to adult perception and action. He takes him from anomie and despair, helps restore his memories of a violent past, and guides him finally to a confrontation with his wife. Hunter is the most transformative figure in Wenders' films. With a persistence and calmness only available to the idealized and idolized figure of the child redeemer, he reverses an adult's despair and begins reconstituting domestic structures by enabling the father to become a healer of patriarchal wounds.

Hunter is also the most conventional of Wenders' children, most like the old Hollywood image of the adult in a small body. At the same time, he is a kind of unworldly emanation of the cinematic fantasy that envisions the child as angelic intercessor. There is small wonder, in retrospect, that in his next film, *Wings of Desire,* Wenders would go straight to the angels themselves, attempting to redeem childhood in a literal passage from eternal innocence to human experience. Jonathan's son in *The American Friend* is named Daniel. The angel played by Bruno Ganz, who played Jonathan, is named Damiel. He is adult and child in one figure, embodying two phases of a dialectic of innocence and experience, fathering his own childhood and, as an adult child, preparing himself for adulthood.

Wenders' characters are propelled by a complex personal, cultural, and historical unease, which they attempt to counter through physical motion and uncertain companionship. The narratives that construct them do not, by and large, allow self-pity or even massive acts of self-examination. Rather, they permit the characters to play out their despair by passing through the signifiers of modernity: the road and its isolated communities. Unlike classical road movies, Wenders' characters find no solace or completion, or any real end to their quest. In some of the films, there are moments of mute recognition and, in *Wings of Desire,* an opportunity offered to satisfy desire through the formation of the romantic couple. But even the romantic tumescence that ends this film does not spill fully into melodramatic closure. The film ends with a title, "To Be Continued," that, for all its banality, still offers more hope than the films that came before. That hope seems somewhat abandoned in *Until the End of the World,* where the attempt to confront childhood becomes a threat to sanity and redemption seems possible only if one literally leaves the world. The film ends with Claire in outer space! However, in space Claire celebrates her birthday, the feared-for apocalypse never comes, and the film ends with a sense of new, if whimsical, possibilities.

Wenders' major works are all gestures of continuation. Small acts of transition, episodic narratives in which characters advance and retreat, seen amid strange and touching bits of highway rubble, composed against passing trains and road signs – they stand themselves as road signs of a composite roadside culture, historyless and rootless. Through these signifiers of modernity, Wenders posits the child as a figure of hope and promise.

Wenders' children, neither tabulae rasae nor – save for a few exceptions – miniature adults in the classical Hollywood mold, represent the self-possession and security his adult characters must work toward repossessing or keep from losing as they make their way in the symbolic realm of the inchoate world

Contemporary anti-establishment politics entering Wenders' cinematic space: "BRD [West Germany] = Police State," scrawled on a wall in *The American Friend*.

around them. The child figures as a point of certainty – oblivious, self-sufficient, and innocent of history. The burden of that history, which, in Germany, forces amnesia, makes the loss of innocence inevitable and breaks up a sense of completed adult subjectivity. The marks of the fissures and torments in modern German history cut into the adult consciousness and make the adult world numbing and indescribable. The marks appear in Wenders' films – Wilhelm's confrontation with Laertes, an old Nazi, in *Wrong Move;* the Berlin Wall, omnipresent in *Wings of Desire;* Bruno's confrontation with an old cinema owner who can no longer even remember the initials of the National Socialist Party; the graffito "West Germany = Police State" near Jonathan Zimmermann's apartment building in Hamburg. One cannot talk of words and things and the comfort of images. All comforts are compromised and no meanings are securely, authentically attached to words. Not so for the children, for whom gesture, word, and thing remain whole, for whom history is irrelevant, and for whom the act of simple description constitutes a statement of power. The child, for the moment, is king of the domain – the adults, kings of the road.

3
Kings of the Road
Motion and Emotion

Wenders' films explore the movements of his characters, in the course of time and across the expanse of the road, as they search for self and a usable identity. Their wanderings follow their desire to encounter experiences that may deliver them from exile and bring them to a reconciliation with the inexorable condition of their solitude. Whether the exile is forced upon them or self-imposed, these characters inhabit their journeys, comfortable and with assurance, as if their quest were a laying claim to the existential reward of a secure position in an adult world. They put themselves in a transient state, choosing an itinerary or subjecting themselves to whatever might come along (a state Wenders himself often claims for his filmmaking when he insists, as he does for *Kings of the Road,* that the narrative was made up on the road as the film was being shot). In their transience, they yield to the inevitable or struggle against it in a curious combination of passivity and motivation, inertia and energy.

To some degree, these figures are small reflections of the travelers of myth, sent on odysseys seemingly as unending as their yearning for an arrival. But unlike the wanderers of mythology, they are driven less by the detached movements of fate as by the drives and uncertainties of contemporary culture and its disquieting legacies of the past. And in their reduced state, they bear similarities to the contemplative figures of eighteenth- and nineteenth-century fiction imported into the image-bound postwar world. (Handke and Wenders based *Wrong Move* on Goethe's *Wilhelm Meister's Apprenticeship,* the bildungsroman that set up the paradigm of the middle-class hero in search of an identity.) These are figures of sensibility and desire, informed by literary models but given form by cinema. They exist by virtue of the gaze, their own and ours. The narratives of myth and literature give way to the restructuring of cinema, the art of the visible in a divisible world. The gram-

59

Wenders' central image: on the road, from *Kings of the Road.*

mar of fixity and motion, of movement within a determining mise-en-scène that constitutes cinema, also constitutes the lives of these figures. They are our image and they depend on images. The image on the screen sets our horizon; we gaze at them as they attempt to fix their diminishing horizons with a photograph placed in front of them on the windshields of their cars. Underlying the release of movement is the desire for stasis; the propulsion of narrative is entertained only because it promises closure and rest. Wenders' wanderers turn into moving subjects who seek arrival and delivery from their journeys of exile and freedom. The viewer (a static subject) follows their trajectory and examines the images that give them existence, seeking rest (as do the characters), but charged, even more than they, by interpreting the characters' stories, reading their images, rendering the horizon articulate.

This interaction of viewer and text is, in Wenders' films especially, a prolonged, interdependent process. The movement of style and theme is consistent, as if each work were part of the director's life process and the viewer's assent to that process. Near the beginning of *Wrong Move*, Wilhelm, a repressed, directionless, and quite likely untalented would-be writer, burns with desire to leave home. He smashes his bedroom window with his bare fist, bicycles to the beach, and gazes at the empty seashore, looking especially at a house on stilts on the beach that blocks the expanse. The composition of that house is similar to the one of the lifeguard stand on the beach that Philip photographs at the beginning of *Alice in the Cities.* Wilhelm walks the streets at night. He visits his girlfriend, Janine, in front of a motion picture theater projection booth. Janine is played by Lisa Kreuzer, who will show up as the ticket seller at the cinema in *Kings of the Road* and later as Jonathan Zimmermann's wife in *The American Friend.* After a brief, apparently pointless interchange between the two, Wenders cuts to a shot of a large ship moving through the water, the camera sweeping around its hull, and then dissolves back to Wilhelm, asleep and talking. He murmurs, "Im Lauf der Zeit" ("in the course of time"), the title of the film Wenders will make after *Wrong Move* (and that will be called, in English, *Kings of the Road).*

At the end of the film — all his wanderings, romances, political discoveries, and disappointments unable to bring him to the point of writing — Wilhelm, more willing to create a mise-en-scène for himself than do the actual work of creation, goes to a mountaintop where he assumes the pose of a typical figure in the paintings of Caspar David Friedrich (1774–1840) — the lonely romantic seer, facing the distance, his back turned to the viewer. Still disappointed (it's not snowing as he had hoped it would; his fantasy mise-en-scène is still incomplete), he looks out and says, in voice-over, that he cannot find the proper experiences he needs, cannot make the right move. The film leaves him there, stranded, unable to transcend his petty self-obsessiveness, gazing, his back turned on the viewer who shares with him the look at the great expanse of the snowy mountain tops.

"I was completely satisfied with Rüdiger's performance in the film," Wenders says. Rüdiger Vogler plays Wilhelm in *Wrong Move,* Philip in *Alice in the Cities,* Bruno in *Kings of the Road,* and shows up in a small role in *The Goalie's Anxiety at the Penalty Kick, Until the End of the World,* and in Peter Handke's 1978 film, *The Left-Handed Woman,* an imago of the Wenders–Handke sensibility. "But," Wenders continues, "I wasn't completely satisfied with the image people connected with him afterwards, as the introvert. That's one of the reasons I decided to make *Kings of the Road:* I didn't want to leave him up there on the mountain top."[1]

It is certainly not unusual for a director to see his or her work as prolonged narrative, variously articulated, with the characters moving in and around, changed and shifted by the variations on the basic themes and patterns. Jean Renoir said that a director simply makes one long film

Men on the road: dying or in desperation, from *Same Player Shoots Again* (*above*) and *Kings of the Road* (*facing page*).

throughout his or her career. Neither is it unusual for a filmmaker to use one actor to play various representations of a single type from one film to another. (Think of the ways in which John Ford used John Wayne or Martin Scorsese, Robert De Niro.) What is unusual is Wenders' ironic stance toward his own text, his ability simultaneously to embed himself in his films and to objectify them, to speak of his characters as if they had actual life in real space and time, while consciously manipulating them and voicing concern about the viewer's response to their behavior. Wenders' auteurism shows signs of a particularly intense involvement in his characters as if they were acting out vital concerns of his own, as if the films were somehow long photo albums of the filmmaker's desires in the course of time.

Unusual too is the way Wenders generates one film out of another. Perhaps he had no idea that the sleep murmurs of a character in one film would become the title of the next. But the evolution of Wenders' filmmaking and the interrelatedness of the individual films give evidence that he works from a principle of linkage. He links not only each film with its predecessor and successor, but the audience's perceptions of the character, the structure of the character himself, his own life experience and how it can be cinematically validated, and the narrative and visual style. "Im Lauf der Zeit," the words

Wilhelm murmurs in his sleep, is perhaps the film dreamed by Wilhelm, and in turning it into *Im Lauf der Zeit*, the movie, Wenders is reconsidering his own dream of Wilhelm and remaking his character. *Kings of the Road* is, on one level, a disputation with *Wrong Move* and *The Goalie's Anxiety at the Penalty Kick*. It is, at the same time, an attempt to rethink, rework, and extend the student films and *Alice in the Cities*. It is an act of recuperation of the road, with a change in travel plans and a new sense of being on the move. *Goalie* and *Wrong Move* suffer (perhaps because of the collaboration with Handke on both works) from an overly intense and self-obsessed subjectivity, which fails to attain clarification or satisfaction of desire. *Kings of the Road* recoups a more defined subjectivity of the traveler – the self-contained searcher – whose movements combine personal and cultural history in a quest for place and peace.

Kings of the Road also consummates a style, a method of inflecting significant form in such a way that configurations and repetitions of structure consolidate into a distinct pattern, which marks the work with signs of the recognizable. Through repetition and coherent signification, style inscribes the author into the work and the work into the viewer's consciousness. Images and narrative are charged with reliability and with the meaning that is born of consistency and, in Wenders' case, of authenticity. They become marked with personality, insofar as personality is signified by repeated, recognizable, meaningful indicators of coherent thought and emotion. This coherency is *discoverable* through critical analysis; it must be accounted for and observed, and its process charted as an important meaning-making element of a filmmaker's work.[2]

The image of the driver on the road is, as we have been saying, central to Wenders from his earliest work. The repetition of the image turns it into a key representation that gathers up the filmmaker's obsessive concerns with restlessness, isolation, and cultural uprootedness counterbalanced with the yearning for refuge, self-containment, and rebellion. *Kings of the Road* raises this representation to the level of cultural and subjective symbol. With the wanderings and adventures of Bruno Winter and Robert Lander, Wenders forms major cultural signifiers out of the instabilities of postwar German politics, the uncertainties of postwar German intellectuals, and the collapse of cinema. By situating these events in a geopolitical area both significant and peripheral (at least in 1976) – the countryside and marginal small towns along the East German border – he further expands and enriches the representation. The concept of frontier – and it is very much a "concept" for Wenders as he does not directly deal with politics, geo- or otherwise – not only alludes to the realpolitik of Germany in the seventies, but to the frontier of the American Western. It is as if the closest thing to the borderline of civilization conventionalized by the American West was the border dividing the two Germanies. But this frontier is restrictive and bounding, and the two riders do not find new lands as much as they discover new uses for the past. This is a frontier back into history, not out of it. It does not represent a myth of expansion, but of contraction and denial, understanding and self-realization.

Contraction and denial are also present through another referent indicated by the small towns and their provincial inhabitants. They allude to the locations and conventions of the German *Heimatfilm*, the popular, reactionary genre that evades contemporary realities with idyllic images of rural simplicity. The travelers in *Kings of the Road* attempt to reclaim their place in *Heimat*, to discover in its banalities their own roots and ways of understanding the past. By moving through the country, they discover ways of getting out, knowing more, but evading less. They are very much like the travelers of the ultimate late-sixties American male-bonding road movie, *Easy Rider*, a major influence on *Kings of the Road*, and one that helps Wenders link the myths of the American West, the politics of the sixties, and the personal quest for identity and place. He manages to transfer the energy and dynamics of the Hopper–Fonda film, while avoiding its superficiality and self-adulation.

In its time, *Easy Rider* was a major countercultural statement: a self-satisfied cry against the dominant ideology and a self-pitying acknowledgment that it could not be overcome. Like all American road movies, it was an attempt to find images of release and freedom, held in check by familiar objects and the built-in confines of the road. *Easy Rider* conjoins these contradictions with the rock music Wenders finds irresistible, and so it stands for him as a cultural monument. The fact that it is also propelled by an oedipal narrative, a rebellious movement against the patriarchy, makes it more useful still. However, the oedipal trajectory of the road movie affirms, finally, the very status quo its characters attempt to escape. Whether in *Easy Rider*, Fritz Lang's 1937 road movie *You Only Live Once*, Arthur Penn's *Bonnie and Clyde* (1967), or Ray's *The Lusty Men*, the attempt to escape the law of the father results in the death of the rebelling child. Wenders' road movies attempt, for a while, at least, to point further down the road to a place where the status quo might be successfully challenged, where a new father figure might be established in an altered patriarchy.

All of the narrative and generic structures that infiltrate and influence *Kings of the Road* – each one complex and rich in political, cultural, aesthetic, and psychological ramifications – are articulated through a precise and felicitous mise-en-scène. *Kings of the Road* is, beyond all the other elements just listed, a film about space and movement, motion and emotion. In the tradition of Welles, Ray, Antonioni, Godard, Bertolucci, Ozu, and Tarkovsky, Wenders creates a work whose intensity and emotion emerge from the construction of figures in a landscape, from the way his characters' search for self is placed, composed, and observed within images that articulate states of mind and place.

In the school films, the fragmented images of people riding in cars and walking streets lacked continuity and spatial articulation. Disengaged from story, these films indulge in relentless motion, a lack of finality within a lack of coherence. They are driven by a haunted sense of movement that forces their characters to wander about and strive for self-possession while, at the same time, being unable to overcome a prevailing sense of alienation. This alien self is situated in the collapse of spatial connectedness, as the elusiveness of time and the anxiety of motion suspends the notion of identity. *The Goalie's Anxiety at the Penalty Kick* extends all of this by experimenting with the spatial components of point of view, often replacing conventional continuity of perception with a cut or camera movement that indicates the central character's inability to connect an absent subjectivity with an arbitrary – and on his part, unwanted – objectivity. World and self slide by each other. In the subsequent films, this exercise in spatial incongruity will prove less desirable to Wenders than a more complex effort to differentiate the viewer's point of view from that of the characters, and to compose them in large, defining landscapes that call for comprehension and emotional response. Rather than indicate the disorientation of the characters through cutting, he chooses to establish their potential coherence through developing an enticing mise-en-scène that entreats the viewer to perform an act of perceptual and narrative integration.

Alice in the Cities, the film that initiates the visual and narrative style of *Kings of the Road,* extends the spatial functions of the school films. The film searches for the right image, the right space in which the characters might dwell. Starting as drifters and wanderers, Philip and Alice become searchers, looking for the house of Alice's grandmother. The search is based on a photograph the child owns. Propped up on the windshield, it is the still point in their movement. (A similar photograph is on the dashboard of Robert's car at the beginning of *Kings of the Road,* as if one character had dissolved into the other in the subsequent film.) At a climactic moment, a house they find matches up perfectly with the photograph, but image and reality do not converge, for Philip and Alice discover that the grandmother, the major person representing family and childhood security for Alice, has moved. While the images are untrustworthy substitutes for reality, they are the only things available most of the time. Wenders' characters will, time and again, make images, hold onto them, and search for the reality they depict. The picture of grandmother's house proved to be a disappointment insofar as its reproduction of the actual house could not satisfy the characters' desire to find the person formerly housed in this "real" building. Yet Alice and Philip continue their search, which is given new purpose by a policeman's information that the grandmother is now living in Munich. In the last shot of the film, they are in a train heading toward that city. In *Paris, Texas,* memory of Travis' childhood is, at first, available only through a photograph: a fuzzy color snapshot of a barren piece of land with a barely legible sign posted on it, which serves as a point of departure for Travis' recollections of his past. The photograph is of a piece of property purchased by his father. Here there isn't even the image of a house, merely geographic space that has to be filled in. (Later in the film, Travis' immediate past and lost domesticity are represented in the wobbly, faded images of 8mm home movies.)

While Wenders' characters use photographs of themselves as a means of freezing their identity, here the photographs are attempts to hypostatize space that exists other than in the cinematic space the characters inhabit. Photographs represent the space of memory, with which the characters attempt to define themselves, their past, or present. But despite their apparent ability to retrieve a sure reality, the photographs provide only an illusion of a space already known – or not known. "In reality," the photographs are visual inventions as are all the other images, still and moving, in the films. Within the narratives, they function for the characters as the film itself does for the viewer – triggering memory and desire, setting character and viewer on a search for meaning within the familiar and unfamiliar: "All images are polysemous," Roland Barthes writes; "they imply, underlying their signifiers, a 'floating chain' of signifieds. . . . Polysemy poses a question of meaning and this question always comes through as a dysfunction."[3] Wenders' characters turn to photographs as a way to heal dysfunction. But they usually succeed only in creating greater dysfunction, relying on images whose relation to reality is slippery, illusive, and allusive. The main photographic space – the film itself – that the characters inhabit is also allusive, though somewhat less slippery. The film and the narrative it creates has an immediate presence – for the viewer if not for the characters, who rarely acknowledge they are only a function of the film. The filmic image has an allusive function as well, calling upon other films, referring to other images, confirming intertextuality through the fact that the memory of cinema is cinema itself.[4] Through allusion, iteration and significance, continuity and coherence, the filmic-narrative space establishes notions of reality, of the immediately seen and the apparently comprehended. Though the polysemy of meaning remains, memory becomes presence. As Barthes says, "The *having-been-there* gives way before a *being-there* of the thing."[5]

This presence, or "being-there," of the narrative image is true, of course, of all narrative films. Wenders, however, articulates his cinematic space so that both characters and things stand in a relation one to another that is both immediate and tentative. They stand in a state of relative isolation, exhibiting an estrangement that is filled with longing and desire. The erotics of the gaze allows Wenders to create a space in which the characters are defined by what they do not have but wish to see, where they were and wish to return, what they recall and where they wish to go. The viewer's desire is to see with the characters and beyond, for we see not only the characters, but their surroundings; we see the characters in ways the characters can never see themselves. Despite this, the engagement is lacking in finality. Wenders allows viewer and character only limited vision. Each searches for a consummation of the spatial and emotional dynamics set up by the film that remain resolutely incomplete and, therefore, each is filled with the desire for completion and the pleasure of completion withheld.

The episodic structure of *Kings of the Road* visualizes the interaction of motion and emotion. From the concrete images that make up the narrative, an emotional intensity is produced that resonates beyond the adventures of

Bruno and Robert on the road along the border. When they are in motion, Bruno and Robert are largely transfixed and relatively uninvolved. When they are at rest, they become introspective. When fixed in space, they move inward. At the beginning of their first night together, Bruno pulls his enormous truck – which serves as transportation, home, projector repair shop, and warehouse – off the road. Robert leaves the truck to contemplate the railroad tracks outside. Bruno is in the cab, alone, impassive as he most often is, still not responding to the presence of a companion. Robert moves to the front of the truck, standing in profile, as Bruno and the illuminated figure of the Michelin Man (who is attached outside the cab above Bruno) are in soft focus behind him. Robert walks toward the misty landscape and there is a cut back to Bruno in the truck, rubbing his face, now looking tired and spent. Another cut reveals Robert, looking as a train roars by. (We do not see the train until the camera pans left, somewhat skewing the point of view: the train is passing by Robert's left side, rather than directly in front of him.) Robert, in an action reminiscent of the childhood game of placing a coin on the train track, picks up an object run over by the train, tossing it from hand to hand, staring at it, and returns to the truck. These are idle moments, pieces of dead time, in which the characters keep to themselves.

The next cut elides time: both men lie in bunk beds inside the truck. Bruno is illuminated below, while Robert lies in darkness above him. Bruno reads William Faulkner's *The Wild Palms* in English. He asks Robert what a loon is. "Crazy person," Robert answers in English. There is a pause, and Bruno responds that it doesn't make sense. There is a cut to a shot outside, of the moon over a stand of trees in the darkness. The image is no one's point of view, but rather a decision on Wenders' part to complement visually the interaction of the two men and the prose that Bruno begins to read: "There was a grey light on the lake. And when he heard the loon, he knew exactly what it was. Listening to the raucous idiot voice . . ." Midway through the reading, Robert turns and looks out the window. A shot from Robert's point of view pans a train going past silently in the night. Over this shot, Robert explains in German that the word means a bird, a diving bird. On the shot of the train, the scene fades to black.

Unlike the preceding moments of solitude, this passage cradles both characters and viewer in a different kind of isolation. It is characteristic of Wenders at his most precise, counterpointing the stillness of the figures with the movement of the train and the more subtle movement of cultures and languages through the Faulkner novel. As the characters approach a moment of tentative proximity, for the first time in the narrative, Wenders alludes to the natural world (the moon over the trees) as a protective and harmonious

Men in limbo: Robert and Bruno "being their stories" in *Kings of the Road.*

presence, suspending the sense of exile so pervasive at other times. The montage is an homage to Yasujiro Ozu, whose films Wenders was just beginning to absorb. Ozu's films are continually punctuated with shots of natural and man-made objects – rocks, trees, trains, roof tops – that counter the lives of his characters with images of stasis and movement, comfort and yearning. They express an ultimate, or promised, or hoped-for tranquility and ongoingness that the characters within the narrative may themselves be unaware of. Here the montage of sky and train further enlarges the space embraced by *Kings of the Road,* a film in which cinematic allusion and cultural layering illuminate the characters' isolation and at the same time point to the potentials of redemption, of reconnection in a secure place.

Bruno and Robert, like all of Wenders' characters, are men in limbo, at a point of personal, cultural, indeed existential crisis. But crisis does not necessarily mean melodrama, contrary to what American film insists. American melodrama's interior mise-en-scène of anguish, desire, frustration, sacrifice, and collapse played out in an external domestic scene of family dynamics gone awry has long since substituted for more ordinary forms of doubt and change and, more important, for alternative methods of cinematic perceptions.[6] Wenders moves the gaze from the internal psychology of his characters to their physical and cultural environment. While sometimes concerned with domesticity (rarely in the early films, almost exclusively in the later), he often places the domestic scene within a larger context. More accurately, context, environment, character, and movement become inextricable. His characters suffer through crises of being-in-the-world, in an almost Sartrean sense. Carrying the burden of existence, they are figures of history and culture, seeking ways to carry that burden.* Subject and object, in Wenders' films, intersect at a radical level, at a more basic point than allegory and on a more complex level than symbolism. They exist on the level of *being seen* and are defined by the way they are seen. In constant movement, restless, in despair or fleeing from or to something, these characters are measured by our looking at them. Their own introspection is usually mute (certainly in the films up to *Paris, Texas;* in that film as well as *Wings of Desire* and *Until the End of the World,* they begin to talk more fluently and frequently, though their communication is perhaps not as successful as in the previous films). Eloquence and feeling become a function of perception.

On their second day together, Bruno and Robert approach a kind of intimacy and are frightened by it. They experience a moment of freedom, by becoming cinema, in the rear-screen pantomime they put on for the children. The transmutation of introspection into cinematic spectacle liberates the two men − at least until they are finished, sitting on the floor, noticing a rope tied like a hangman's noose swing passed each of them. The children, easily accepting the spectacle without consciousness of its artifice, honor it with their laughter. Later in the day, however, the incident wears on the men − on Bruno in particular. He is unhappy at the way he was *seen.* Standing by a roadside sausage kiosk (an old van painted white in the middle of a field by the road, like something in a Walker Evans photograph − another intercultural, visual allusion), he tells Robert that he was uncomfortable at the way Robert stood above and looked at him. He felt angry and helpless. Robert tells him he felt the same way, and Bruno cannot quite manage the shared response. "Cut it out!" he yells angrily at Robert, defending his isolation against the intimacy that Robert's gaze threatens, against the childlike openness they both displayed in the movie house.

Once back in the truck, Wenders composes them in a two-shot inside the

---

* In an almost too obvious existential allusion, Wenders has Robert suffer a nausea and sickness unto death. In a pause on the road, early in their relationship, Robert and Bruno go into the washroom of the VW plant in Wolfsburg. Robert is in despair − indeed he has just tried to commit suicide. He smells his old, rank clothing and throws up in the basin.

Reinventing cinema: Bruno and Robert perform slapstick to entertain the children, from *Kings of the Road*.

cab. The shot contrasts with the previous one in front of the sausage van. There, physical stasis was a backdrop to tentative emotional movement. Here, physically in motion, they only look straight ahead, separated from each other by the expanse of the cab itself and the windshield frame between them. When night falls, reflections of highway lights slash across Bruno's side of the window; reflections of trees across Robert's. Bruno begins to inquire about Robert, who starts to tell his story: he is a pediatrician (we later learn that he is actually a psycholinguist who studies language acquisition in children) and left his wife in Genoa. Bruno is impatient with this. "I want to know who you are," he insists. "I am my story," Robert responds.

The pretentiousness of the remark is undercut by Wenders. Before Robert says these words, Wenders cuts to a shot of the Michelin Tire Man attached to the front of the truck's cab. The sudden appearance of the glowing, jolly, unchanging advertising figure serves to reduce Robert's evasive overstatement, and at the same time, as a reference point – similar to the trees and passing train in the earlier montage, or the moon and clouds seen through the truck's skylight later in this sequence – it deflects our concentration, widens the spatial context, defuses the moment. Robert's story – at this point at least – is his life with Bruno, traveling the border country, attempting to escape his past and establish his present. Story and image, as we have seen, are Wenders' essential concerns, and the banality of the advertising logo (as well as Robert's remark) is transformed into the existential surround of his travelers' quest. Robert and Bruno are indeed their stories. They exist only as they are seen in action, only as they are *told* by Wenders' film. Their quest to authorize, indeed to justify, themselves is their existence. "Stories only exist in stories," says Friedrich, the film director, in *The State of Things*. Friedrich attempts to escape storytelling, and it costs him his life. The fictional character and its creator simply cannot exist without the drive of narrative, event, and change. Bruno and Robert work themselves into narrative.

Their story is their drive out of stasis. Each experience they face on the road places them back into the center of their unhappiness and mistrust and then permits them to move a bit further on. Robert at first envisions no movement for himself; he wishes to undo the past and dreams of his life as a perpetual rewrite, a continuous act of inscribing his story with a special ink that erases what he has just written. "Dreaming was writing in circles," he says, "until I dreamed up the idea of changing the ink." Robert works to emerge from the abyss of self, to write himself into presence, erasing the past, while still being unable to textualize the future. But even presence proves itself illusory, as the cinematic image attests, for its space is a representation of what was but now exists only as photographic memory: Its inhabitants dream of their creation; their very life is given by the willing or unwilling presence and assent of the film's spectators. Despite the illusion of the being-there of the image, it is, finally, only an image. The narrative of Bruno and Robert promises the immediacy of emotion, the certainty of presence, the offer of change. In actuality, it is a tenuous collection of visualized possibilities, a piecing together of a story in the space, time, and sound of the film. Bruno and Robert are representations of character and history, figured through a series of events that pull them into their own past and the culture's. They move through stages of tranquility and despair, edging toward enlightenment, but always just skirting it. They come from an abyss – the emptiness of nonexistence preceding their creation – the abyss of melancholy opened by each successive encounter.

This *mise-en-abîme* is given a body in the episode that forms the core of the sequence we are discussing – as moving a representation of domestic despair as Wenders has ever created, and as sharp an indication of emotional emptiness as exists in the film. In the middle of the night, Robert is awakened by an insistent noise from the rock quarry where they are parked. He discovers a man at the top of the quarry, sitting in the dark, dropping stones down the metal troughs. (The man is played by Marquard Bohm, one of Rainer Werner Fassbinder's stock players, who brings to the sequence the distressed melancholy and repressed violence of Fassbinder's films.) Invited into the truck, the man tells Robert that his wife killed herself by driving into a tree. In a series of tight closeups – Robert leans against a jukebox stored in back of Bruno's truck; Bruno, awakened by the voice, listens in the darkness; the man sits at the edge of the bed – he tells a disjointed, Handke-like story of a woman driven to death by an existential ennui brought about by the oppression of the domestic. " 'I'm fed up,' " the man recounts his wife's words. " 'Fed up with the bed, the washbasin, the kitchen, the lamp, the painting.' " The smell of the kitchen suddenly drove her to suicide.

She seems to have suffered the very overload of the everyday banal that drove Josef Bloch to murder in *The Goalie's Anxiety at the Penalty Kick* and the domestic fury that drove Travis to chain his wife to the stove, in the story he tells in *Paris, Texas*. In no instance does Wenders actually represent the violent reaction to the ordinary. The spareness of *Goalie* only suggests Bloch's response to his existential disgust. *Kings of the Road* and *Paris, Texas* suggest violence only in verbal language rather than visual images. Wenders is rarely interested in portraying acts of domestic violence, but rather the emotional reaction to it, the grieving of the man responsible for the action; the act of grieving itself is the hopeless act of recuperating the past in a present bereft of the power to change it.

The idea of mourning itself, *Trauerarbeit* – the work of coming to terms with the country's past – has preoccupied many German intellectuals for decades.[7] The representation of mourning in *Kings of the Road* may not point directly to such larger cultural concerns, but the fact that the man who grieves acts to promote the possibility of mourning, of memory, proved by the changes in Robert and Bruno's lives following his visit, indicates that his presence has more than local melodramatic purpose. Mourning cannot change the past but helps to overcome the paralysis the past causes by recognizing it and then ushering it into the present and future. This is what lies at the bottom of the problem of *Trauerarbeit*. The story of the man who grieves has a catalytic power. Like the crazy man on the bridge with whom Travis makes brief contact in *Paris, Texas*, or the good samaritan who bandages Jonathan's cut head in *The American Friend*, he is a point of emotional recognition and – especially in this case – a direction sign to emotional alteration, a way out of the abyss. That is why Robert and Bruno seem to react so little to his story. Robert does not even want to let him stay with them until his wife's car is removed. Bruno, softening on this point, cannot

The difficulty of mourning: the grieving man, production still from *Kings of the Road.*

bear to be in the man's presence and wanders off, climbing a high tower that stands nearby, where, like Wilhelm on his mountain at the end of *Wrong Move,* he escapes to an isolation that gives him the illusion of control.

The apparent indifference of their reactions belies the force the story has on them. In fact, a chain of responses is set in motion that alters their lives. In the middle of the sequence of the grieving man, Robert reads a film magazine, and his attention is drawn to a production still from Jean-Luc Godard's 1964 film *Contempt.* A key figure in the still is Fritz Lang, and it is his image to which Robert returns after the grieving man leaves. He cuts out Lang's image from the magazine. Lang is one of Wim Wenders' own paternal spirits, the ghost of German cinema and the figure who stands for the violence inflicted upon the inheritance of film by postwar Germany. (His image will appear again in a photograph behind the theater owner who proclaims, in the name of her father, the end of cinema in the next-to-last sequence of *Kings of the Road;* Friedrich will visit Lang's footsteps in the Hollywood Walk of Fame in *The State of Things.*)[8] The resonances of the grieving man widen and deepen. Wenders' own consciousness and grief intersect with his

74

characters', creating a wider configuration in which personal history, cultural history, and cinema come together. The echoes of patrimony move from the film's creator to his characters and back out again. The idea of the father and the tension between father and child spread into the fiction so that, when the grieving man leaves, Robert goes to visit his father, a newspaper man in Ostheim. It is another major turning point in the film and marks not only Robert's movement, but the movement of a generation toward confrontation with and resolution of all their fathers have done.

With his decision to visit his father in Ostheim, Robert makes a move toward rediscovery of a self that has been overwhelmed and repressed from childhood by patriarchal structures and by history. From his first encounter with children (before his spectacular entrance into Bruno's life, driving his VW into the river) to the episode with the boy at the railroad station near the end of the film, there is constant movement within Robert to recuperate his damaged childhood, silence the overbearing paternal voice, and go on to develop a new adult sensibility, a respect for women, all within a more supple and responsive patriarchy. This utopian ideal is held in potential within the various decisions Robert makes and the confrontation with his father that he seeks. All of the dangers and uncertainties on the way are symbolized in a gesture he makes before leaving for Ostheim. He walks to the end of a ramp in the quarry that juts over the rocks and into an empty space, unconnected to anything on its other end. It is perhaps an obvious gesture, for with it Wenders calls upon the stylistics of Michelangelo Antonioni to represent his characters facing a void in their lives. Yet it is powerful, and further indicates how Wenders can manipulate the space surrounding his characters and make the interaction eloquent.

The father and son reunion is strained and painful, and almost turns violent. The father is a weak and seemingly broken man. Wenders plays upon our sympathies, allows us momentarily to feel affection for the old man, and then forces us to break that sympathy in order to comprehend who he actually is, what his role is in his son's life, and, symbolically, indeed historically, to expand that role into a generational statement.* Robert must gather as much power as possible to confront this old man. He refuses to allow him to speak. Out of his anger at the way his father diminished him

---

* Wenders' portrayal of the father–son conflict feeds on an important tradition in German literature, notably the depiction of the generational conflict in Expressionism. Franz Kafka's works come to mind, particularly his stories *The Judgment* (1912), *The Metamorphosis* (1912), and the seminal *Letter to His Father* (1919), in which seemingly weakened father figures rise up to prevail over their sons, who are – unlike Wenders' characters – incapable of overcoming them in open confrontation.

75

and his mother under the oppression of the paternal voice, out of his recognition that this voice is carried and broadcast through the newspaper his father writes, Robert forces his father to assume the mute position of the oppressed. And as he pushes the old man out of language, he attempts to appropriate it for himself. Robert silences the father's language so that he alone may speak it, perhaps in a less destructive discourse. As his father sleeps, Robert composes the front page of a newspaper, using his father's own medium to subvert it. He works on his new edition, his manifesto of the new child becoming a new adult, through the night. When morning comes, Robert leaves, reluctantly accepting his father's embrace and presenting him a copy of his newly found language. The headline reads, "How to Be Able to Respect a Woman" (*"Wie Eine Frau Achten Können"*).

The resonances here grow very complex. The grieving man had set in motion not only a desire for reconciliation of husbands and wives, fathers and sons, but also a process of inquiry into gender and sexuality. Nestled within their general malaise, Wenders' males carry a sadness about their sexuality, an inability to behave with intimacy toward men or women, a crisis of gender. They have lost most traces of male aggression, yet have not discovered enough identity to give themselves to women without feeling desolated. They can only mourn sexuality, as they mourn everything else. The grieving man, acting out his desire for closeness with his wife, wears her blood-stained coat, covering himself with the sign of her pain and his inability to comprehend it. This incomprehension is almost a wound for Wenders' characters. "I have always felt only lonely when inside a woman, lonely down to my bones," Bruno says in his final confrontation with Robert near the end of the film. He finds the contrast between physical union and unfulfilled desire, between bodily contact and longing for emotional redemption excruciating. The grieving man, with his gesture of wearing the coat, recognizes, on a level of mute despair, this loneliness and also his responsibility for it. His own self-annihilation intertwines with his wife's. As a mark of his grief, he leaves the coat behind when he leaves the truck — an act that illuminates his companions and the viewers of the film alike about the pains and enigmas of intimacy.

The sexual paralysis of all of Wenders' characters is analogous to their paralysis in history. Passive in the personal and public sphere, easily distracted by the road, they avoid commitment of any kind. When passion intrudes, they react according to their own needs, sometimes bravely, as in Robert's visit to his father, and sometimes with greater passivity. When Robert goes off to see his father, Bruno meets a woman — named Pauline in the script, though without a name in the film itself — apparently by chance in

Innocence and ignorance: Hitler as legacy and kitsch object, from *Kings of the Road*.

his circuit through the decaying cinemas of the border towns. Their meeting and the events that follow are carefully intercut with the sequence of Robert and his father, so that the two meetings play counterpoint with each other – confrontation with patriarchy and confrontation with sexuality becomes mutually intertwined. Bruno and his friend act with a peculiar nonchalance and guarded desire that seem to indicate an old acquaintance. But informality here appears to be only an indication of the lack of emotional energy.

They come together at a fun fair. The woman has just won a candlestick in the shape of Hitler's head that she carries under her arm. This odd object that reduces a figure of terror to an object of kitsch has little apparent effect on Bruno. She asks him to light it for her, then he asks her to light his cigarette with it, and almost in bewilderment, he makes a joke, "Fire from the Führer!" (*"Feuer vom Führer!"*). "Here, hold the old fellow," she says, handing him the Hitler candle and then taking a ride on the bumper cars. After her ride, Bruno lights her cigarette with Hitler; she takes the object and places it under her jacket.

Bruno later goes to the cinema where, coincidentally, he finds Pauline working as a ticket seller. The movie being shown is one of the many pornographic films that flooded the German market in the seventies, financed partly with the money that was supposed to subsidize the work of young German cinéastes.[9] The corruption is aggravated. Not only is such a film being financed and exhibited, but it is exhibited badly. Watching the movie, Bruno discovers that the screen image is dark in the middle. He goes up to the projection booth to correct the problem and finds the projectionist masturbating to the film that he has projected on the back wall of the booth by hanging a small mirror in front of the projector lens. And like his seed, the film is spilling onto the floor.

Bruno's professionalism overcomes his distaste (and bemusement) over the film and its projection. He takes over the booth, removes the mirror, and changes reels with a delicate and assured mastery over the equipment. He is in his element. At this point, a subtle but spectacular event occurs in the structure of *Kings of the Road*. Wenders – who, like most postwar European filmmakers, tends not to use editing as an expressive device – makes one of the most interesting edits in his work, a dissolve that links Bruno's actions with those of Robert in his father's print shop and connects two actions of communication. From Bruno, turning the controls of the projector, making a smooth, professional reel change for a film that isn't even worthy of being shown, Wenders dissolves to Robert, turning the controls on the linotype machine in his father's office, composing – as his father sleeps – the words he cannot tell him directly. The connection of these images not only is an example of the creative structures of cinema, but is *about* those structures, about the power of film to speak about life and make connections. The edit is also about the active and vital aspects of these two characters, who, despite their diminished emotional life, still have a measure of control and skill in the world.

Robert composes at his father's linotype; in the movie house, Bruno composes in the projection room. He edits parts of a trailer for a pornography film into a continuous loop, a piece of film that will run nonstop in the projector. "Brutality, action, sex! Ninety minutes of film that television cannot show . . . ," the sound track says over and over again, while images of a rape, a house collapsing in flames, and a woman's breasts heaving repeat in an obsessive return of the degraded and degrading image. Watching this grotesquerie of sex and violence in the theater, Bruno and Pauline, who started their evening in a playful, even flirtatious mood, can only fall back into the despair of their loneliness and the recall of other sadnesses. Pauline remembers a couple in the theater who could not withdraw from intercourse and had to be carried away in an ambulance. He recalls a woman he saw seated in front of her house under a hair dryer. And he remembers the man who grieves, who told him, "The only thing there is, is life." "But which . . . ?" Bruno now asks. His desire is so fragmented that he cannot quite focus on the possibility of a coherent, emotionally integrated life, one that might allow traveling the road, seeing a pornography film, and meeting a women who holds a bust of Hitler to make some integrated sense.

Bruno continues to move above the abyss. His professionalism works with his emotions, and he turns the degradation of the porno film into an expression of his own despair. The result is only more pain and uncertainty. Robert, meanwhile, uses his linguistic skills and his father's printing machines (his machines of representation) to express his own emotional turmoil. While his father sleeps, he toils through the night, composing his antioedipal newspaper. In the middle of the night, Robert's father awakes to tell his son that his own mother had died during childbirth. Later there is another awakening: Pauline awakes from a dream and asks Bruno for pen and paper to write it down (they are sleeping together, though nothing indicates they have made love). Bruno gives her a strip of photographs from a booth in Wolfsburg. He tells her to write her dream on the back of his picture, permitting the verbal representation of her desire to mark the visual representation of his, keeping their bodies safely apart. Later in the morning they face each other, she cries, and Bruno touches his finger to her tears and then to his face, quietly attempting to acquire feelings. But his neurasthenia prevents any lasting, unmediated contact. He leaves her and rejoins Robert on the road.

Wenders' characters go on the road for a variety of reasons – they all have different stories. But the master narrative that drives each of them is the story of desire. As withdrawn and lonely as they may be, they yearn to talk, to be companionable, to slip easily into history, to be themselves, could they only know who those selves are and where history could be found that was not terrifying. They desire intimacy, but their fear of sexuality – of closeness on any level, physical or emotional – forces them to escape the very stability and responsibility that intimacy, however briefly, requires. Wenders' men seem responsible only to their own ongoing attempt to authenticate their existence. Other language, the language of the feminine, for example, is unheard, untranslatable, or in the later films, utopian. Women occasionally point out how self-absorbed the male characters are. The woman to whom Philip Winter goes for a place to sleep in New York in *Alice in the Cities* tells him that he is too caught up in finding the proof of his own existence to

recognize the existence of others. Thérèse in *Wrong Move* complains of Wilhelm's lack of emotion and commitment. But the men are never responsive to the language of their lack. Instead, they look to that lack as a reaffirmation of their solitude. At best, like Robert, they can only proclaim, through the mediation of language, that women ought to be understood.

Over and over again, they turn to children or to other men for respite. Children act as their mute alter egos, the representation or confirmation of their own difficulties in passing into the adult realm. The children are mute not in the sense that they cannot talk (although the never-seen figure of the murdered deaf and dumb boy haunts the characters in *The Goalie's Anxiety at the Penalty Kick,* acting as an invisible double to Josef Bloch's own tattered perceptions). Rather, children simply do not respond in threatening ways; their simplicity and directness hold the male figures down to earth, keep them within the history of the visible and knowable. Children do not especially have to be befriended. Their simplicity makes them always available, whether they are strangers or not; they are the mirrors of immaturity, backward-looking mirrors. As long as Wenders and his characters accept the myth of the child as a simple creature living in imaginative plenitude, in the simple fullness of words and meanings, they are trapped in a situation that

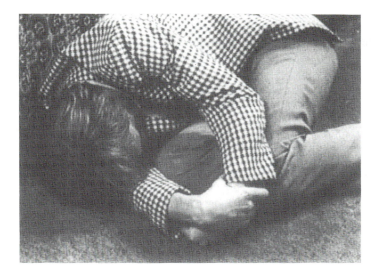

Gender relations: Josef Bloch after Gloria's murder (*facing page*) and retreating into the fetal position (*above*), from *The Goalie's Anxiety at the Penalty Kick* (1972).

slows their transformation to functioning adults. The simplicity and directness of children is, for Wenders, a key to adult redemption. In reality, it is a nostalgia that continues to defer his characters' access to history, something Wenders seems to recognize in *Until the End of the World*.

The male friendships of Wenders' characters are especially intriguing. The tensions that occur between his men are caused by the same problems of intimacy that affect their relations with women, but in another register. The men behave with each other as if sexuality were not a question. Their relationships continue to suspend them over an abyss of sexuality, yet permit them the illusion that their lives are going on as if that abyss did not exist, or could be ignored. Male friendship seems easy, seems to make fewer demands than a heterosexual relationship; it replaces loneliness and routine and, for awhile, appears to be simple to control. The characters never quite see it as a substitute for other kinds of intimacy or as an excuse. They are permitted to inhabit a homosocial realm (a realm not uniquely created in Wenders' films but one defined and confirmed over and over again in literature and film), which appears safe, natural, unthreatening.[10] And it *is* safe because women and the difference they present (sexual, physical, social, cultural difference) are denied, the discourse seems uniform, and emotions appear to be kept well in check. The safety is illusory, of course. Homo-sociality is a construct within a world that is inalterably defined by hetero-sexuality, homosexuality, or bisexuality – gendered, in short, with all the cultural and ideological problems of power, fear, and repression that gender entails. The homosocial is the fantasy of a world without sexual difference or desire and, therefore, creates its own annihilation at the moment it is brought into existence. Annihilation of difference does not, in Wenders' hands, set up an alternative to patriarchy, or even make patriarchy un-problematic. In fact, male friendships confirm patriarchy and male ex-clusivity. But for Wenders' characters, they provide an illusion of escape.

The gender-related uncertainties and depressions suffered by these men are very much driven by the periods and cultures in which Wenders works. In the seventies, shifts in gender relations were significantly reshaping societies and ideologies on both sides of the Atlantic and affecting Wenders' personal life as well. He notes the signals of changing times in comments made in 1977, after *The American Friend* had been screened in Cannes. He states, perhaps from a situation of self-protection, that women know more about the problems of identity than their male counterparts: "No other narrative," he maintains,

> treats the idea of identity with greater urgency and justification than cinema. Because no other language is capable of addressing the phys-ical state of things. . . . Hence, the idea of identity is a new one, as it can no longer be taken for granted. Often it seems to me women already know more about this than men. And children when they haven't been deprived of anything. Cinema will bring all of this to light.[11]

The privileging of self-knowledge in women and children may be an act of special pleading or even disingenuousness on Wenders' part, an excuse for his inability to deal with women in his films. Certainly "the idea of identity" is hardly new, to film or literature or philosophy. Perhaps the enforced rethinking of gender-based identity going on at the time made him more sensitive and more evasive.

Feminism in the seventies pressed in upon male certainty and self-content-ment, and Wenders' men reflected this. As his men slip further out of con-fident subjectivity, they slip further out of satisfying relationships with women. This dispossession of self had been Wenders' fate as well as his characters' from the very beginning. In his predominantly male world of drifting questers, women were not a factor but a felt absence. And these absences are filled with women who played roles in Wenders' own life. The woman Hans visits in Munich and Robert visits in New York is played by Edda Köchl, who was Wenders' wife for a brief time in 1970. The friend Hans sees in Berlin is played by Libgart Schwarz (who appears in *Goalie* as well), the wife at the time of Peter Handke.[12] Lisa Kreuzer, who appears in *Alice in the Cities, Kings of the Road,* and *The American Friend,* was a longtime "friend" of Wenders. His abrupt departure from her caused a brief scandal. He was briefly married to Ronee Blakley, who sings and is seen in *Lightning over Water.* His new relationship with Solveig Dommartin leads to a wholesale remythologizing of romance in *Wings of Desire* and *Until the End of the World.*

We do not mean to monger scandal here or fall into the sexist trap of reading the male artist's success and failures through the women in his life. What we are trying to affirm is that, for Wenders, as much or more than any contemporary filmmaker, the personal becomes the cinematic and the cultural becomes an excuse to plead emotional poverty for a decade – women demand much, have stronger personalities, are surer of their identities than men – and then, when the crisis seems to have passed, celebrate emotional liberation in the mideighties. The desire to seek the self, sequester it, and be kind to women without wounding one's own identity becomes connected with the notion that women are somehow stronger and therefore beyond sympathy for men's problems. This leads to an abandonment of emotions and delayed, mislaid fulfillment. It is safer simply to ignore women and the pain and loss they inevitably bring to lost, identityless selves. To Wenders' credit, his male characters try to correct the oppressiveness of male domination on the local, everyday level, though they find it difficult to achieve a leveling heterosexuality or a liberating homosexuality that will allow domination by neither party. After all, Robert, whose domestic unhappiness leads him to a spectacular, if halfhearted, attempt at suicide, finally finds the words to conquer his father, even though they are a tentative, cautionary, "How to Be Able to Respect a Woman." When these words are, in the end, attended to in Wenders' films, the attention is at the expense of domesticity in *Paris, Texas* or through the resurrection of romanticism in *Wings of Desire.* In *Until the End of the World,* respect for a woman allows Wenders simply to turn her into another road wanderer, assisting her man.

While the men struggle, the women mostly remain passive. The grieving man wears his dead wife's coat and Bruno's friend puts Hitler under hers. Both are acquiescent gestures: one uses the memory of woman as self-protection and self-realization, while in the other the woman acts as a nonchalant cloaker of history, protecting Bruno and the viewer from the full resonance of what the Hitler candle stands for. In their passivity, Wenders' women are sometimes the targets of violence, especially in *Paris, Texas*, though here, the violence done to Jane is less important on the narrative level than the effects of that violence on the emotional life of the man who committed it. Women sometimes cause violence indirectly. In *The American Friend*, Jonathan's wife decides to bring her husband back into the domestic fold by helping him fight the gangsters who have used him. As a result of this redetermined domesticity, Jonathan betrays his friend Ripley and dies while driving the car, as his wife sits beside him pained by her helplessness. Jonathan's death is, finally, unconnected with her desire to save him.

So amid the shared pain of unhappy heterosexuality, Wenders' men seek solace with each other and attempt to find the oedipal roots of their unhappiness. They finally look past women to the search for their father and, through their father, toward Germany's history and its manifestation in cinema. For cinema, as always in Wenders' films, is the mediation through which his characters attempt to discover themselves and the expression of the possibilities of their salvation. As Wenders said, "No other narrative treats the idea of identity with greater urgency and justification than cinema." *Kings of the Road* begins, ends, and is saturated throughout with references to film so all-encompassing and moving that they turn cinema into affirmation and consolation.

Near the end of the film, Robert and Bruno spend the night in a place of emotional, cultural, and linguistic confusion — an old hut on the East German border, formerly inhabited by American soldiers. American graffiti cover the walls. Robert tries to rig up a telephone left behind in the hut in order to get to his wife, but hears only the voice of an American phone operator on the other end. He talks to Bruno about language and recalls a child who saw letters as animated, personalized creatures. Bruno, in a rare moment of self-revelation, finds his own voice and speaks about his terrors of intimacy. Gunfire is heard outside — sounds of the effects of realpolitik in the distance, allowed to intrude only so much. They both get drunk and talk at length about their fears and insecurities. Robert confronts Bruno with his emotional deadness and they fight — an almost predictable masculine response to emotional openness. (The characters are photographed almost entirely in one-shots during this sequence, as if to anticipate their readiness to go their own ways. The fight is one of the few times they are observed together; but even here Wenders needs to pull back and expose their separation from each other and his own discomfort with their sudden, physical closeness: he cuts to a shot of them from outside the hut, the camera looking through a window.)

Their dialogue on sexual fear, on the terror of losing themselves, their independence, and their hopes for change should they ever give themselves up to a woman is, of course, redolent of the insecurity that grew out of the resistances to male security set up by feminism in the seventies. It is also touchingly adolescent and provides enough catharsis for the characters to stimulate some further movement in them, as if, having opened themselves to each other, they can now move on with their lives. Robert leaves and meets the boy at the railroad station who refreshes his understanding of childhood and language. Bruno visits the aging movie house owner who talks of the death of cinema (in a sequence where he is surrounded by photographs of scantily clad movie stars, while behind the women there is a picture of Fritz Lang).

It is of great importance that the redemptive images of cinema – the projection room, the old woman, Fritz Lang – and not the emotional coming to life of two characters are what lead the film to closure. This narrative of lost emotions that were, in fact, never present, of the vitality of the road and the stimulation of cultures, has from its inception to its end been authorized by the cinematic imagination and the personality that fuse it. Wenders is quite aware of his success and the fact that the redemption his characters seek is at last given to him through the imaginary of his art. In the last shot of the film, Bruno mounts the cab of his truck as a sad lyric plays on the track, a vocal version of one of the country/rock compositions that have molded and emotionally charged the narrative throughout. He quietly tears up his itinerary. On the truck window are reflected the letters "WW." They are the initials of the Weisse Wand Lichtspiele (the White Screen Cinema) that he is just leaving. They are also the signature, the authorizing presence, of the film's maker. The camera cranes up, picks up the neon WW on the marquee and the few working lights on the theater front that make up the word "End."

Closure comes not with Bruno's moderately liberating gesture of tearing up the routine of his life (in fact, the camera begins craning away from him as he does this, and the act is not highlighted in the composition), but with the masterful movement of the camera and the purely cinematic play on the letters left burning on the movie house. Closure derives from a kind of self-satisfaction and self-possession, a reassertion of the very qualities that have kept Wenders' characters going through all the films to his point. The satisfaction is with saving the cinema and the self through cinema, in the very midst of both their demises.

Kings of the Road is a ballad (quite literally, given the musical motifs that support the narrative) of male unease told in images of such clarity and eloquence that this unease is itself made easy. A film about coldness and loneliness, it is made warm and communal by its dependence on and confidence in the salvation of the image. The pain of male defeat is palliated by the support of cinema's victory. The filmmaker is redeemed by his art and cinema becomes father to the man.

4

The State of Things

If, for Wenders, cinema is the great affirmation, the authenticating imaginary, where the desire of the imagination finds its object in the history of film, it is also the source of discontent and anger. The place of images is insecure because it is under constant attack, debased by commercial interests, and diluted by its very heterogeneity and omnipresence, finally as unstable as the history images record and represent. Almost as often as he makes fictional narratives about young men attempting to sort out their existence, Wenders makes quasi-documentaries about himself in which he attempts to authenticate his belief in cinema and his own stake in it.

Tokyo-Ga (1985), for example, is an effort to track down the physical and cultural remains of one of his great patrimonic guides, the Japanese filmmaker Yasujiro Ozu, in order to discover whether the world of Ozu's films can be found in the chaotic and unsettling imagery of modern Tokyo. The film is a sometimes overwhelmed observation of the city, which becomes, through Wenders' perceptions, a distantly seen urbanscape, sharply outlined, pristine, pastel, cold, and almost incomprehensible. He is taken to the point of obsession with the simulacra of Western life created by the Japanese: the pachinko games, the golf driving ranges set up on a rooftop, the fake food displays in restaurant windows. He observes with maddening detail the work of the factory that manufactures the food and notes with amusement that the factory let him film everything but the employees eating. The Japan seen by Wenders is all representation, a postmodern world where nothing is real but everything is seen. The world of the degraded image.[1] (During his travels, Wenders meets Werner Herzog atop the Tokyo simulation of the Eiffel Tower. Herzog tells him there are no more images on earth that correspond to the images inside him. He will have to go on a NASA space flight in order to find the images he needs. Wenders says that he hopes to find something usable closer to home. Less a romantic than Herzog, he believes the images of the world may not correspond to those inside him, but may at least validate them. However, as if recalling, or parodying, Herzog's remark, Wenders sends Claire into space to observe the earth at the end of *Until the End of the World*.)

Against the odds of the visible, he seeks out the "real" Ozu, the filmmaker who, after the war, attempted to preserve the rhythms and traditions of Japanese life when many Japanese were themselves moving away from them. Wenders seeks the images that Ozu employed – the trains, rooftops, children at play – to punctuate the narratives of his own films in order to create a harmony of things-as-they-exist. Through interviews with Chishu Ryu (the actor who, as a young man, played the old father in many of the director's later films) and with Ozu's cameraman (who demonstrates how he set up compositions and weeps at the memory of his old master), Wenders attempts to achieve belated intimacy with a filmmaker far beyond his own culture, yet apposite, Wenders believes, in desire. He visits Ozu's grave and discovers a blank marble slab with the Chinese character that means "nothingness." The dead refuse to speak; the world they attempted to represent and imagine exists only in their images.

Wenders discovers everything but the real Ozu, the real image maker, the real images. He is moved to contemplation: "We gasp and give a start when we suddenly discover something true or real in a movie, be it nothing more than the gesture of a child in the background, or a bird flying across the frame, or a cloud casting its shadow over the scene for but an instant. It is a rarity in today's cinema to find such moments of truth, for people or objects to show themselves as they really are." (As he makes this comment, he is photographing his own reflection in the window of a moving train.) This contemplation is typical of the reflective mood he enters in his documentary films. Here, as well as in *Reverse Angle* (1982) or *Chambre 666* (1982) or *Lightning over Water,* he examines or simply mourns, in something close to a depressive state, the decay of the image-making capabilities of the film-maker, of the image-perceiving talents of the viewer, or, in the latter film, the death of cinematic patrimony itself, from which he hopes to regain the legitimated desire for artistic purity.

The documentaries speak, in another register, about the same problems as the fiction films. But the redemptive opportunities sought by the fictional characters are more easily created by the interventions available to the documentary maker. Wenders' characters barely control their destinies; Wenders, the subjective filmmaker, can at least turn to his medium for assurance more directly than he can in the narrative films. Amid the pastiche of images in

Tokyo and the disappointment over not being able to find authentic remnants of Ozu, Wenders creates a moment of enlightenment. He makes a cinematic discovery that allows him to merge with his Japanese master. After the sequence at Ozu's grave, he goes at night to a street filled with bars, like those that appear in many of Ozu's films, "in which his abandoned or lonely fathers drown their sorrows." He composes and shoots the street "like I always do." The image is interesting, as are most in this film, for its exotic content: a small alley with street lamps arching over. A woman walks past. Then Wenders changes the lens on his camera. In voice-over, he comments that he puts on a 50mm lens, the kind Ozu used in every shot he made, the kind that gives a slightly telephoto quality to the image. The content of the shot is the same, but the composition and mise-en-scène are not. The angle is now slightly low, the buildings close on each side, a street crossing close on the horizon. Suddenly, Wenders has recreated an image from an Ozu film. "Another image presented itself; one that no longer belonged to me."

In a world without adequate images, a world whose mise-en-scène has been used up by television and advertising and movies without imagination, and where the filmmaker, orphaned and without place, wanders through yet another culture to find paternal nourishment, survival comes through cinematic oedipalization. The son – by the act of changing a lens – becomes the father. Ozu is discovered and revived in an image. And lost again. Redemption occurs through representation, which by its very nature is not the thing itself, so that the redemptive act becomes futile, even inauthentic. Wenders finds a father, seems almost to see from behind his eyes, but realizes that, finally, the patriarch's images are not his own.

The moment of the lenses confirms the notion we suggested earlier, that Wenders' films can be understood to a great extent as existing beneath the superimposition of images from the work of other filmmakers. The sequence in *Tokyo-Ga* makes this fact more trenchant by clearly expressing the desire of the filmmaker to efface himself through the very technical reproduction of another filmmaker's images. At a loss to find in the world the images he desires, Wenders finds himself in the images of another. The surrender of self is both positive and negative: he discovers a community with his aesthetic forebears but must deny himself at the same time – these images "no longer belonged to me." The act and his response indicate the discomfort he experiences with the modernist-humanist tradition to which he is heir. We must examine this tradition for a moment in order to understand more fully the ways Wenders deals with cinema and why he continues seeking out its patrimony.

Historically, modernism allowed the artist to merge his or her work with an ongoing creative collectivity without giving up subjectivity or claim to individual imagination. Modernism is the site of inquiry, where the artist positions him- or herself within the flow of signifiers, selecting, rearranging, creating new configurations, and denying old meanings. In the modernist enterprise, representation is an act of mediation, exploration, and de-stabilization that authenticates the self through imaginative activity. Wenders, coming at the very end of the modernist movement in cinema, begins questioning the power of representation. He falls back on modified realist premises, believing that, with care, the cinematic image can permit "people or objects to show themselves as they really are," but cannot authenticate or even simulate the authentic self.

At the end of *Kings of the Road,* Wenders indicates that cinema could have redemptive possibilities, but at this point in his career, he is already moving away from modernism to a position of postmodernist critique. He is becoming increasingly aware of the fracturing of image and meaning, signifier and signified, the dispersal of individuality, creativity, history, and the authentic, all of which are dissolving amid the pastiche of images and sounds generated by communications media – images and sounds that are static, unredeemed, without patrimony or lineage, past or future.[2] In time, he will move from critique to an embrace, creating, in *Wings of Desire,* one of the significant postmodernist films of the eighties. During the late seventies and early eighties, however, he was still caught up in inquiry, still trying to prove the authenticity of cinema while at the same time observing the breakdown of that authenticity. He still *demands* that cinema have redemptive power, though he may be less optimistic that it can retain or maintain it.

The transitional films of this period each examine the components of the romantic-modernist-postmodernist position and his own uncertainty within it. *The State of Things, Tokyo-Ga, Reverse Angle, Lightning over Water* are specifically about filmmakers and filmmaking. *Reverse Angle* is a depressive meditation upon the bad experiences Wenders had making *Hammett.* Here the artist is presented as victim, the wanderer whose images no one wants. *Chambre 666* is an exercise in self-effacement and revelation: at the 1982 Cannes Festival, Wenders invited, one by one, Jean-Luc Godard, Michelangelo Antonioni, Steven Spielberg, Werner Herzog, Rainer Werner Fassbinder, and other contemporary filmmakers to his hotel room, turned on the camera, and left the room, allowing them to deliver monologues on the state and future of cinema in response to a questionnaire he gave them to study. *Lightning over Water* is Wenders' last attempt to confront and make peace with another cinematic father figure, to discover in the death of the father the authorial integrity of the image. Unlike *Tokyo-Ga,* the quest is not one of retrieval, but of annihilation. By turning the last days of Nicholas Ray into an emotionally charged oedipal drama, Wenders hoped to correct the history of film, Ray's place within that history, and his own struggles with bad faith and an obsession to control events. The attempt backfires and Wenders is left with nothing but inauthentic, if sometimes haunting, images, a dead filmmaker, and no redemption. He attempted to reedit the film twice,* removing, finally, its most excruciating sequences in which he lies in Ray's hospital bed and, later, forces Ray to face the camera, keeping it running while the dying man asks him to cut.[3]

Lightning over Water is almost offensive in its manipulativeness and its naïveté that borders on callousness, no matter how much Wenders attempts to mitigate his manipulations of a dying man by foregrounding the artifice of his deeds. The film is constructed by intercutting rehearsed sequences with "documentary" videotape of the rehearsals and filming. With this structure, Wenders attempts to gain some distance from his subject and to emphasize how much emotion emerges not out of direct experience, but out of experience mediated and meditated by cinema. What he discovers is that visual manifestations of pain and death are, in the end, impossible to mediate, more difficult still to be made instruments of reflexive gestures.

Foregrounding the means of cinematic production is certainly not a unique act and is essential to modernist practice. Wenders acknowledges this in the structure of *Lightning over Water* – the acknowledgment is simply out of place here. It is perhaps the particular provenance of modernism to transform the romantic's obsessive desire for individual creativity into a no less obsessive desire for linking that creativity with other works, while revealing how the specific forms of painting, poetry, film, or music are differentiated from one another as well as from other forms of discourse. The romantic evokes the uniqueness of Art; the modernist evokes aesthetic community and struggles with and against structure and convention. The struggle may provoke an "anxiety of influence" or may – as in the case of modernist filmmakers – result in a celebration of influence, a cinematic consciousness that joyfully acknowledges its traditions and revels in foregrounding the machinery of its construction.[4] Wenders is one of the most celebratory filmmakers in the modernist tradition. But his celebrations are marred by his demands that the films and filmmakers he celebrates be made to account for his own presence and authenticity as a filmmaker. The romantic self-

---

* Wenders reedited the film after its Cannes premiere and then, apparently, for its American release. The sequences referred to are present in the printed cutting continuity of the film, but not in the American videotape version. There are other differences as well.

assertion or desire for self-validation compromises the modernist impulse to defer subjectivity to the aesthetic community.

Modernism spoke to the breakdown of content, the loss of meaning, cultural consensus, and traditional political hierarchies, and the illusions of coherence in the wake of the First World War and the Russian revolution – the very matters that the New German Cinema attempted to address in the late sixties and seventies in the face of its own history. But Wenders desired more personal assertion than modernism allowed – more emotional directness (short of melodrama) and sense of patrimonial connection – in order to heal subjective and historical rifts. His desiring gaze is aware of the political world, observant of the ways politics and culture interact, but interested, finally, in local, personal responses to that interaction.

Wenders sees himself at the center point of his work and the work of cinema as a whole. Far more than his predecessors or contemporaries, he attempts to assuage his anxiety of influence by begging both forgiveness and authority from those who came before him. *Lightning over Water* and *Tokyo-Ga* are each subjective supplications to admired figures – one dying, the other dead – for recognition and for independence. We have seen this desire for authenticity in the fiction films – the "WW" reflected in the window of Bruno's truck at the end of *Kings of the Road*, for example. We have pointed out that Wenders often makes brief appearances, not as a way of exposing the mechanisms of cinema and toying with the audience as was Hitchcock's wont, but seemingly as a way of signature, of proof, almost, of his existence. This is nowhere more clear than his appearance in the middle of a short piece he made for German television ("Die Insel," one of two segments he directed for a 1974 series called *Ein Haus für Uns*). The film is a rather straightforward narrative about a lonely little girl. At one point she and her parents go to the movies. Wenders places himself in the movie house where the characters go, watching his own film, *The Scarlet Letter*. For anyone who recognizes him, he manages to upstage the central characters and bring the narrative movement to a stop. In a reverse angle, a cut to a shot in which the viewer sees what the characters in the theater are gazing at, his becomes the authorizing point of view for the film everyone else is watching. His gaze controls the mise-en-scène entirely; he has created it as director and directed himself to be the one who validates and is validated by it. We recall the comment he makes in the introduction to his book *Emotion Pictures:* "I was watching movies, but as much as I was looking at the screen, I was also aware of myself as the observer. . . . I was not reflecting *upon* movies, I was reflecting them, period."[5]

At least until *Paris, Texas,* Wenders insists upon such acts of self-authentication, of seeking and owning cinema, of *trying out* himself as film-maker, of putting or inscribing himself in the scene, making auto-biographical marks. In a sense, Wenders is his mise-en-scène; the space of his films his own consciousness, more romantic than modernist. Werner Herzog put himself in physically demanding situations to prove his powers. ("Post-Nietzschean" is a term that comes to mind when thinking of Herzog.) Wenders goes further, putting his very subjectivity in danger to prove his cinematic worthiness. As a final effort to absorb himself into his art, in an effort to consummate the oedipal process by removing that part of subjec-tivity that rebels against cinematic authority, he figuratively kills himself off, first by surrendering himself to the anonymity of Hollywood production and then by making a film in which a director, unwilling to surrender to Holly-wood, is murdered by the very forces he tries to resist.

The crises of both romanticism and modernism occur when ego and sub-jectivity fail or are proven inauthentic or incapable, when the culture itself is no longer satisfied with the products of the subject, when either form or reception become entirely resistant to the subject's imagination. This occurs when subjectivity is withered by other forces – history, economics, taste – that either ignore or overwhelm it. In the late seventies and early eighties, Wenders suffered his crisis, indulging in the ultimate act of self-authorization through self-annihilation. He went to Hollywood to make a film. This was the state of things: *The American Friend,* made in Hamburg, Paris, and New York, much of it in English, drawing upon the generic imperatives of the early fifties gangster/domestic melodrama/film noir and the chase thriller, gave Wenders greater coin in the international film market than he had found heretofore. The film, in short, was something of a commercial success. At the same time, Francis Ford Coppola, an American filmmaker who was running out of creative steam and had no financial acumen, decided that he wanted single-handedly to become a modern incarnation of the Hollywood mogul. He set up his own studio and, among other projects, decided to become the American producer-distributor for some European filmmakers. He was, like many people in America during the late seventies, enamored of the New German Cinema and worked out a deal with Wenders to film Joseph Gores' novel, *Hammett,* in San Francisco and Los Angeles.

Historically, there are three different groups of European filmmakers who came to America to work. One is the group of émigrés to Los Angeles in the middle and late twenties, F. W. Murnau being among the best known. The second is the group of refugees that arrived before or during World War II, Fritz Lang being a prominent figure among them. Each group faced the necessity, with varying degrees of success, of absorption, acculturation, and adaptation to the Hollywood style. Some did not survive; others, like Lang, slipped into the Hollywood mode of production with little difficulty. The third group is the most troublesome, for it concerns the independent "art" directors of the postwar period, who decided, for a variety of reasons, to accept either the challenge or the blandishments of Hollywood. They are relatively few in number, for as much as European cinéastes admired and learned from American film, they knew well enough that their methods of working and notions of how cinema should be made neither fit nor could survive the American system. Those who tried and did well had to work through the most trying compromises. Michelangelo Antonioni came to America in the late sixties to make *Zabriskie Point,* struggled with MGM, and made a film so visually rigorous and intellectually banal that it was despised by everyone. Bernardo Bertolucci, while never actually filming for an American company in America, has, with *The Last Emperor* and *The Sheltering Sky,* become, for all intents and purposes, an American director. Volker Schlöndorff, an important early figure in the development of the New German Cinema, whose narratives always had a sufficient linearity and conventional realism to make the transition, moved easily into Hollywood production with *Death of a Salesman* and *The Handmaid's Tale.* Wolfgang Petersen, whose film *Das Boot* was the rare phenomenon of a film in German that became a success in America, came over for *Enemy Mine* in 1985. He also had little difficulty assuming the demands that story predominate form. Percy Adlon, who made an extraordinary film about Marcel Proust's housekeeper, *Celeste* (1981), teamed up with actress Marianne Sägebrecht for one film in Germany, *Zuckerbaby* (1983). He went on to the United States to make two more films with this actress, *Bagdad Cafe* (1987) and *Rosalie Goes Shopping* (1990). Both of the American films retain a certain eccentric style. The popularity of *Bagdad Cafe* was such that it was turned into an American television sitcom.

Jean-Luc Godard and François Truffaut were often tempted by Holly-wood. Truffaut was, at one time, asked to direct *Bonnie and Clyde;* Godard actually prepared a film to be made in the United States with Robert De Niro and Dianne Keaton, but never came to do it. (Coppola did distribute his *Sauve qui peut [La Vie]* in 1980.) Fassbinder threatened to leave for America, but never did. Herzog, apparently never tempted, preferred the South American jungle to Beverly Hills and left it up to Coppola to remake his *Aguirre: Wrath of God* as *Apocalypse Now.* But Wenders, whose cinematic style, methods of working, personality, and high moral regard for cinema made him the least likely candidate for Hollywood filmmaking, did not resist. Seeking the completion of his oedipal journey, he went into the heart of the cinematic patriarchy, which repaid the favor by forcing on him the language of the American father figures he emulated. Under duress, he gave up his images, his editorial rhythms, his control, his subjectivity. *Hammett* was quite literally a twice-made film. The project was begun in 1978; the first version was made in 1980, the second, final version was completed in late 1981 and screened in Cannes in 1982. Each credit for the film has two names, except for the writers, of which there were three; there are also three "assistant" directors.[6] The first version has never been seen, and the remade film is a hybrid of the original in which most traces of directorial style are removed. Coppola did not like Wenders' conception, narrative form, mise-en-scène, or pace. He made him – like a father a bumbling child – do it over again. The result is a rather indifferent film, an homage to *The Maltese Falcon,* an invocation of the late thirties – early film noir, a failed attempt to capture the complexities of a writer's imagination and the despair of the creative act.

What is left to admire in *Hammett,* as Kenneth Michael Mashon points out, is the continuation of Wenders' struggle with the idea of storytelling, with the necessities and structures of narrative and not only the way stories are told, but the way they shift perspectives on life in the telling. While the generic forces of the detective film do not force the film into important revelations of contemporary culture, as the conventions of the fifties gangster film did in *The American Friend,* the centrality of the writer and the confusions of "fact" and "fiction," perception and the authenticating positions of perception, fit well into Wenders' ongoing concerns.[7] But the *results* of the film are, finally, more interesting than *Hammett* itself. Attempting to keep his imagination and esteem intact, driven to greater lengths of self-examination and self-authorization, and forced to examine his basic preconceptions about cinematic practice, Wenders made four films about filmmaking during and immediately after *Hammett:* two short documentaries, a full-length, quasi-documentary on Nicholas Ray, and the most amazing film of his career, the fiction film that retells the making of *Hammett: The State of Things.* This film is a cry of anger at an unresponsive industry and at an artistic temperament that cannot yield to that industry; it is both an image of the director's martyrdom and an act of redemptive suicide, the adult's desire to kill the child who wants to maintain an imaginary simplicity and self-possession – the child who believes that the accurate, adequate, and valid image can redeem loss, absence, and amnesia.

The State of Things is also the most insightful film about filmmaking since Godard's *Contempt,* made twenty years earlier. The subject is hardly new to film. Hollywood has always enjoyed making films about itself, often con-

The hero in a bind: Wenders' first "American" film, *Hammett* (1978–82).

templating its own ugliness in the process. But the Hollywood version of reflexivity is not structured by a consciousness of structure; filmmaking is merely part of the apparatus of plot and not a determining narrative force which – in the modernist, reflexive film – turns the film in on itself and, in so doing, foregrounds its moral and aesthetic structure. Of course, all modernist film does this, whether or not the subject of its story is cinema. Modernism is, on one level, the drive to specify the formal creation of meaning. But films that are about filmmaking on all their levels – whether they be elegiac, like *Contempt,* celebratory, like Truffaut's *Day for Night,* angry and full of hurt, like Fassbinder's *Beware of a Holy Whore,* or meditative, full of doubt, pain, and loathing, as in *The State of Things* – raise the ante of the reflexive act. Filmmaking becomes subject, site, beginning, end, future, life, death, and the determinant of individual identity – a perfect Wenders situation.

The State of Things is more fully made of cinema than any other of Wenders' films. Driven by the experiences of *Hammett,* its immediate cause was the production of another film. Raul Ruiz, the prolific Chilean exile, was in financial trouble, making a film in Portugal called *The Territory* (a bizarre and silly film about a group of hikers unable to escape their locale, turning

Self-reflexivity: Sam Fuller as Joe, Friedrich Munro's cinematographer, from *The State of Things* (1982).

to cannibalism to survive – Buñuel's *Exterminating Angel* by way of producer-director Roger Corman). One of the actresses in the film, a friend of Wenders, called him for help. He brought down some raw stock left over from *Lightning over Water* to help out his fellow cinéaste. He liked the location and decided to turn the predicament of a crew stuck without money or stock to finish their film into his own screenplay (with the help of the former radical filmmaker Robert Kramer). He flew to New York to arrange financing, kept the location, cast, and crew of *The Territory* – including its master cinematographer, Henri Alekan – and made a film that constituted his response to Coppola, to the questions raised by the desire for a subjective cinema and the overweening conflict of art and commerce.[8]

Every aspect of *The State of Things* is grounded in cinema. Roger Corman, the man who gave Coppola, Scorsese, and other recent American film-makers their start in the business, suggested to Wenders that the film being made by the crew of *The State of Things* should be a remake of a little-known 1961 science fiction potboiler –*Most Dangerous Man Alive* – by the American film pioneer Allan Dwan.[9] (There is much confusion on this point. Everyone who discusses *The State of Things* repeats some version of this story, and in the film, the producer, Gordon, alludes to the fact that the film within the film, "The Survivors," is indeed a remake of Dwan's last feature. We were unable to locate a print of the Dwan film, but plot summaries do not indicate much similarity between *Most Dangerous Man Alive* and "The Survivors." Kenneth Michael Mashon suggests that a film that does seem to bear a similarity is Roger Corman's own 1959 *The Day the World Ended*.) Corman appears briefly in *The State of Things* in the role of Gordon's lawyer. Sam Fuller, writer-director of odd, energetic, anticommunist films in the fifties and early sixties, and much beloved by the French New Wave (he plays a small role in Godard's *Pierrot le fou*), has the role of Joe Corby, the cameraman in *The State of Things*. John Ford's *The Searchers* saturates the film explicitly: Friedrich Munro, the director and main character in the film (named after Friedrich Murnau and called Fritz, after Fritz Lang), reads from the novel by Alan Le May that was the source for Ford's film. The passages of solitude and rootlessness that he is taken with form a reference point between Wenders' film and Ford's, creating a cluster of intercultural and interlinguistic references. Friedrich dresses like Doc Holliday from Ford's *My Darling Clementine* and quotes Mose Harper from *The Searchers*. The name of Ford's film appears on a movie marquee in Los Angeles. A shot in "The Survivors" – the film within the film – echoes a shot from inside a cave in *The Searchers*. Even more, the core narrative movement of *The State of Things* echoes Ford. The search for place – the struggle to find a knowable ground upon which the rituals of order and domesticity can be celebrated, friendship and security elaborated and made dependable – has its base in Ford's film, as does the sense of homesteading in alien territory practiced by the film crew on the Portuguese coast.

While *The State of Things* is not a film explicitly concerned with domesticity or friendship on the level of plot (it is more about betrayal, the obverse side of male companionship, the dialectic to the domestic scene), "The Survivors" is a postapocalyptic vision of a small group of pioneers attempting to find the remnants of community on their trek across the nuclear desert. The film crew in Portugal, living on the edge of the world, overlooking an abyss of gray ocean, finds only dissolution. Ford's homesteaders are here broken into two groups: those who heroically seek a new place in the wilderness (in the film within the film) and those who succumb to it.

The film's dialectics are intricately constructed around three events: the making of "The Survivors," the stranded crew waiting in their hotel for money to finish their work, and Friedrich's trip to Los Angeles to find his producer. All of the conventional narrative elements, a simple linearity, continuity, psychologically motivated characters, a defined and "realistic" space through which the characters move, melodramatic closure – those elements that Coppola and his producers persuaded Wenders to adopt in the second

Cinematic apocalypse: the film within the film, "The Survivors," in *The State of Things.*

version of *Hammett* – are negated in *The State of Things*. The "plot" of the film is minimal, and the narrative denies the rhythms demanded by classical American film form. The first version of *Hammett*, Wenders says, was made mostly of long shots, a structure that creates a slow and meditative rhythm. This method was "much criticized by the studio, who found the tempo not to American taste."[10] He remade the film so that it could be cut to that "taste" and, in *Reverse Angle*, gives us a scene in which *Hammett*'s three editors, in three rooms, sit with pieces of the film, cutting it in the linear, shot–countershot style that gives American cinema the form that makes it "realistic" to the minds of filmmakers and, supposedly, more accessible to filmgoers.

The State of Things, one imagines, recoups *Hammett*'s original style. Made mostly in single – though not especially long – shots in a black and white that captures a spectrum of gray tones no longer seen in contemporary film (which has lost the ability to model light and shadow in monochrome), its structure, especially during the section in the hotel, is fittingly slow and deliberate. Wenders has never before been so desirous of simply gazing at his characters, observing them in their dailiness. Each of them, waiting in the

99

Love in limbo: *The State of Things*.

broken-down Portuguese hotel at the end of the earth, is given one or more small sequences and enclosed within a cell of filmic life, without a story to move them forward or sufficient psychological motivation to draw the viewer completely into their sphere or into a narrative movement. In a way, the first part of *The State of Things* harks back to Wenders' school films, with their minimal budgets and minimal narratives of isolated individuals who, like monads, moved through rooms or along the road. The cast and crew of "The Survivors" are given more definition and articulation than those earlier characters, and like all Wenders' creations, they are self-sufficient and self-possessed. Living in limbo, they sleep, have love affairs, masturbate, play music, ruminate, tell long stories. They are neither joyful nor in despair, only passive and (rather unlike the characters in the previous films) physically static, moving around themselves in narcissistic circles.

Like the characters in the film they are making, they inhabit a world threatened by death; like those characters, they are survivors. But unlike them, they do not actively seek to revive the land and save themselves. Prisoners not of nuclear annihilation, but of film economics, they wait for their release while at the same time practicing their lives, sustaining themselves through small acts and large thoughts. The seemingly distant world does impose on them, however, almost as an act of fate. The effects of the outside world are both indirect and inescapable, such as the death of Joe Corby's wife in Los Angeles. The distance of this event is so great that it distracts no one but Joe himself (and the viewer, who understands the sense of long-distance loss through Joe's phone calls to Los Angeles and his growing anxiety and passivity).

A more abstract, almost cosmic, imposition occurs when Friedrich, asleep and dreaming about Gordon, is startled by a large chunk of driftwood hurled through his motel window by the wind, scattering pictures of his children in a rain of images. This sudden upheaval from the natural world serves as a catalyst for Friedrich and an omen. He reads a passage from Le May's *The Searchers,* about the discovery of a dead piece of juniper in the desert that looks like a man and is an omen of death. Abutting this sequence, connecting omen and event, is a shot of Joe, in his room, listening to the endless drone of a clock with a mechanical voice. The passage of time is the only connection he has with his dying wife; the violence of nature and the passage in *The Searchers* are the only inkling Friedrich has of the disaster that awaits him. In between, the concern with making cinema holds everyone to a dead center. As Joe listens to the sound of his clock, the camera observes him in his stillness and then drifts past him to strips of film hung on a lightbox by his bed.

A stillness before apocalypse, premonitions of endings. The visual structure of *The State of Things* expresses Wenders' desire to make images that tell nothing and show everything – in this instance a world and its inhabitants waiting quietly for something to happen. The narrative structure goes a bit further, attempting to examine his own experiences as a European filmmaker of limited emotions caught in the Hollywood mill that refuses his aesthetic and his very presence. It speaks of the death of cinema, especially the death of the European art film. The strips of film that hang over the artificial light in Joe's room and the dead tree that crashes through Friedrich's window constitute the play between form and difference, surprise and control, emotion and intellect, the tension of creation and passivity that structure the film and, we daresay, Wenders' life at this point.

His experience with Coppola must surely have convinced him that the time of the art film and his previous life as a sensitive, subjective filmmaker were over. His attempts to maintain his sensibilities and cinematic raison d'être against the Hollywood machine were done in for good and all by his *Hammett* experience – unredemptive and fruitless. *The State of Things* is, in effect, a determined stand, a purification through defiance, that attempts to claim – perhaps for the last time – the moral integrity and imaginative vitality of a cinema that foregrounds form and the auteur's imagination over story and commercial interest, that focuses on the character as defined in time and place rather than events, and that claims black and white as film's essential form.

Black and white cinematography becomes, in fact, a central issue of the aesthetics of *The State of Things,* a central point of its story, and the matter over which Friedrich and Gordon lose their lives. "You can see the shape of things" in black and white, one of the actors in "The Survivors" tells Joe. "Well," says Joe, "life is in color, but black and white is more realistic." Joe/Sam Fuller expresses something of a commonplace in the history of American cinema, especially in the fifties. During the years when color filming was becoming prominent, the conventional wisdom was that small, dramatic, "serious" films should be made in black and white, because it was considered more realistic. "Realistic," of course, refers to convention, to the way filmmakers and viewers were used to visualizing reality. Everyday life, as Joe recognizes, is in color, but film history dictated black and white as the serious medium because, until the late fifties, color was used almost exclusively for musicals, some Westerns, costume dramas, and fantasy films.

Wenders' defense of black and white is stated in more general terms in a later sequence with Kate — Friedrich's girlfriend — and one of her daughters. Kate is attempting to draw the seascape around the barren hotel and is in tears because she cannot capture the lights and darks: "Nature, everything," she says, "is just lights and darks . . . the only way you can paint this is by putting the lights against the darks, otherwise it's nothing, everything is lights and darks, shadow and light . . . that's what gives it form." There is an almost desperate quest for the primal structures of art in such a statement, a desire for self-assurance by seeking the roots of an aesthetic, a simplicity of form that might redirect cinema back to the imagined purity of its origin.

We have pointed out how Wenders despairs over the degradation of the image in film and television (where even black and white is made banal when used for rock videos and other commercials, where films that were made in black and white are colorized, and where films made in color fade beyond recognition). He wants the image to be more articulate than words and story, direct and full of nuance, but he finds visual complexity shunned in commercial cinema because it may prove an unwanted distraction. Black and white cinematography becomes a symbol of the last stand against cinema's decay. Friedrich is filming "The Survivors" in black and white in defiance not only of the conventions, but of the economic forces of commercial cinema. This defiance causes Gordon to stop production, flee Portugal, leave the crew stranded, and, finally, bring about his own murder and Friedrich's.

Joe (played by Sam Fuller) and Friedrich Munro, the filmmaker and director, from *The State of Things.*

The sequence of Kate and her daughter painting the rocks and ocean intervenes as a reflective moment at a point of extreme transition in the film, for it occurs between the meditation on the static lives of the stranded crew and Friedrich's comprehension of his betrayal by Hollywood. His revelation leads to his fatal trip to Los Angeles. First, he breaks into Gordon's villa in Lisbon, its interior an odd combination of Norman Bates' house in *Psycho* and the projection room in *Citizen Kane,* with Expressionist lighting reminiscent of *Mabuse, Metropolis,* or *M.* Dusty and dark, illumined by two shafts of light from low, circular windows, it is more decayed mausoleum than home to a producer on location. There are two things of special interest in the room: the figure of Dennis, the screenwriter of "The Survivors," lying on the bed in the dust and dark, and a computer. Dennis had appeared as the most unhappy of the stranded crew and will now be revealed as Gordon's lieutenant and something of an intellectual thug. The computer will become the sign of Friedrich's lost independence. The camera slowly tracks the room from Friedrich's point of view as the haunting chords from "The Survivors" play on the track.

Dennis and the computer, it appears, have been in control of the film from its inception. (We find out later that Dennis' money is partly backing the film.) Dennis refers to the computer as "a piece of Gordon's mind," and indeed it contains images from the film, its storyboard, its budget, but also the graphic of a hand – the trademark of Fritz Lang. The computer also contains the personal and artistic life of Friedrich, including a list of his films, a curious amalgam of half-made-up titles that reflect on Wenders' work and his admired forebears. That Friedrich's aesthetic history and sensibility are captured by a computer signifies a frightful reduction for Wenders. The digitalizing of imagination by a machine and the control of that machine by a frightened writer, whose loyalties to the film's producer undermine the director's art, represent for Wenders the mechanization and displacement of form, imagination, and subjectivity. In the haunted house in Lisbon, filmmaking is reduced to a mere icon of the age of mechanical reproduction, an expression not of subjective reasoning with the structures of an art, but objective control of its external, commercial forms.[11] Gordon's computer is only the latest tool for rationalizing production, yet its place in the systematic process of diminishing imaginative autonomy seems particularly disturbing in its cold deliberateness (and its gothic setting). The computer is the mausoleum for cinema's corpse.

The list of Friedrich's films that comes up on the computer screen forms a synthesis of lost works and broken dreams of German exiles, Hollywood outsiders, and patrimonic figures. (One title, "A Stranger Here Myself" – a line from *Johnny Guitar* – places Nicholas Ray among the exiles – as an American who exiled himself from Hollywood.) These are the people who were enticed by the dream of American filmmaking, sometimes crippled by it, but always standing proof that "artistic integrity" and "individual imagination" are difficult to maintain in a system that counts upon the mass production of images to survive. Wenders understands this, but it would be incorrect to read *The State of Things* as *only* a lament for the creative individual at odds with the Hollywood system. From mourning comes understanding, and the film becomes a rather complex suspension of conflicting responses. Wenders is, finally, neither to be confused with his character Friedrich nor disassociated from him entirely. He is saddened by the state of contemporary filmmaking, mourns the commercial degradation of the image, and was no doubt stunned by his experiences with Coppola in the studio system. At the same time, he is aware that the part of him that responds to cinema the way Friedrich does must be reconsidered or even expunged. *The State of Things,* then, is an act of cleansing for Wenders as much as it is a denunciation of the Hollywood "system." The film becomes a cathartic way for him to eliminate unyielding and perhaps unfruitful aesthetic obsessions by reflecting them in a work that is about that very preoccupation, a way to achieve the redemption lost in the making of *Hammett*.

The film, in fact, denounces Friedrich for being too cold, for insisting on a purity of narrative in his films that drives out life. "Life goes on in the course of time without the need to turn into stories," he insists. But one of his actors, an admirable and amusing storyteller who delivers a hilarious monologue about his Los Angeles adolescence, reminds him that "life without stories isn't worth living." The story of the death of Joe's wife, which is carried on offscreen, goes all but unremarked by Friedrich, who, in his own despair to find Gordon and finish the film, forgoes the opportunity to attend her funeral and comfort his friend when he is in Los Angeles. Friedrich's remoteness is contrasted to Gordon's energy. Even in his desperate flight from the mafiosi who want their money back, Gordon remains a witty and spirited character, a storyteller, and indeed more streetwise and full of life than anyone in Wenders' films.

Gordon – played by Allan Goorwitz, a very talented contemporary character actor – is a spent, frightened, hysterical, ironic, profane, and funny producer at the end of his rope: the Hollywood producer as intelligent, paranoid schmuck, hanging on to his life by wit and the last remnants of the energy of the dealmaker. Certainly, Gordon is a more sincere, more human character than the profit-hungry moguls Wenders sets out to chastise. His is the energy of a person with a mission and pragmatic goals – finish the film, give Friedrich what he needs, the backers what they need, and survive. He succeeds with none of these, partly because Friedrich is so unsupportive in his unyielding aesthetic obsessions. Friedrich permits himself a dangerous luxury, he feigns ignorance of cinema's economic realities and betrays Gordon as much as he does Joe. He insists upon his own artistic purity and refuses to yield to another person's desire and need – a problem shared by very many of Wenders' characters. Friedrich, who thrives on isolation, unwittingly forces the gregarious Gordon into isolation as well, and Gordon rails and jokes against his imprisonment in a way unimaginable to Friedrich or the inhabitants of the hotel in Portugal.

As if in defiance of Friedrich, Wenders turns the narrative against him in the last part of the film: he makes him take part in a story. What had, in the Portugal sequence, been an exercise in the kind of filmmaking Friedrich likes – simple images of people in the course of time – becomes, in Los Angeles, a thriller of sorts, a quest for Gordon and a flight from their pursuers. There is, suddenly, action, story, and closure, very final closure.[12] The mise-en-scène changes as well. Hollywood is made into a stark urban place, almost

Driven by desire and fear: Friedrich on the run from the mob in Los Angeles, from *The State of Things*.

unpeopled, a noirish dreamscape of city streets and billboards, a gray menace, an urban wilderness that might well appear in "The Survivors," but at the same time, curiously, a place of life. The Portugal sequence ends with a montage of the cast and crew at their various tasks of time filling, of Friedrich and Kate making love while the children look on with amusement, of sea and rubble – still lifes in a place out of time. The music accompanying the montage is one of the mournful passages heard throughout the first part of the film. The cut to L.A. – from a shot of the screenwriter's typewriter overlooking the sea in Portugal – is made to the sound of rock music. The new urban space Friedrich enters is simultaneously devoid of apparent human activity but filled with anticipation, dread, pursuit, and representations of power.

In Los Angeles, Friedrich is seen from high-angle shots, isolated in his car. Buildings and billboards dwarf the few people seen on the street; telephone and power lines form something of a visual motif: they loom over Joe's house, where Friedrich makes a brief and unresponsive visit. At one point, Friedrich sits in his car in an empty parking lot. Reflected in his side mirror is a utility pole in the shape of a cross. Church bells can be heard on the sound track. The image resonates, in an almost surreal fashion, back to Ford's *My*

Darling Clementine (already referred to earlier in the film) in which the image of the steeple of an unfinished wooden church at the edge of the wilderness signified the movement of human community into the desert. In contemporary L.A., civilization in the desert has encroached back in upon itself, turned into another kind of wilderness, a wasteland of roads, billboards, parking lots, and telephone poles, images that seem here to be the dead end of Wenders' obsession with the car on the highway.

No longer representing a forced freedom, an opportunity to escape for a while from despair, the road is now an ominous sign of omnipresent, oppressive solitude. The very way Wenders now composes the car on the road is different from images in his previous films. Friedrich drives through the night and the camera is placed low next to him, gazing up so that his impassive face is dominated by the glare of passing street lamps. Elsewhere, there is a high-angle shot of him in his car eluding his pursuers, as if caught in an urban maze, seen from some disembodied, threatening point of view. Friedrich finally discovers Gordon hiding in a huge mobile home, a dark, imprisoning version of the truck in *Kings of the Road* that was Bruno's comforting work space and home. The cavernous, mobile shelter has become here a modern day Kabinett of Dr. Caligari.

These images introduce an uncommon paranoia into Wenders' work. Most of his wanderers, even Josef Bloch in *The Goalie's Anxiety at the Penalty Kick,* seem secure on the road, as if protected by their very freedom to move while being on the run. But in *The State of Things,* the commercial necessities of filmmaking – the thuggery and philistinism that Wenders had already acknowledged in *Kings of the Road,* but thought he could overcome – is recognized as an inescapable force. The powers that make film possible have no interest in its aesthetic productions, but only in self-perpetuation and profit. Los Angeles is the center of those powers, and the paranoid landscape Wenders creates around Friedrich and Gordon proves as deadly as it looks. He literalizes the mise-en-scène and then turns the literal back into metaphor.

When their business deal turns sour, Gordon's money men do not shy away from using force to protect their interests. By having Gordon and Friedrich killed by some unseen mafia henchmen, banal physical violence comes to stand for the realities of a more subtle economic censorship of the arts that victimizes both the commercial viability and the aesthetic aspects of the cinema. "Market forces" effectively control the stories we are told. The thugs who kill Gordon and Friedrich are simply the most obvious indicators of a larger complex of cultural domination and control. Perhaps this helps explain the omnipresence of utility poles and advertising billboards in this part of the film. They are shorthand images of the communication and media culture manipulated by a system that requires submission and enforces conformity. Based upon the images of gangster-style assassination and the suggestion of a greater cultural hegemony maintained by the system, it would be no exaggeration to suggest that what Wenders perceives here are the mechanisms of cultural fascism.

At one point, he makes a sly connection between dominant cultural power and fascist control. During their ride together, Gordon says to Friedrich: "I don't believe this . . . I'm sittin' in a fuckin' mobile home, about to get blown away, maybe, and I'm sittin' here with a fuckin' deaf-mute German. . . . I'll tell you, I never thought I'd live to see the day when I'd be working with a German director, right? A Jew from Newark, New Jersey, and a German, picked up at the fuckin' Chateau Montmartre. What the fuck are you and I doing with each other . . . ?" What, indeed? We may recall the sequence in *The American Friend* in which Jonathan Zimmermann, urged on by Ripley, makes contact with a French gangster, who urges him to assassinate an alleged American mafioso, "an American Jew from New Jersey." And he does it, in a chase sequence through the Paris Metro that somewhat disguises what Wenders is doing: demonstrating how easy it is for a German petit bourgeois to become a tool in somebody else's scheme and reenact the past political crimes of his culture, abandoning conscience, reason, and humanity.

The situation is not so different in *The State of Things*. Jonathan Zimmermann was a craftsman, Friedrich Munro thinks himself an artist. Both represent – as do so many of Wenders' characters – that ruined postwar generation of Germans, so anesthetized by their past and present they can barely feel. Jonathan, while acting out the role of provider and protector of the family, is lured out of his passivity by the promise of adventure and money. Friedrich is an artist, clinging as hard as he can to his subjectivity and integrity, driven, finally, by the threat of economic disaster to his crew and film to pursue Gordon. The "deaf-mute German" is passive beyond measure; he is victimized by Dennis, the screenwriter, and by Gordon, who, like Ripley, is victimized in return. This Jew from New Jersey gets killed because Friedrich is an aesthetic purist, whose willful ignorance of the necessities of cinema production puts both of their lives at the mercy of the culture industry's thugs. The aspects of fascism here are quite dispersed. Friedrich's impassivity and unyielding sense of aesthetic order, his aloofness from the realities of life and cinema, make him susceptible to domination by less well meaning figures. Gordon, who did, after all, support Friedrich's project of making an unusual film counter to present commercial interests, also becomes a victim of powers that brutalize culture. Fascism as a violent force appears within the larger structure of corporate authority, which takes advantage of the innocent and unwilling alike, and whose minions would as soon kill the German and the Jew both rather than bother with their attempts to work out a compromise on the shooting of "The Survivors."

Clearly, Wenders is not making a wholesale attack on Hollywood here. Gordon is a small-time producer who seeks out small-time, hoodlum backers (the parallel between Gordon and Coppola is interesting, though stretched). But Wenders is hinting at larger issues, theorized by the Frankfurt School of cultural critics in the early forties (Adorno, Horkheimer, Kracauer), who spoke to the overwhelming power of the culture industry and the extent to which individual imagination and small artisanal efforts are endangered by it. The analysis of the Frankfurt School is, like Wenders', deeply pessimistic. They see in mass society little opportunity for the individual to escape dominant political and ideological forces. "Life in the late capitalist era," Horkheimer and Adorno write, "is a constant initiation rite. Everyone must show that he wholly identifies himself with the power which is belaboring him." And that identification is forced upon the individual by the culture industry, which provides the manipulative and seductive means and images of compliance through the master narratives of culture. "The miracle of integration, the permanent act of grace by the authority who receives the defenceless person – once he has swallowed his rebelliousness – signifies fascism."[13]

These theories of cultural oppression have formed the prevalent critical assumptions that popular culture is empty of content, manipulative and deadening in its all-pervasive structure (theories that are under attack by the contemporary school of cultural criticism developed by such writers as Raymond Williams and Stuart Hall). Wenders, even while subscribing to these tenets, finds himself in a curious position between the Frankfurt School critique and his own position as an artist in a popular medium. He has always defended certain aspects of popular culture – rock music, American films – while, at the same time, espousing a high cultural status, quality, and purpose for cinema. His critical writings, the statement of the cinema owner at the end of *Kings of the Road* that "the way it is now it's better that there is no cinema than a cinema the way it is now," and his own comments in *Tokyo-Ga* about the degradation of ordered and translucent images by television, as well as the experience of *Hammett* and the making of *The State of Things*, indicate a desire to protect cinema from the subversive powers of the culture industry.

But Wenders, like his alter ego Friedrich, must work for that industry, or must find a way to work *in* it while maintaining cinema as viable subjective expression. The dilemma is compounded by the fact that, by the late seventies, a supportive film culture had all but disappeared in both Europe and the United States. The audience for alternative cinema of any but the most accessible, popular, and conventional kind was disappearing; the possibilities for distribution of subjective films continued to diminish; the New German Cinema, as an active, quasi-collective undertaking, was waning, its knell sounded by the death of Fassbinder in June 1982 (shortly after the completion of *The State of Things*). An adequate space for authentic, thoughtful filmmaking was no longer to be found. The modernist movement was over. For Wenders, the choice (in retrospect) was clear. He needed to find a way to condemn and compromise, to rail against the fascism hidden in the spirit of commercial filmmaking and continue to be a commercial filmmaker at the same time. He had to accommodate both Friedrich, who, like himself, was insisting upon just and valid images, and Gordon, who, like Francis Coppola, is driven to make a commercially viable film.

"I'm at home nowhere, in no house, in no country," Friedrich complains, summing up the state of rootlessness and ennui suffered, to various degrees, by all characters in all Wenders' films. He might have added "in no cinema" and completed the litany that he himself seems to comprehend was edging into the borders of bad faith. For in fact, Wenders, despite the sense of exile from authentic filmmaking, was indeed making an enviable space for himself in the ashes of modernist cinema; he needed only to clear away some of the self-indulgent romanticism of the wanderer and adjust some notions of the narrative. The final confrontation of producer and director at the end of *The State of Things* does both, by balancing out the needs of the imagination, the needs of the money men, and by extension, the needs of the audience. Gordon tells Friedrich that the loan sharks who are now trying to kill them are only looking for a story, a support, a place in which to put the characters. Friedrich insists that the space between characters – the kind of space Wenders provides in the first part of the film, for example – is enough to carry the load. "All stories are about death," says Friedrich, fearful that the linear representation of narrative events will bleed the vitality out of the camera's erotic gaze. Gordon responds by singing his sorrowful Hollywood dirge, "When did you learn you were dead, my friend, when did you learn you were dead, in Hollywood?"

Death, for Gordon – at least insofar as his business is concerned – is not an aesthetic matter, but a commercial necessity, "second best only to love stories" – sex and death. Gordon and Friedrich are shot before they can think of redemption, the third most popular story in Hollywood, and the

Black and white in Hollywood: Friedrich, the filmmaker, and Gordon, the producer, in Gordon's mobile home running from the loan sharks, from *The State of Things*.

one quite likely on Wenders' mind as the dialectical third part in his struggle as a filmmaker. Wenders had looked to the very act of filmmaking as his redemption. For him, the ability to define the spaces between his characters and their movements within those spaces was more articulate and energizing than any story of love and death. But now, in the early eighties, he found himself in a dilemma. Caught in the transition from modernism to postmodernism, from the concept of art as a clarifying and redemptive mediation of history to the idea of art as spectacle that vacates history and dissolves subjectivity, he discovers that purity and aesthetic pleasure are no longer valued commodities. He cannot redeem film in a purely elitist tradition, because film as mass medium is essentially an art of populist appeal that pulls the profane into its narrative heart and defuses its imagery with the banal and everyday.

As a filmmaker, Wenders is not in a position to change his audience radically. The most he can do is create films in good faith and hope to maintain a structural balance between his and his audience's desire. This is perhaps the most difficult task any filmmaker must confront, and at this

A violent death: the killing of nonconformist cinema – Gordon and Friedrich being shot, from *The State of Things*.

juncture the only way Wenders seems able to face it is by killing off the two opposing forces of Friedrich and Gordon, perhaps with the hope that their death will result in the birth of a third, compromising force. But the obsessive urge for instant redemption cannot quite be assuaged by the desire for compromise. Friedrich videotapes his own murder. The event recalls the news cameraman in Patricio Guzmán's *Battle of Chile* (1975–9), who filmed his own murder by the army. By linking Friedrich's theory that all stories are about death with a film about revolutionary struggle and the self-documentation of a cameraman's last shot, Wenders hopes to set up an apotheosis of the filmmaker. The redemption, unfortunately, turns out to be in bad faith. Friedrich is not quite involved in the political struggle that Guzmán's film captures, nor is his death real.

Perhaps, in the end, we can read *The State of Things* not as a redemptive act, but rather as a rite of passage – quite literally, as a way out of the bind in which Wenders found himself during the shooting of *Hammett*. By destroying both Gordon and Friedrich and, with that act, indicting the sinister forces of commercial filmmaking, he enables himself to emerge less encumbered and doubt-ridden. Less pure, as well, for he seems to discover that the only hope for redemption may be in yielding to the recognizable cinematic *conventions* of redemption. This means, finally, that to be redeemed in and by cinema is to be redeemed *with* cinema, seeking a renewal of self in its patterns of love and death, heroism and sacrifice – its stories, which turn out inevitably to be so reduced by the ordinary and typical that redemption becomes elusive. So after *The State of Things,* Wenders begins a descent from modernism into melodrama and then into the postmodern mode. *Paris, Texas* and *Wings of Desire,* the fiction films that follow *The State of Things,* explore the limits of domesticity and the triumphs of love, the despairs of loneliness and the renewal of the romantic couple. *Until the End of the World* recapitulates the journey on the road, questions the permanence of romantic renewal, and interrogates technology and its images in a pastiche that suggests the postmodern itself can barely offer even an illusion of redemption.

From wandering the lonely roads of existence, paying homage to his cinematic fathers, Wenders now examines the tentative restoration of communal relations by revisiting the domestic. In *Paris, Texas* and *Wings of Desire,* Ford and Ray press home their patrimony more fully than ever as Wenders begins to search for images of reconciliation, which lead him to an agony in the desert and a journey to heaven.

5
Paris, Texas
Between the Winds

Paris, Texas is a crucial text in Wenders' career and a vision of hope – unlike *The State of Things,* which is a stark, brooding text about crisis and despair. The modernist structures of the previous films, with their spare, suggestive, open-ended narratives, apparently disappear here, while the image making, the desire to see the ways in which environment and figure interact and define each other, grows more intense than in the previous films. But at the same time, there are more ordinary compositions, more conventional dialogue and expository sequences with a greater dependence upon Hollywood cutting patterns than heretofore. The allusive activity, so prominent in the previous films, peaks at the film's beginning and then quietly vanishes. Marked as it is by *The Searchers, Paris, Texas* brings the allusionist urge of modernism to a climax and marginalizes it as a mode of self-conscious interrogation of cinema. The film is very much a response to the questions raised by its predecessor.

Wenders was conscious of the nature of this response. "I've made quite a number of films that were more concerned with reflecting themselves than reflecting anything that exists apart from movies," he said in an interview. "And I think that's a really serious dead end for something that I love very much, which is movies. . . . At the end of *The State of Things,* there was no other choice than to redefine, or find again, or rediscover what this is: to film something that exists, and film something that exists quite apart from movies."[1] And so Wenders looks for a story and for closure, a narrative structure that seems to speak of "something that exists quite apart from movies." But a contradiction remains. That something turns out to be domestic melodrama, the conventions of which were developed not out in the "real world," but out of nineteenth-century theater and then the movies. To consummate his break with his modernist past, he takes on one of the most cinematic – not to mention most conventional – subjects he could find: home and family. His would-be escape from modernism turns out, in the end, to be another examination of the structures of cinema, even though he seems to think otherwise.

As a result, *Paris, Texas* appears as conflicted as its predecessors, seeking a classical, invisible storytelling form, but still inflected with the cinematic template and mediations that mark the previous works. The film does not solve the modernist crisis of self-consciousness of imagination and form; it does not cross the border into postmodernism. *Wings of Desire* manages that with its mixtures of style and tone, its pastiche of high-art cinema and banal, pop-operatic romanticism, its moving observations of everyday life, its highly stylized poetic dialogue, its melancholic and reductionist notions of German politics, and its coy naïveté about angels and love. *Paris, Texas* is, in effect, the end of Wenders' first major cinematic journey. Summing up all his work to date, it weaves together images and narrative ideas from *The Goalie's Anxiety at the Penalty Kick, Alice in the Cities,* and *Kings of the Road;* it solves Friedrich's dilemma in *The State of Things* by observing the spaces that exist between people and by permitting story to creep into those spaces; it partly resolves – or more accurately, restates and transposes – the crisis of domesticity examined in *The American Friend.*

That film, as we noted earlier, is driven by early fifties domestic/gangster films noir. At its core, however, is another fifties film of the terrors of domesticity, Nicholas Ray's *Bigger Than Life*. There, James Mason's schoolteacher Ed is pulled from his family first by disease, then by its medication, which turns him into an egomaniac. The overwrought plot is overdetermined by a mise-en-scène of domestic containment, of dreams of individual potency gone bad. (Ed was a football player and works for a cab company after hours to make more money for his family.) Ed's house is full of travel posters that are representations of frozen motion and depleted energies, like the model trams and pictures of steam engines in Jonathan's flat. Ed's escape is through a monstrous exaggeration of paternal control, brought on by pills (on the level of plot) and by the repressive force of fifties domesticity (on the level of form and ideology). Jonathan's escape is through the more generic route of gangsterism, Ed's by the attempted imposition of a godlike ego. *Bigger Than Life* suggests the inescapability of domestic oppression. To escape it, the father can only become a destroyer, attempting, in the end, to kill his son. But Ed gets better and returns to the family, in the same circumstances in which he left it. Both films show how the lack of self-perception and the impositions of the domestic can cause violence and lead to a family-threatening situation in which myths of potency seem to be the only possible routes of escape. Both Ed and Jonathan delude themselves and justify their actions as part of their role as family provider. But in both instances, Ed's exploding ego and Jonathan's fascination with the hitman's life are justified only as responses to the rigidity of the domestic.

For Nicholas Ray, and many other American filmmakers in the fifties, domesticity was itself a kind of abandonment, a slippage into the comfortable and necessary at the expense of male freedom. Wenders stretches this ambivalence across the poles of his characters' despair. They remain, even more than Ray's characters, lonely and hopeless in solitude or in domesticity; adventure exists only as momentary and inauthentic respite. "Pity the poor immigrant," Ripley sings (recalling the old Bob Dylan song) as he sits abandoned by Jonathan, who has gone off with his wife to die, alone on the beach near Hamburg – like Philip Winter on the Jersey shore at the beginning of *Alice in the Cities*. The Wenders immigrant walks the borders between home and isolation, often finding both in each, until *Paris, Texas*, in which solitude is a cathartic prelude to the overcoming of alienation through the discovery of self and identity and a rethinking of domestic politics.

Unlike Wenders' other wanderers, Travis, the central figure of the film, follows a carefully made narrative trajectory. He appears first as a mystery and seemingly concludes as a clear-thinking, responsible adult. In the middle, he learns, changes, and in turn changes other people. He behaves, in fact, like any good psychologically motivated movie character. He is first seen walking through the desert, like Ethan Edwards in *The Searchers*. (It is Wenders' most open and direct visual allusion to Ford's film.) But where Ethan rides to the welcoming door of a desert homestead, Travis walks through the wastes until he gets to a roadside café, where he passes out. Ford always presented the grace and protection of house and family to his wanderers as potential respite, even when, like Ethan, they are incapable of accepting it. Neither Ethan nor Travis is able, finally, to accept domestic comforts, and each will return to the desert having exorcised some internal demons, Ethan free to "wander between the winds," Travis quietly to depart the scene of reconstituted domesticity. For Travis, though, an important part of his life comes to a productive conclusion. He is elevated to a level of understanding – of self, of others, and of domestic realities that makes his return to the road suggestive of a new beginning.

Both Ethan and Travis begin with somewhat similar pathologies: an inability to comprehend and deal with otherness, with racial or sexual difference. Ethan Edwards acts out a particularly violent racism, a hatred of Indians, compounded by their destruction of his family and kidnapping of his niece. He is filled with anger, a terror of miscegenation, and an obsessiveness that leads him almost to the point of destroying his niece when he finds her. His actions are determined by the history of the West and that history's ideological reconstruction in literature and film. Community in the Western was restricted to the white settler, who brought a petit bourgeois Eurocentrism into the desert and a firm sense of order and place. Savages were understood as remnants of the wilderness who must be destroyed or segregated to permit the constitution of a domestic space, which women nurture and men protect. Ford attempted, in *The Searchers* and elsewhere, to mitigate this ideology somewhat by depicting the Indians as misunderstood and the white man's zealotry as bordering on the psychotic.

Wenders and his co-scenarist, Sam Shepard, start from a position considerably different and more advanced than Ford's.* In *Paris, Texas,* there is no domestic enclave to protect, only one to rebuild. The racism and sexism that inform Ford's work are less of a given and not displaced by generic imperatives. Wenders and Shepard begin with an understanding of the violence inherent in the patriarchal family and the need to expunge it, even if that means the family must exist in an altered form. Whereas the act that originally drove Ethan from the community is never quite clarified (love for his sister-in-law is suggested, illegal activity is hinted, some acts of violence are alluded to), the act that drove Travis from human community was his violence against his wife, Jane. Seized by a kind of savagery, overcome by jealousy, and fearful of losing his prized possession, Travis chained her to the stove, acting out a crude superiority in the gestures of a master–slave relationship. This incredible act of gender violence – to which Jane responded by setting her husband afire – drove Travis from human community. His attempt to run away from his act and finally to undo it drives the narrative proper of the film.

By playing with the conventions of the Western genre in 1956, Ford could, with only the slightest manipulations, make a film that seems to condemn both racism and sexism on the level of plot, while continuing to uphold contemporary ideologies of the inferiority of women and racial minorities on other, more subtle narrative and structural levels. Wenders also deals with

---

* Wenders had tried unsuccessfully to get Sam Shepard to write the screenplay for *Hammett* and later drafted an adaptation of his short-story collection *Motel Chronicles.* Shepard took over as scriptwriter for *Paris, Texas* and produced a screenplay in close collaboration with Wenders. Halfway through the shoot, Wenders changed the ending they had originally intended and called upon Kit Carson to help develop the concept of the dialogue in the porno parlor that makes up the central part of the second half of the film. Shepard provided the dialogue for this sequence. (See the interviews with Wim Wenders and Sam Shepard in the updated reprint of the script of *Paris, Texas.*)

contemporary attitudes, and his film seems unambiguously to condemn patriarchy and male domination, though it too goes on to confirm them in subtle ways. Ford's Western creates a mise-en-scène in which the ambiguities of white power and its attendant psychoses are held suspended throughout the narrative and past its closure. John Wayne's Ethan remains a heroic figure in a heroic landscape despite the questions about the dark side of heroism Ford gently, almost reluctantly, poses. Neither the landscape nor the heroism exist for Wenders in the early 1980s. Indians are no longer usable signifiers of savagery. The southwestern landscape, as remarkable as it appears to Wenders as it does to other European filmmakers as diverse as Michelangelo Antonioni and Percy Adlon, becomes a grand symbol of barely habitable wilderness. It is a representation of the untamed that is safely contained by a thriving, modern culture, a memory of the past and the past within the past. (At one point in the film, Travis and his son stop at a desert tourist attraction made up of enormous sculptures of dinosaurs.) The small adobe outposts, the mean motels in the heat, the pastel neon and fluorescent glow of desert towns, the endless roads and railway tracks express yet another path for Wenders' desire, another space for peripatetic despair. But no Fordian hero emerges from the dust, just another lost soul in the purgatory of adulthood, seeking a new childhood.

The quest narrative of *Paris, Texas* is psychological and cultural. A man seeks to recuperate himself back into domesticity and to redeem himself, in the usual Wenders fashion, by aligning himself with the innocence of a child. The narrative also sets forth a cultural quest (though this is understated and never quite concluded) that pursues another Wenders concern about the interleaving of America and Europe and the dissolution of cultural specificity. The very title of the film, which refers to the place of Travis' conception and the location of his desire for paternal confirmation – pictured for him in a photograph of a barren piece of land with a "For Sale" sign on it – combines the name of the ultimate civilized city (from an American point of view) with the name of the ultimate in American frontier violence (from a European point of view). In the cultural oxymoron of the film's title, these signifiers are placed in tension so that the central character can reconstitute himself between them and presumably find a stability for his innate violence within his own culture. By film's end, Travis reaches an insight into the primary function of civilization: the containment and redirection of natural aggression. (This is, after all, the story that movie Westerns have always been telling.) He accomplishes his apprenticeship to civilization by absolving himself of the violence he has committed in the past, acquiring a language with which emotion can be spoken rather than acted on, and by exploring the problematics of the family. Travis' ability to channel his anarchic passion, discover compassion for others, and recognize his need for community drives him to resolve the disquieting legacies of his past conflicts. Like Ethan Edwards, he glimpses the domestic, and it has a momentary effect. Like Ethan, he discovers no place for himself in it.

Travis wandered the desert because he betrayed the domestic imperative through his inability to maintain patriarchal order, self-discipline, and control. Unlike Ethan, who was always outside of that order — a maddened heroic figure who appears simultaneously to threaten and protect domestic space — Travis appears at first as a motley, unheroic, distracted apparition who partakes of different worlds. His dirty suit, white shirt, and faded yellow tie suggest a businessman lost in the wilderness; his worn shoes, ill-fitting red cap, untrimmed beard, and ragged hair suggest a homeless man. His initial appearance is both incongruous and indicative of a life riddled by conflicts and inconsistencies. This is the mad fool, an unlikely and even threatening figure. At his point of entry into the narrative, he does not even possess language. In fact, far from the threat to domesticity he later alludes to when he and his wife retell the story of their violent relationship, Travis proves to be one of its ruins, something akin to Ed in *Bigger Than Life* and to Jack Torrance in Stanley Kubrick's *The Shining,* who, maddened by patriarchy, become its avenging destroyer.[2] But unlike these figures, who proceed into madness and violence in the course of the narrative, Travis' violence lies in the past — accessible only through memory and language — which he must recover and reconstruct in the course of the film. The process of the narration, more complex and more carefully developed than in Wenders' previous films, reconstructs Travis' past, has him articulate it, and places him in the adult realm, the symbolic realm of language in which the self is ordered and controlled by patriarchal hierarchies. Travis' journey takes him to self-knowledge that is finally the knowledge of the culture's ruling patterns, which he then becomes capable of obeying or deserting.[3]

Like so many other of Wenders' characters, Travis goes through an existential quest that is informed by oedipal desire. But few other characters have done so in such a schematic fashion. Formerly, the discovery of a male friend, a child, a slight reordering of individual priorities, sometimes death, all within a narrative and mise-en-scène that reached, via allusion and quotation, into the protective patriarchy of cinema, seemed to serve these figures as a passage out of solitary self-absorption. Travis moves through stations of the oedipal journey in a more rigorous fashion, ending not (like Josef Bloch in *The Goalie's Anxiety at the Penalty Kick* or Wilhelm in *Wrong Move*) paralyzed and in despair, or dead (like Jonathan in *The American Friend* and

His brother's keeper: Walt (right) and Travis (left) on the edge of closeness and separation, from *Paris, Texas* (1984).

Friedrich in *The State of Things*) or (like Bruno in *Kings of the Road*) with a simple recognition that he has to change his ways. Travis emerges with a clear understanding of complicity, guilt, and the necessity of taking definitive action. Coming out of the desert, mute and all but unseeing (though he is *seen,* by the camera, of course, and the viewer, but also by an animal, a hawk who responds to his passing, as if Travis were himself part of the natural landscape and potential prey), he then falls literally into the world of language in the clinic of a German doctor in the town of Terlingua – the language of the earth. These two immigrants, the German doctor and Travis, start the process of his self-recognition.

The actions of the doctor, as the first agent of Travis' rebirth into human community, do not bode well. He is a peculiarly corrupt individual (on the one hand reminiscent perhaps of his Nazi predecessors, on the other a straightforward representative of greed), switching from aid and comfort to exploitation, using his position to blackmail Travis' brother Walt for a ransom to get his brother back. Walt, however, is neither corrupt nor greedy. He is the first major guide for Travis' movement out of the wilderness. A prototypical middle-class man, he is secure in the adult realm, placid, indeed somewhat passive — his brother's keeper. Walt's unquestioning place in the world of the ordinary is figured through his job, literally. He is a maker of signs, advertising billboards in particular, and is first seen standing before a huge photorealist painting of a modern building, with a billboard-size photo of Barbra Streisand at his feet. Wenders had experimented with this kind of trompe l'oeil in *The State of Things,* where the actors in "The Survivors" pass before an enormous backdrop of a natural scene. There, the imagery was part of a formal inquiry into perception and the demarcations between human form and nature. Here, it is part of the play between the natural and artificial, wilderness and family, the untamed and the domestic that makes up the narrative underpinning of the film. Walt is a kind of American extension of Jonathan Zimmermann in *The American Friend* (before Jonathan is lured away from his domestic moorings) and, like Jonathan, a maker of artifacts.

This association of the two figures does place some suspicion on the goodness of Walt's character. His particular occupation makes him more suspect still, for we know Wenders' opinion of commercial image making; and the fact that his name alludes to Walt Disney further suggests that he is trapped in the world of derivative and degraded images.* Like Jonathan, Walt is in a precarious position. The nature of his vocation fosters conformity and reflects the emptiness of his social values. His character is moored in unquestioning domesticity, his life stable and seemingly untroubled. In Wenders' view, he has little of his own that is authentic, and he does not, certainly, produce original images. In the end, he loses everything, including his place in the narrative. Like Jonathan, he loses his patrimony (false to begin with, because his "son," Hunter, is really Travis' child), and when Hunter leaves him to travel with his father, Walt disappears from the film and is never more referred to.

But in the beginning, he functions as a double parental figure, to Hunter and to Hunter's father, treating the latter with understanding and with increasing impatience in his attempt to bring Travis into the adult world. Travis' refusal to talk receives, finally, a strong and effective rebuke: "I'm getting a little sick of this silent routine. You can talk! I can be silent, too, you know. I'd just as soon that both of us keep our mouths shut for the

---

* If Walt, the maker of advertising posters, is associated with Walt Disney, Travis' name is probably suggested by the Robert De Niro character in Scorsese's *Taxi Driver,* a madman who attempts to destroy the culture to which he cannot adapt. In the clinic sequence in *Paris, Texas,* Wenders' visual treatment of Travis lying on a cot echoes the way Scorsese observed his Travis in the earlier film. Travis also suggests "traverse," the "moving across" that is the central activity of Travis, the wanderer.

whole rest of the trip." But Walt expresses a paternal care as well, buying Travis clothes and yielding to his obsessive behavior, for Travis begins in complete withdrawal and then slowly emerges – on the road and in motels – as a child, fearful, obsessive, lost. He will only sit in the back seat of the car; he won't ride a plane for fear of leaving the ground; when another car is rented, he insists it be the same as the last. Walt's annoyance is provoked by the "silence routine," while his patience provides the support of male companionship that Wenders finds, in film after film, so important for the healing of a broken spirit.

But the relationships between the various characters in *Paris, Texas* are more intricate and more conventionally dramatic (perhaps due to the interventions of Shepard) than in any of Wenders' previous films. This conflict between relational complexity and conventional melodrama is part of the transitional status of the film we alluded to earlier – the interlacing of modernist exploration and more traditional narrative development, the sequestering of new positions in old conventions. No certainty exists in *Paris, Texas,* no security of emotional connection. Although the film explores and searches for an authentic domesticity (or a domesticity authorized by cinema), that exploration leads continually to the uncertainty of the domestic, just as in Nicholas Ray's best films. At each stage of Travis' entry into the adult realm, he learns more and finds more difficulties because of what he learns.

Travis' contact with Walt gives him back language, the first instrument he needs to reenter culture. The next stages of his movement into the symbolic introduce him back to gender and childhood through his son and Walt's wife, Anne. She is as strong, complex, and intriguing a female character as Wenders has ever created. Being French, her marriage to Walt echoes the cultural tension of the film's title and recalls Travis' tale of his father's desire for a French wife. Anne is transitional in all senses, as a mother, as a central female character. She responds subtly to Travis, his presence seemingly awakening her domesticated eroticism. Yet she remains down to earth, ordinary (except for her foreignness), and she passes on to Travis a certain basic sense of feminine strength and familial intimacy. When Travis gains his son's confidence and the two head back through the desert to find Jane, the Henderson family is essentially broken up, and Anne, like Walt, disappears from the narrative. This seems to be an almost natural conclusion to the film's epic structure. After all, the wanderer is someone passing through, although this time he takes along a prized possession. In *Paris, Texas'* Fordian antecedent, Ethan Edwards reconstitutes the remnants of his broth-

Travis reenters the domestic sphere. Anne comforts him while Walt is looking on, from *Paris, Texas.*

er's family. Here, Travis reconstitutes part of his own family but at the expense of his brother's.

Travis' stay with the Hendersons provides him with a reentry into the domestic. There is a certain gentleness, even playfulness, early on, represented by a shot of the family's feet under the dinner table, a simple metonymy for a family at ease together. But Travis' uneasiness lingers; he spends his sleepless nights shining the family's shoes; he converses with the maid, from whom he learns some basic rules about being a father. And like Ripley in *The American Friend,* he introduces, quietly, unobtrusively, a seductive element into the domestic scene, to which Anne responds by divulging the secret of Jane's whereabouts, something she had withheld from both her husband and her adopted son and that finally results in the dissolution of her foster motherhood. As if aware of the tentativeness of her own domestic space (a tentativeness imaged in the location of her home in the Los Angeles hills above the airport), she responds to Travis by provoking its dissolution. Her feminine sensibility offers qualities that prepare Travis for the trials of encountering his violent past and a place of rest where he can calm his savagery. But her insecurity and dependence, the passivity, perhaps, that results from the deadpan of the domestic, seems to leave her vulnerable. Walt, as if in compliance with the social conventions of his gender, relinquishes his claims on Hunter because Travis is his brother, not because he is convinced that Travis can handle the challenge. For Walt, giving up Hunter is like yielding the right of way, while Anne yields partly because she is seduced by her brother-in-law (another allusion to *The Searchers*) and simply too weak, or too guilty, to maintain her fragile domestic scene.

It has been argued that, in his quest for a perfect domesticity, Wenders simply cannot permit the "artificial" family of Anne, Walt, and Hunter to survive.[4] While he passes over the opportunity to authorize an alternative family structure, this is not his primary focus in the narrative. The alternative nuclear family and its dissolution is simply less important for Wenders than observing Travis' discovery of domestic peace in the recuperation of the repressed. The process of discovery, as we noted, is a heavily mediated re-oedipalization of Travis, stages in a passion play in which he realizes paternity and responsibility and makes the transition from the desert of self-contempt and the childhood of self-indulgence into the world of responsible adulthood, a journey into the heart of ideologically safe human rectitude, if not plenitude. He does not discover a fullness of domestic peace for himself but does bring about a mother and child reunion. In the process, he learns what being a father is about – and what Wenders considers being an adult is about. He momentarily transcends the violence of his past and redeems paternity, if not himself.

Part of this redemption involves appearance itself, the very spectacle of fatherhood that Travis has lost in his descent into himself. The Hendersons' maid, Carmelita – the next guide in his journey – responds to his question about how a father looks by picking out for him a dandyish three-piece white suit and hat. She then asks a provocative question: how does he wish to carry himself, like a rich or a poor man? "There is no in between," she tells him. This small interlude has strong reverberations within the film. On one level, it appears to be an almost stereotypical comic interchange in which the wise servant advises her master, momentarily reversing their standing in the social hierarchy. But Wenders has, in fact, created a subtext in *Paris, Texas* that subverts the stereotype. There is seemingly little class distinction between Carmelita and Travis. For one thing, Travis is of Hispanic descent. His mother's name was Sequine, and her father was Spanish. Travis is intimately connected with things Mexican: part of his four-year journey was spent in Mexico. At one point during his reentry into the domestic, he stands at the kitchen sink (the camera is positioned outside the window, gazing at Travis) singing in Spanish a song that expresses a longing for his roots, his birth and origins:

> On the day on which you were born
> All the flowers bloomed
> And in the baptismal font
> The nightingales sang.
>
> Dawn is breaking
> And the light of day has begun.
> Arise now
> Morning has broken.

The multiculturalism of the film is rooted in its very origins. Co-written by an American and filmed in the Southwest and in Los Angeles by a German filmmaker backed by European funds and distributed by an American film company, it must, almost by its nature, examine the various cultural strands that make up its central character. Travis, part violent redneck, part sensitive wanderer, son of a man who wished to hide his wife's Spanish roots by fabricating her French descent for the sake of sophistication, stands just off-center of the American cultural mix. It is as if Wenders was attempting to rethink the stereotypes of the melting pot, from Travis, who tries to come to terms with his complex heritage, to the lower-middle-class directness and simplicity of Walt and the blonde, blue-eyed simplicity of Hunter and Jane (who is played by a German-born actress attempting to maintain a Texas accent). The allusions to cultures and their representations turn up not only in such direct confrontations as that between Travis and the maid and the indirect references to the characters' lineage, but in more subtle forms, often in background images. For example, in the alley behind the Houston porno house where Travis goes to find Jane, the camera picks up a wall painting of the Statue of Liberty with African-American features. When Travis returns for the long confrontation with his wife, Wenders cuts away from their conversation back to the alley to a brief shot of Hunter. As the camera pans with the child across the screen, the viewer can just make out the words "RACE, BLOOD, LAND" written on one side of the wall before the composition settles upon an enormous mural of the head of a native American woman. The three elements (all presumably on the same wall, though seen at different times) – the African-American Statue of Liberty, the native American, the American neo-Nazi slogan – seem to create for Wenders a triptych of cultural conflict.

But cultural conflict does not translate into racial or class conflict.

"Race, Blood, Land": Wenders on the set of *Paris, Texas* (*top*); Hunter, in the same scene, turns his head to the image of the native American woman (*bottom*); the Africanized Statue of Liberty on the wall brings the issue of diversity to the American myth (*facing page*). From *Paris, Texas*.

Though it attempts to describe the great mix of cultures and investigate the interconnections of Europe and America in a somewhat unconventional way, *Paris, Texas* finally only refers to these issues, primarily through the mural images, without ever confronting them. This is not unusual. Wenders is not particularly interested in matters of class anywhere in his work and rather tends to look instead at individuals – most often lower-middle-class individuals – moving through their environment in search of personal redemption. The historical, social, and economic components of their personalities and their quest are only suggested, only present in the recesses of the text.

Earlier, we spoke of how Wenders, along with his contemporaries in the New German Cinema, was obsessed with finding images for Germany's past. In the course of our study, it is clear that this obsession is not so much with history itself or even the individual's place in that history, but rather with discovering paths to individual salvation in which a character could transcend history by rediscovering simplicity and breaking old habits. The representations sought by Wenders are those of subjective change, not historical understanding. Travis, therefore, is not so much a lower-middle-class American, caught up in the turmoil of a violent, divided culture, as he is another Wenders character on the road in search of the refuge of knowable self. The stations of his journey are personal, if not political, oedipal, if not social (though the social, the political, and the personal intersect at every instant). It is not surprising then that Travis' brief conversation with the maid goes unquestioned or unremarked (is looked on, in fact, as a positive, helpful encounter) and that the next step for his newly burgeoning personality is to confront, understand, and be led by his son.

Hunter is the final guide in Travis' oedipal drama – a drama that seems to work in reverse. Struggling against his father's ennui, repression, and vulnerability, Hunter becomes a paternal figure, the son as father, the guide to Houston, the city where the mother can be found, the city in the desert that, through NASA, guides explorations into the universe.* But before the final journey can be undertaken, Wenders creates three specific moments in the narrative that become, in effect, rituals of preparation, symbolic turning points for the character and summations of some of Wenders' key imagistic concerns. The first is the moment that Travis walks through the streets of L.A. after learning about Jane's whereabouts from Anne. This is a straight, purposeful walk, similar to how he was seen coming out of the desert, but here with less blankness in the eyes, less hysteria. The camera tracks him laterally in full figure, similar to the long shot of Hans at the end of *Summer in the City,* confirming a movement that combines clear direction and a lingering uncertainty. He walks through the night into the dawn, coming finally to a bridge over the freeway. A voice begins to be heard, incoherent, full of the frenzy of a deranged street person. As the ravings become clearer, words can be made out, about prophecies, about threat and doomsday. Travis slows as he approaches the mad man above the huge expanse of highway. He stops and makes a moment's eye contact, the camera a little bit ahead of him, as if urging him to move on. "You will all be extradited to the land of no return," the man yells, as if seeing into Travis' past. Travis puts out his hand and touches the man on the back, walks around him, and leaves; the camera tilts up slightly to compose Travis among the hills and power lines above the highway. The mad man takes no notice of the brief, humane intervention into his madness and continues his apocalyptic harangue. But Travis has seen something: himself – or the image of the person he might

---

* Hunter is surrounded by *Star Wars* and NASA paraphernalia; he wears a NASA jacket and, on the road to Houston, talks to his father about the creation of the universe and travel through space. One of his monologues is reminiscent of the lecture on the vastnesses of space given in the planetarium in a famous sequence of Ray's *Rebel Without a Cause.* There, cosmic awareness was a matter of despair, diminishing the presence and potency of the troubled teenagers in the face of an impersonal vastness. Here Hunter's excitement about the universe is a sign of a child's enthusiasm and naïveté in seeking abandon in the realm of fantasy and expansiveness.

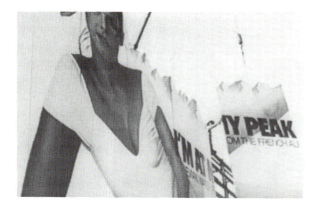

"I'm at my peak": the body as commercial commodity. Evian advertisement, from *Paris, Texas.*

have become had he not returned from the desert to confront his past. His gesture is one of recognition, acceptance, and resolution.

Like the man who grieves in *Kings of the Road,* the madman over the highway is a kind of mirror image for the main character. Linguistically malformed, with violence so profoundly repressed that it is expressible only as prophetic ravings about the end of the world; uprooted, talking of the vastness of ruin just as Hunter talks about the vastness of space; trapped permanently by his madness above the highways that lead to that vastness, the man is Travis' insane other. By touching the madman, Travis admits his kinship with the lunatics and the trapped. The madman over the highway is the *possible* image of all Wenders' characters were they to lose their self-possession and be absorbed into their isolation. He is the collective sign of the uprooted and displaced, living precariously in a world over the abyss.

The second symbolic turn is a sequence in which Travis confronts his brother Walt. He joins him on a huge billboard being erected by his company. The enormous image of a reclining woman in a leotard, advertising Evian water, is being put into place piece by piece by a crane. The words on the billboard read, "I'm at my peak." Travis conquers his terror of heights and joins Walt on the scaffold, telling him he is off to find Jane. He looks at the highway beneath them and remarks that things look clearer from this height. His clearer vision is, of course, not merely external, and his new comprehension of himself and his past are echoed in his position above the highway and in front of the sign. The billboard behind him reveals, to the viewer if not the character, some aspects of his violence against his wife. It echoes an earlier episode when the photo of a nude, hung on the wall in the desert cafe, served as a backdrop to Travis, who, coming in from the desert,

Bonding beneath the freeway: Travis and Hunter decide to search for Jane in Houston, from *Paris, Texas (above)*. Wenders on the pickup truck, trying out the scene (*facing page*).

promptly collapsed from exhaustion. The nude on the barroom wall and the reclining woman on the billboard represent the woman as a vaguely pornographic object, seen in fragments, objectified and two-dimensional. These are images of social commodification and degradation, representing critical problems of gender relations that inform Travis' history of violence against his wife.[5] In a wider sense, the ordinariness of the billboard image (Travis takes no direct notice of it; Walt puts it up as part of his job) makes the ready availability of images of women used to sell merchandise obvious and indicts the generalized exploitation of women and the prevailing misogyny in the society. Part of the cultural mise-en-scène, Wenders merely has to include it in the frame, draw brief attention to it, and its resonance is set forth.

This attempt to pack a great deal of meaning into a composition that includes both human and graphic figures is similar to the sequence of the wall murals we discussed earlier. There, the signifiers (the native American, the Statue of Liberty, the neo-Nazi slogan) bore too much weight, more than the narrative cared to support. But here, Wenders has more success, for the sequence is well integrated into the narrative; the image on the billboard – its panels set into place by a huge crane piece by piece – is closely related to his own often-stated critique of degraded images, his willingness to confront matters of gender in ways he had avoided in his earlier work, and prepares

130

the narrative for the final revelations about Travis in which the degradation of his wife plays a major role.*

The third sequence of transition occurs when Travis and Hunter make their first stop on the road to Houston. They sit in the back of their pickup truck under a sweeping architecture of highway overpasses. The composition and cutting supply some important information, for the construction of the sequence differs from the typical Wenders' road scene. It is static: although traffic moves around the characters, they and the camera observing them are still. The shots that make up the sequence place Hunter in a dominant position. He sits above Travis in the back of the truck and is more centered in the frame than is his father during the one-shots of each that make up most of the dialogue. Travis is placed in the left corner of the frame, against the cab window; behind him a hill and a portion of the overpass can be seen. (The composition connects with earlier shots of Travis driving with Walt from the desert to L.A., where again he is placed on the far side of the frame,

---

* The sequences here and in the pornography parlor where Travis finds Jane bring together a number of references to images of nude women that appear throughout Wenders' films. We have discussed the pornographic film loop that plays a major role in *Kings of the Road;* in that film there are also pinups glimpsed in ticket booths and projection rooms. In *The American Friend,* Ripley gives Jonathan a little peep show device that demonstrates cinematic lighting styles by means of images of naked women.

cramped against the side window of the car, the space of highway, also cramped, to the side of the composition.) The highway does not surround Travis here; Hunter is the figure set against the sculpted figure of the overpass. The road has become less threat than means, recouping its significance from Wenders' earlier work, where the highway helped his characters mediate their solitude. The mise-en-scène here shifts the center of the narrative to the child as paternal guide for the childlike father, providing him attention, support, and purpose, expanding his language. At lunch in the back of the pickup, Hunter teaches Travis some French (they are eating cheese, and Hunter has Travis pronounce its name, "La Vache qui rit"), completing the circuit of references to France, to an ideal culturation, the civilizing of the external and the psychic wilderness. Hunter is the child of the past and the future, giving Travis memory while he, himself, looks forward to the trip to Houston. His eagerness and openness further the relaxation of Travis' oppressed spirit and help lead him on to the recuperation of the family.

Through all of this, Wenders continues to follow the narrative model of *The Searchers* by marginalizing the disruptive figure – the lone, violent male – and re-creating the domestic space. Travis is, in effect, directed by Hunter, nowhere more clearly than in the sequence under the highway and, again, later, after Travis' first meeting with Jane, when he flees in despair to a bar outside of Houston. There, with Hunter at his side, he loses his nerve and gets drunk. Hunter takes charge and literally supports him as they walk into the waiting room of an all-night launderette. In a moment of mutual trust, treating his son as if he were older than his actual age, Travis talks about fancy women and his own mother, who was plain and good, and his father who made himself believe she was from Paris. Throughout the scene, Travis lies on a couch and Hunter sits in a leather chair beside him, in a parody of analysand and analyst. As in the psychiatric situation, transference occurs. Hunter becomes still more the paternal figure of understanding as Travis yields to him and edges toward the confrontation with his past behavior. At this point, the oedipal space, as strangely off balance as it seems to be, is actually becoming clarified. The son – momentarily playing the father – is poised in a position to return to his mother, and Travis, still dependent and childlike, is made ready to assume the role of independent adult.

But independence cannot occur until Travis confronts his past on his own, an event that occurs in the long monologue with his wife in the porno house where she works. The confrontation and its accompanying revelations are heavily mediated. Neither Wenders nor his character can quite bring off a direct confrontation. This is not necessarily to imply some unconscious obstacle on the director's part; the scenes between Travis and Jane are quite methodically constructed. Wenders, as a filmmaker, is simply more comfortable with mediations, which he layers in these scenes by means of the one-way mirror and telephone in the booth of the porno house, devices that serve as protective barrier, movie screen, and confessional.[6] The dialogue serves as yet another layer, through the elaborate narrative about his past that Travis creates for Jane's benefit. Travis can absolve the psychotic version of domesticity that he lived before the narrative of *Paris, Texas* only by distancing his confession as a story told in the third person. This intricate set of mediations serves as a kind of mutual protection, charging the distance and space it creates between the events, characters, and audience with recollections of exploitative, violent eroticism and suggesting that a direct communication of such primitive emotions would destroy the characters and fail to make a reasoned impression on the viewer. The sequence inverts Friedrich Munro's concern, expressed in *The State of Things,* that when stories are told, life flows out. Here stories are an attempt to recuperate lives by filling a bad memory with words that might be healing and restorative.

However, the delicate balance Wenders attempts to set up is threatened often during the two sequences that make up the confessional. The mise-en-scène that situates husband and wife in a porno house in which the woman, at first, thinks her husband is a client and later is made to listen to a confession of violent abuse, suggests a sexual hysteria that carries a potential of overwhelming, rather than clarifying, the narrative. Indeed, the notions of woman as whore offered here seem to smack of the very misogyny Wenders has been working against. Some of this can perhaps be laid to the imagination of Sam Shepard, though Wenders is responsible for the mise-en-scène, and we must speculate on the levels of service to which it is put. We stated earlier that the representation of woman as pornographic object serves, partially at least, as a sign of penance, if not redemption, for the male character within the film and for the male maker of the film, who had been mostly evading and denying the issue of women and sexuality up to this point. The recognition of women's degradation functions as a step toward correcting images that degrade. Such representations also serve as a function of Travis' guilt. The man who tied a cowbell to his wife's ankle and chained her to a stove, and who was in turn set ablaze by her in an act of desperate resistance, returns to find his wife in the position that he, in effect, always wanted her to hold: subservient, without identity, at his mercy — an object of sexual power kept safely behind a one-way mirror. Throughout the scenes of confrontation, she seems unable to transcend this oppression, and he can only address it through a mirror, over an intercom, in the third person. His desire to recuperate domesticity from the violence both he and Jane commit-

The confession booth: Jane and Travis recounting their story, from *Paris, Texas*.

ted is therefore compromised by her transgressive role as sexual object in the porno parlor and by his own recognition that the language and actions of domesticity will forever elude him. Despite this, some contact *is* made: Travis lights his face so that Jane can see him, and at one point the reflection of his face on the glass merges perfectly with hers on the other side. While they achieve no intimacy, no direct communication in the way estranged couples often do in American film, their words and gestures offer the potential of rational discourse about emotions.

With the distancing devices built into their reunion, Wenders holds back a sense of emotional fulfillment. He recognizes that his characters exist only in images, that they are, finally, fictional characters in a motion picture (something alluded to earlier in the film when Travis watches home movies of himself, Jane, and Hunter at Anne and Walt's home), and that they exist only as their story. All they can do is render to the viewer an opportunity to transform these images and stories back into life – emotionally, cognitively, aesthetically – and to make sense of how destructive patriarchal structures may be transcended.

Within the narrative, Travis' journey back to domesticity is, finally, incomplete on a number of levels. The characters cannot, of course, escape

The oedipal moment: Hunter is reunited with Jane, from *Paris, Texas*.

their status as representations; it holds them within the bounds of the mise-en-scène, within the frame of the visible and within the restriction of their stories and the way they tell them. On the level of culture, Travis and Jane cannot transcend their own limits or those that the patriarchy has structured for them. Jane tells Travis that every man that speaks to her has Travis' voice. He has, therefore, never really left her. Despite his brutality to her, he, and what he represents, have become internalized. He remains patriarchy's agent, holding his place while being physically distant, a cogent force even while he was himself disintegrating under the pressure of his own guilt. And as far as Travis is concerned, he remains at the periphery even as he tries to reenter the domestic realm, like a spirit facilitating the reunion of mother and son, Madonna and Child, a new holy family without his presence.

In a Houston hotel room, Hunter and Jane embrace, the child climbing upon and grasping his mother with his legs in a passion that has curious sexual overtones. Perhaps, having performed the service of oedipal guide to his father, Hunter must now reverse the path, possess his mother, go through a stage of innocence, and come back as an adult. He must certainly transform her from a sexual commodity – the wife who in her shame and distress took work in a porno parlor – to a parent. He makes a mock gesture of clipping her hair, as if to diminish the cheapness of her appearance as a dyed blonde who suggested availability and attractiveness to her customers. The gesture is complicated, a combination of reduction and transformation. It indicates that Hunter can make his mother into the image of her that he needs; but it seems, along with the intense embrace, also a gesture of potential ownership and diminishment, of a reconciliation that, ultimately, will place Hunter on the path to male domination.

Travis observes all this from the outside (he had already recorded a farewell to his son on an audiocassette, Wenders again pointing to the role of language as mediation), standing next to his Ranchero on the large, empty roof of a parking garage surrounded by the sharp-edged Houston skyline. He observes from a distance what Wenders shows us close-up; he is pleased with what he has brought about and then proceeds to drive into the sunset. The last two shots of the film – a close-up profile shot of Travis in the car and the car itself on the highway, leaving the city – inscribe Wenders' signature. Not literally, as when his initials appeared reflected on the windshield of Bruno's truck at the end of *Kings of the Road,* but through the reiteration of his primary cinematic signifier, the male driver on the road. On the highway stands a billboard that reads, "TOGETHER WE MAKE IT HAPPEN. Republic Bank." The signature images of the poet of the road, the language of advertising that ironically reflect on the events of the narrative (Travis and Hunter found Jane at a Houston bank), and the near banality of a happy ending collide. Travis has thwarted his own melodrama by removing himself from the domestic scene at the moment he has created it. Wenders has reckoned with the history of patriarchy, alluded to its violence, and resolved it (presumably) by reuniting mother and child, allowing the violent element to disappear. Travis, it would seem, finds redemption in a new beginning. The man who drives away has achieved a higher level of understanding of his own self and others. Like Ethan Edwards, Travis has completed his initial itinerary and is free to move on. But finally, very little is altered. The world of the advertising billboard and the images of repressed and oppressive sexuality are unchanged. And even though Travis seems to have abdicated his violent obsessions, he – like his namesake in *Taxi Driver* – drives into the night still full of threat in a culture that cultivates and supports men who are possessed by their desire to master women.

We suspect that the closing shots of *Paris, Texas* are intended to express the enduring sadness of the now enlightened man who purposefully, perhaps even heroically, removes himself from the temptations of violence in the domestic scene. But in the context of Wenders' other films, they constitute a continuity of the self-disrupted, self-sufficient life in transit that has been the staple visual and contextual theme of all his work. Up to this point, Wenders seemed unable to find a point of rest for his male characters, a way for them to make subjective and cultural peace, a way to get off the road, to enter history. The cluster of works that include *Hammett, The State of Things, Paris, Texas, Lightning over Water,* and *Tokyo-Ga* – all of them made outside of Germany – seem, among other things, to admit to Wenders' defeat in coming to terms with his own culture. They make up the traveler's escape from his country and a search for support and stability in another. They constitute as well the continuing escape from heterosexual commitment and the refusal to admit homosexual possibilities.

Without home, history, and secure sexual commitment, Wenders' characters (and Wenders' own persona in the documentaries) continue to move from skyline to skyline, until their creator decides, in the film following *Paris, Texas,* finally to invert the line of travel, to fantasize a way of coming to rest that, in effect, evades subjectivity, history, and politics and, through the masquerade of spiritual romance, goes beyond the concept of *Heimat* – the simple and comforting home – into a curious version of romantic melodrama. *Paris, Texas'* America is a fantasyland, a place of striking images, a mise-en-scène of desert and city sometimes barely hospitable to the human figure and in which it must struggle to create a comfortable space. Articulated by Sam Shepard's intense, sometimes hysterical, family melodramatics, the film moves almost schematically toward a proper melodramatic closure, in which the warring, destructive elements of the domestic seem to collapse into the illusory harmonics of the status quo. Wenders pulls the conventions up short and therefore still leaves himself an open space. His character back on the road, he has yet to find a resting point. If, finally, Wenders realizes, as Nick Ray did, that the conventions of domesticity are simply unworkable, then he has to turn to others. This he does, with a vengeance, by moving to the romanticism of spiritual melodrama in which the suggestion of a holy family present at the end of *Paris, Texas* becomes a new mythology of domesticity in *Wings of Desire.*

6

Wings of Desire

Between Heaven and Earth

Wings of Desire is made up of at least three interleaved texts: first, an intertextual web of allusions that infiltrate the film; second, an experiment in perception – the creation of a quasi-documentary of Berlin, a way of seeing the (at the time) divided city as a pastiche of individual lives, whose murmurs and acts of despair constitute a painful vision of modernity; and third, another installment in Wenders' inquiry into the possibilities of domesticity (how to get off the road) and yet another attempt to solve what is still for him the mystery of gender.[1] As always in Wenders' films, allusion provides the textual weave, the material from which the text receives its support and nourishment. He dedicates the film to three "angels," one long-gone and two recently dead filmmakers: François Truffaut, Andrei Tarkovsky, and Yasujiro Ozu. As we have seen, Ozu has guided Wenders' films at least since *Kings of the Road* with an idea of domestic order and the presence of a mise-en-scène that counterpoints figure and world in a delicate and acceptable balance.

The films of Truffaut – especially the moments that involve children – have always touched Wenders' work. Though Truffaut's children are less symbolic creatures than are Wenders' (which enabled the French director to elicit more simple, direct performances from them than does Wenders), the two share an attraction to the spontaneity of the young. Other elements in Truffaut's work, particularly the director's ability to capture small, seemingly insignificant moments and observe them with a meaningful gentleness, feed into Wenders' desire to observe the everyday, small motions of his characters and the "dead times" in their lives. Though Truffaut would never film anything as intimately physical, the scene in *Kings of the Road* where Bruno walks to a sand dune and defecates is made in the kind of offhand, matter-of-fact way that Truffaut often uses to observe his characters. That the sequence

Divine icons: the "human" angel and its representation, from *Wings of Desire*.

in *Kings* is not offensive (or perverse, as it perhaps might have been had Luis Buñuel filmed it), but merely startling and human, is indicative of the ways in which Wenders appropriated the significant offhandedness of Truffaut. The "good boy" of the New Wave, Truffaut refused the political inquiry of Godard, the Hitchcockian perversity of Chabrol, the narrative intricacies of Rivette, and the conversational obsessions of Rohmer. His celebration of adult eagerness and the spontaneous perceptiveness of children no doubt appeals to Wenders, who is also driven to find the authentic and sincere – sometimes, like Truffaut, at the expense of depth and complexity.

The nomination of Tarkovsky as one of Wenders' angels is interesting. Why the Russian filmmaker and not Rainer Werner Fassbinder? Fassbinder's political commitment and artificial style, his refusal to indulge in an authenticity that might simply be a cover for banality, the unrelenting irony in his turning the everyday into a mirror for melodrama and the defraction of subjectivity in his films (away from his own personality and toward class and historical determinism) puts him at some remove from Wenders' own approach to filmmaking. But he was, after all, a major figure in the political economy of the New German Cinema. "The bastard died on us," Wenders once said about Fassbinder in an expression tinged with some obvious anger.[2] In *Chambre 666,* the film Wenders made at Cannes in which he offered a number of directors an opportunity to speak alone in a room about cinema, Fassbinder is introduced with an image of an enormous tree and the same portentous music as *The State of Things*. The grudging acknowledgment of Fassbinder's power and presence places him in a quite unangelic position; he is recognized by Wenders, but clearly not as a member of his pantheon. But then, in matters of style and mise-en-scène, even of content, Tarkovsky is also quite distant from Wenders.

Tarkovsky is a filmmaker of large moral and aesthetic meditations, with mystical leanings in the tradition of Tolstoy and Solzhenitsyn. He indulges in great romantic statements of art and the individual, in arguments on freedom and moral necessity.[3] His films are made up of spectacular, complex images in a neo-Expressionist mise-en-scène built out of long takes that deny editing as anything more than a way to move from one set piece to another. Great, decaying, water-filled rooms, religious icons and machine guns under running brooks, horses and German shepherds, levitations, deliriously slow tracking shots of men moving across dark landscapes are repeated throughout the Tarkovsky canon. Thematically, Ingmar Bergman is the closest comparable filmmaker in the West (Tarkovsky's last film, *Sacrifice* [1986], was made in Sweden with one of Bergman's actors, Erland Josefson), though Tarkovsky's visual and moral complexity far outstrip Bergman's. There is none of Wenders' ordinariness, the observation of the everyday, in the Russian's work. Every image attempts a large, symbolic statement. Both filmmakers, however, look to the cinema as a redemptive force: Wenders, to the faith and support supplied by the films of the past; Tarkovsky, to the revelatory possibilities of the image, to the duration of the gaze that, by looking long enough, will discover the spiritual in the material world.[4]

The gaze of both filmmakers reveals configurations of despair and hope between his characters. Wenders' mise-en-scène often foregrounds the material world as strange and even threatening, but more often as dramatically explanatory of his characters' experience. Spectacle and the uncanny – two major elements of Tarkovsky's vision – are largely absent from Wenders'. But clearly, Wenders admires the presumption of the Russian's images and probably felt sympathetic to his career problems in the USSR and his subsequent wanderings. (Tarkovsky left the USSR after *Stalker* [1979], and made his last two films in Europe.) That he should think of Tarkovsky when he makes his own film about spirituality and materiality is not strange, therefore, though neither is it surprising that he flips the terms of the spiritual and material upside down.

Wings of Desire proposes that redemption occur with a descent into physicality. In this, Wenders comes closer to certain conventions in American

Angelic pietà: Cassiel carrying Damiel before his fall to earth, from *Wings of Desire.*

films – and one British – in which angels (who are most often figured as the dead who are anxious to return to their loved ones on earth) come to earth to guide the living into a fuller life. *Here Comes Mr. Jordan* (1941), *A Guy Named Joe* (1943), *It's a Wonderful Life* (1946), the popular 1990 film *Ghost,* and most important Michael Powell and Emeric Pressburger's *A Matter of Life and Death* (also known as *Stairway to Heaven,* 1946) come to mind as films that attempt to conquer the despair of death by fantasizing a somewhat whimsical afterlife whose participants successfully guide the living through their (usually) romantic trials. In many of these films, the dead demonstrate a certain regret at their state, suggesting that spiritual being is less rewarding than earthly sexual fulfillment. Hollywood film has always represented religion and religiosity in terms of the most egregious piety, of cute, childlike irrelevancy, or acceptable irreverence (the usual posture of movie Catholic priests), or of a restless afterlife in which angels are anxious to intercede for the living. Concerned with the material, in all senses from economic to aesthetic, film has not known what to do with the spiritual and usually presents it as a useful tool to expedite the sexual.

The envy of life on the part of the dead is most clear in *Stairway to*

The angel's gaze and the child's view: complementary visions, from *Wings of Desire*.

Heaven, where the dead make easy transit from a drab black and white heaven to a technicolor earth. (In Tarkovsky's *Stalker,* black and white is used for the everyday, color for the mysterious, potentially liberating, spiritual world of "the Zone.") Wenders finds Powell and Pressburger's reversal of color conventions more appropriate and raises it to structural importance. For Wenders, angelic perception (in black and white) is simultaneously omniscient and limited, and the conflicts between these two states lead to the ultimately insoluble conflict of the film's structure and point of view. Wenders' angels are perfect (though incomplete) humanists. Their center of operations is the Berlin public library. Their chief function is to calm savaged emotions and save despairing lives. They have perceptual access to everyone's subconscious, and the film is at its best when its apparatus – camera and microphone – represents the angelic point of view, moving as if through the air and recording stream-of-consciousness monologues of the city's inhabitants. As Ruth Perlmutter suggests, the angels are cinema; theirs is the ideal ability to record and transmit, to access and represent individuals in their world and to save them from despair. The angels, like an ideal cinema, can intervene to clear a troubled consciousness and give structure to disordered perception.[5]

The sequences of *Wings of Desire* in which the camera takes angel flight, gliding through the Berlin cityscape, into apartments and through the Berlin library, descending to children on the street and accident victims, ascending to suicides on rooftops, recall the middle- to late-twenties German tradition of the *Neue Sachlichkeit,* the new objectivity. This aesthetic followed and modified Expressionism as a means of representing the politically charged modernity of daily urban life. In painting, it is associated with the hard, satiric portraiture of George Grosz and Otto Dix. In film, the style leaned toward documentary observation in works as different as Walter Ruttmann's *Berlin: Symphony of a Great City* (1926) and Bertolt Brecht and Slatan Dudow's *Kuhle Wampe* (1932).[6] In all cases, the Expressionist image of a disturbed or psychoanalytically determined subjectivity was replaced by a more politically informed expression, an "objective" observation of an urbanity strained by the conflicting and violent demands of the middle and working class. *Neue Sachlichkeit* was the last great movement in German art before the Nazis (most of its diverse practitioners fled or were silenced after 1933) and therefore stands as the final attempt to document the first phase of twentieth-century modernity.

The style drives much of Fassbinder's work, although it is reworked through the patterns of Hollywood melodrama. It is barely present in Wenders' films, however, partly because of his political reticence, because of the lack of satiric or ironic drive, and because his cinematic perception is more spatially than figuratively oriented. *Neue Sachlichkeit* depended on the figure in painting and on montage in film. Wenders' mise-en-scène defines the figure within its spatial determinants, in motion, in cars, rooms, and streets. (For example, the early shots of Derwatt, the Nicholas Ray character in *The American Friend,* sitting in a chair, a television set behind him, composed with a wide-angle lens, provide neither narrative nor character information, but rather meditate upon a spatial configuration of alienation and distance.) But the montage sequences of angelic intervention in *Wings of Desire* attempt to capture some of the celebration of the city found in Ruttmann's *Symphony* film and even observe working-class characters in tenements, subways, and streets. Wenders, as we have noted, seems most comfortable with lower-middle-class, as opposed to working-class, characters. Travis and Jane in *Paris, Texas* are about as close to working-class characters as can be

Longing for the physical: Damiel gazes unseen at the object of his desire, from *Wings of Desire.*

found in his films, but their class is not the primary interest. They serve rather as two further examples of the emotionally uprooted attempting to discover a respectable petit bourgeois life. The disenfranchised in *Wings of Desire* are not central characters, but part of the angelic montage.

Perhaps it is a sign of Wenders' discomfort with the class-determined particularities of everyday life that leads him to fantasize a heavenly perspective in *Wings of Desire.* Providing the angelic point of view, the camera descends; it does not observe its subjects as they see themselves, but rather as they are themselves subject to an extraterrestrial force. Wenders' "symphony of a great city" is conducted from on high. His angels are caring but inescapably condescending. When he plies the angels' perspective, he creates a well-imagined, even moving, trope of a city battered by history, torn by politics, and guarded by fantastic figures, who see and hear everyone's distress. In these sequences, his camera is more supple and sinuous than it has ever been, swooping from great heights, entering apartment rooms, wandering and drifting through the city, making divine cinema. But in the end, neither the city nor its inhabitants remain the central objects of his gaze. The film is diverted by a quasi-mystical meditation on romantic love, constructed through the conceit of a male angel who desires to slip out of eternity, into time, sexuality, and domestic love.

A useful way of understanding what Wenders does in constructing the story in *Wings of Desire* is to take a brief detour and examine the role of Peter Handke, who collaborated on the script (or more accurately, who was implored by Wenders into collaboration).[7] The association of filmmaker and novelist goes back to the late sixties when the two indulged their mutual fancy for rock and roll in *3 American LPs.* It was *The Goalie's Anxiety at the Penalty Kick,* however, where the nature of the interaction became clear. Handke's novel, as we have noted, is a modernist narrative that attempts to blend together the various influences preoccupying him at the time: existential alienation and the absurd, derived from Kafka and Camus; an interest in the detective novel and, more generally, with the ways the conventions of popular fiction could undercut the narrative structures of the modernist tradition; and, finally, case studies of war-related schizophrenia as manifested in shell-shocked soldiers.

In the character of Bloch, Handke attempted to explore the disorientation of human existence through the perceptions of a subject detached from reality. By severing the conventions of verbal communication, Bloch becomes a semiotic solipsist. Enclosed in his own perceptual space, he is removed to the point where he commits the casual, unpremeditated murder, of which he seems as much the passive victim as the woman he kills. Wenders, as we mentioned earlier, attempts to create a structure of point of view and mise-en-scène that corresponds to Handke's treatment of linguistic conventions gone awry. He stresses the alienation that envelops the main character as he progressively becomes more passive.[8] Handke's concern for language focused on the problem of the ineffectiveness of representation, as words and meanings, collapsing into the subject, become unalterably separated from each other. Wenders shifts to the more palpable, accessible – and in early seventies European cinema, more common – theme of the impossibility of communication between human beings. More important, in presenting a discordant mise-en-scène, he is able to present simultaneously Bloch's failing perceptions and an ongoing world that seems to exist independently of him. Handke's concern with the difficulty of relating the self to the external phenomena becomes a narrative of subjective stasis and dislocation, which, for Wenders, is part of the development of a long meditation on the male figure on the move, searching for an adequate representation of subjectivity.

The next collaboration with Handke was an original screenplay. *Wrong Move* elaborated on the problem of isolation begun in *Goalie,* this time positing it as the failure of the searching hero caught in his own indecisiveness and passivity. Wenders showed his protagonist in suspension, almost neurasthenic, whereas Handke had intended Wilhelm to find a way to follow his calling and becoming a writer.[9] The stasis of the main character in *Wrong Move* is so antithetical to the filmmaker's usual position that he followed it with *Kings of the Road,* in order to release the character from his solipsism. In 1977, Wenders produced and Handke directed *The Left-Handed Woman.* Here, the tension between language and objects, words and images, is reflected in the social relations of the main character, who, through a sudden illumination, leaves her husband and enters, quite literally and movingly, a space of her own. She sidesteps the patriarchal order that had marginalized her and attempts to redefine herself through language. The film is more fluid and coherent than any of the Handke material directed by Wenders himself. The writer seems at home in the creation of delicate and articulate images that indicate a thorough understanding of the cinema of Ozu. (In case there is any doubt about the influence of the Japanese director, a picture of Ozu hangs in the main character's house and, at one point, an Ozu film is running on television.) Where *The Goalie's Anxiety at the Penalty Kick, Wrong Move,* and, later, *Wings of Desire* suffer a kind of self-consciousness and static dramaturgy not found in the films written by Wenders himself or with other collaborators, *The Left-Handed Woman* uses stasis as a point of negotiation, allowing both character and viewer to comprehend the design of female space and the ways that design can be altered.

It is difficult to determine whether *The Left-Handed Woman* demonstrated a filmmaking skill that Handke could develop further because his subsequent film work, particularly an adaptation from Duras, has not been released in the United States. And our specific interest here is the difference in narrative structure and mise-en-scène that occurs in those films Wenders makes with Handke. Part of that difference has to do with language, obviously Handke's main interest. In his fiction and drama, he adopts aspects of Wittgenstein's ideas of language play (*Sprachspiel*), foregrounding the conventionality of language use and the ways those conventions are able to be altered. His early plays (*Sprechstücke*), which brought him great notoriety in the late sixties, explore linguistic conventions by stressing automatic repetitious patterns that, through their very repetition, reveal the limitations of everyday discourse. In plays such as *Kaspar* (1967), Handke successfully challenged the normative forces that inhibit free language play and lamented the fact that the acquisition of language as part of the process of socialization constrained the individual within predetermined social and linguistic norms – a position Wenders takes when he celebrates children uninhibited by linguistic constraints.

Handke's major project in the seventies, when he and Wenders became proponents of the "new sensibility" movement, was the re-creation of a sensitized poetic expressiveness. Wenders manifests this new sensibility in the delicate interactions of a longing individual in a landscape that both reflects and deflects his desire; Handke does so in the poetization of everyday language, a rarefying of discourse that attempts to give it presence by forcing the listener to attend to it. *Wings of Desire* is a crowning example of his search for otherness in language that distinguishes poetic discourse from the abused verbiage of the everyday world. With this forced artificiality, Handke hopes that language will be able to conjure up the spiritual and mediate transcendence. By unearthing the "poesis" in everyday language, the banal familiarity of commonplace phenomena, the plain thingness of the ordinary reveals an extraordinary singularity, as long as the poetic perceptions discover inner being and hidden beauty and give them voice. Such poeticized speech and spiritual exhortation attempt to infuse *Wings of Desire* with an otherworldly quality, pulling against its images of the everyday. The language is sometimes "exquisite" and often modeled on older elegiac styles. Sometimes, in its poetic excesses, it is postmodern kitsch.[10]

In *Wings of Desire,* Handke and Wenders root their language in the religious sentiments of romanticism, which strove to redeem the ordinary world by elevating it to the ideal. Thus, the dying motorcyclist in *Wings* is comforted by Damiel, who offers him a prayer-like psalm that will carry him from his place and moment of finality to the distant reaches of the spiritual. Emulating the biblical journey out of the Valley of Wails, this hymn moves to the heights of the sun to evoke a universal place. Step by step, the movements of clichéd metaphoric phrases, such as "The Far East," "The High North," "The Wild West," and the observations of such ordinary events as raindrops on the ground, are offered up as a vision meant to be superior to the fear of death. In metonymic fashion, the wonders of the world are exhorted to bring salvation. This encircling of the miraculous aspects of human existence culminates in the dying man's vision of the family tree: father, mother, wife, and child. Handke's transfiguring poetic discourse reveals its indebtedness to the concept of divine domesticity in Genesis and the gospel of creation.

This poeticizing encircles not merely the sequence of the dying motorcyclist, but the film as a whole. A poem celebrating childhood, in the manner of Rilke and Hölderlin, is read and copied by Damiel at the beginning and end of the film. (Its linguistic texture projects an elegiac contemplation that is carried through to the film's final apotheosis of romantic love.) Paul Klee's painting *Angelus Novus* and Walter Benjamin's philosophical exegesis of this image as an icon of the progress of history are further guiding concepts for the film, joined by the folklore of the guardian angel, all linked as further signs of the redeemed male child. These elements overdetermine *Wings of Desire*, which traverses the fields of history in Berlin, attempting to reclaim the innocence and humanity of its central character. Handke's poetry rarefies, even hypostatizes this narrative. It helps lead it, finally, into the self-indulgent, where poetry and romantic desire help turn the film into an act of evasion rather than redemption.

When it works, Wenders and Handke's use of poetic dialogue to weave a rich metaphoric texture allows them to reach far into the imagistic traditions of Western humanism. The biblical concept of the angel as divine messenger is augmented by other religious and classical allusions to angels as both loyal servants and apostates. Damiel's fall echoes that of Lucifer, though his defection from the divine is expressed not as an evil act (and, of course, in Wenders' new age version of spirituality, no God is referred to); rather, his entrance into mortality is provoked by desire and the simple exertion of will, not to power, but to self-realization. The male angel is transfigured by his desire for gender and physicality, human bonding and heterosexual love, and the glories of the everyday. Damiel's human rebirth embellishes, indeed seems to grow out of, the cherubic figure of Daniel in *The American Friend* and Hunter in *Paris, Texas*. The innocent and angelic child-redeemer, whose desire is directed toward his mother and into speculations about outer space, seems to have become a full-grown angel in the figure of Damiel, who desires the female and longs for human reality. In *Paris, Texas*, the unification of Hunter and Jane, mother and child, evokes the holy family. Wenders' texturing of the metaphors in *Wings of Desire* expands and then relies on religious mythology, simultaneously confirming its traditional validity and inverting its images and concepts.

The creation of Damiel as angel of superior spiritual existence and defector from the supranatural plays out a fundamental dualism in Wenders' portrayal of his male characters. Whenever the male self is in a state of pure desire — as are the children in Wenders' films — they demonstrate an innocence of angelic dimension that approaches cliché. Alice and Hunter are able to act as guardian angels of adults struggling to find their footing in this world, as does the child at the end of *Kings of the Road* who points Robert the way to the simplicity of a language that resides in things, enabling him, in effect, to read from the book of God's creation. The angels in *Wings of Desire*, visible only to children and other angels, are adult versions of the children in the earlier films. Given their provenance, they extend and make manifest the spiritual and folkloric dimensions already latent in children themselves. They are truly "guardian angels," compassionate spirits whose

Christ, eros, and desire, from *Wings of Desire*.

job is to protect and even redeem the adults of earth. Damiel furthers this compassion, peculiarly enough, by turning it inward, becoming his own guardian angel and seeking to redeem himself.

In the first library sequence (and it is a brilliant conceit to present the library as the gathering place of the angels), Damiel is seen sitting at a table with children, one of them in a wheelchair. He has his back against a rail, and appears, for a moment, as if he were suspended in space. (The composition is somewhat reminiscent of *The American Friend*, in which Jonathan — played by Bruno Ganz, who also acts the role of Damiel — is seated in the airport in Paris, as if suspended before a huge expanse of building.) His head is turned sideways, his eyes downcast, and his hands grasp the rail behind him. The echo of Christ on the cross is quite obvious. Compared with Robert's playful mimicking of the roadside crucifix in *Kings of the Road*, Damiel's posture shows a straightforward "imitatio Christi." Placed in the library, this representation suggests a bridging of the body, soul, and intellect, a combining of the flesh and spirit within the archive of human memory. (Wenders was probably thinking about Alain Resnais' 1956 documentary on the Paris Bibliothèque nationale, which is called *Toute la mémoire du monde*.)

The combination of human and divine is further worked through in a gesture made by Damiel in the course of this sequence. He takes a pen from the table. The act is coded, cinematically, by the old device of double exposure: Damiel lifts the "spirit" (the "idea" of the pen), while its "corporeal" form stays on the desk.[11] After this act, he once again assumes a cruciform position. Seated on a reading chair, fully clothed in his winter garments – a black suit, gray shawl, and a dark coat – arms stretched out and angled as if pinned to a cross, the white pen resting on his lap, his image suggests that of a redeemer who exists within and without the world, his body containing the instrument of inscription. He embodies it and it becomes part of his own embodiment. By placing it on his lap, it is given a phallic presence, a sign in which writing, language, and the body are unified by erotic desire, logos redeeming eros, the spirit setting the word free. The erotic gesture is even more marked when, later in the film, watching his lover-to-be undress in her room, he lifts a sculptured egg from her table and fondles it as a surrogate for her body.

The expression of erotic desire as a safe, controllable, spiritual, even universal event is a major project of *Wings of Desire*. It seems to be Wenders' act of convincing himself that sexuality will not make a man lonely if it has a spiritual origin and component; it can be as comforting as cinema itself, which, for Wenders, has its own spiritual dimension. Just as cinema acts as a means to redeem the material world, so the invention *in* cinema of a figure who sees, hears, and reclaims the spirit first for others and then for himself becomes another mediating device, another way to step aside from history, culture, and their discontents and find means for the self to survive with its fragility both intact and affirmed. Cinema and the community of images and stories it fathers offers sanctuary to the wanderer and a way to reclaim the self. Damiel, by inscribing himself into the world, reclaiming subjectivity in a newfound body, recreates the cinematic act of giving the world its image and the body its place.[12]

It turns out to be a modern, cinema-driven version of the age-old quest to unite body and spirit. From the very start, Wenders establishes the camera as omniscient eye, reminiscent of an Olympian entity whose godlike stance exhibits the qualities ascribed to the ancient tellers of myth. It attaches that eye to Damiel, who is seen standing on the Gedächtniskirche, the ruined Memorial Church, high above the commercial center of West Berlin, head downcast as if in mournful introspection, watching the city below. The omniscience is verbal as well – Wenders' love of articulate images is balanced by Handke's infatuation with language – so, as if attempting to keep a balance of the spheres, Wenders and Handke give Damiel an earthly counterpart, an old, frail, childlike man named Homer, who lives in the library. Homer assumes the role of the divinely inspired voice of narration who incorporates the spirit of human experience from the old epics to the most

Two spirits of humankind: Homer, the eternal narrator, and Cassiel, the angel of solitude and compassion, from *Wings of Desire*.

recent tales of historic events. If Damiel and Cassiel are the representations of omniscient, spiritual perception, Homer is the representative and bearer of collective memory, the spirit of history. He is also the spirit of Berlin, who laments the vanishing of the city in the war and the cycle of aggression and destruction created by humans throughout its time. Saddened by his burden of mourning, he desires to create the epic of peace rather than of devastating conflicts. Sitting at one point in an old, abandoned armchair in the middle of a desolate urban space, the sweeping curves of an elevated pedestrian bridge and the Berlin Wall behind him, Homer appears as a center point not only of the distant past, but of modernity itself.*

Homer's frailty is an analogue to the tired, perhaps dying city and its inhabitants, torn, despairing, needing relief from history. He is the end of

---

* Images of modernity infiltrate the film, in the architecture of Berlin – so much a part of the film's mise-en-scène – and through small references: in the library sequence the pen that is taken by Damiel is from a music student, who is copying a letter by the modernist composer Alban Berg; lying on top of one of the opened scores is Theodor W. Adorno's book on Berg; in the library one also sees German avant-garde composer Hans Werner Henze's score *Das Ende einer Welt* (*The End of a World*), which happens to be close to the title of Wenders' next film, *Bis ans Ende der Welt* (*Until the End of the World*).

history, its final word. Damiel is the beginning of a new world order, entering time as a modern eros, redeeming history with his love. And just as Homer mediates Damiel in history, another angel, Damiel's companion Cassiel, mediates Homer in spiritual perception. He is the figure of resistance, of eternal disinterestedness and immobility, who looks, guides, but refuses to participate. He is seen first with Damiel in the front seat of a BMW sitting in a car dealer's showroom. This is a remarkable image for Wenders: a car, holding two male friends, but unable to move! The shifting one-shots from one angel to the other seem to point to the separation of the two, for this sequence is not only about the mutual bonding of the two angels (the shooting pattern does resolve into a composition showing both figures together), but about the split in Damiel's nature. Cassiel will retain his angelic state, watching over human activity, reporting events and attempting, sometimes unsuccessfully, to intervene in them. (He is unable, at one point, to save a suicide from jumping from a high rise topped with a Mercedes-Benz logo.)

Damiel states his desire to relinquish the splendid isolation of eternal spirituality in order to enter the human world of time and space. Cassiel expresses his own desire to forever stay within the word. For him, the logos, the voice of the spirit, triumphs over the physical and ephemeral. For Damiel, an angelic deconstructionist, the multifariousness of physical form, the colors of the world themselves, are too inviting. Cassiel remains in black and white throughout the film, ending as a monochrome insert in the background of Damiel's multicolored romance. For Damiel, the desire to inscribe himself in flesh and blood overpowers the omniscience of an eternal point of view. (When Damiel falls to earth by the Berlin Wall, his armor plate smashes on his head, causing him to bleed; he wanders by the wall and asks a stranger to describe the colors of its graffiti to him.) The motionless BMW is a sign of his prison (perhaps this is why Wenders referred to *Wings of Desire* as his vertical road movie), as the gesture with the fountain pen in the library and egg-shaped object in Marion's room are the initial signs of his resurrection.[13]

But it is, after all, an inverse resurrection. The desire of the angelic mediator to change his status and emerge with both sexuality and compassion results in a kind of self-absorption that threatens to become a travesty of spirit and flesh, history and politics, of the material reality of culture. Finally, after the delicate balancing of Christian and earthly myths, of storytellers, seers, and angels, it is as if Wenders' struggle in coming to terms with the place of second-generation, postwar Germans and their culture is resolved here in a heavily mediated, mass-culture joke.

Just before he makes his final leap into the flesh, celebrity and television interfere with the process of memory, and it becomes difficult to sift irony from irresponsibility. Another mediator is created for Damiel in the form of a fallen angel, the only adult who can sense the angelic presence and the only man on earth who can help convince him that his desire to assume the body of the everyday is correct. This character is the actor Peter Falk playing "himself" in one of those Hollywood conceits in which person and persona are merged. Initially Falk's appearance is amusing and touching: the self-effacing, working-class Jewish man, wise without flourish, presents a nice comparison to the pompous angels and the suffering Berliners. His kindness to Damiel, his advice on being in the world, and his calling Damiel "*compañero*" all indicate a humanity missing from the other characters.

The kids Falk meets on the street call him Columbo, and for a moment it is not clear whether Wenders is making a joke or a critique of celebrity and the influence of American culture in Germany. (One might also stretch the religious metaphor of the film and note that "*colombo*" is the Italian word for "dove.")[14] The possibility of the critique is extended by the fact that Falk has arrived in Berlin to play a role in an American television movie about the fascist period in which a detective goes to Berlin in 1945 to find someone. (Media swallows media, and the plot of the television movie is divulged when Falk watches himself being interviewed on television.) Wenders shows the movie set, filled with people in Nazi uniforms or in coats embroidered with the Star of David. Their conversations are overheard by the angels (throughout the film, the audience is privileged to the angels' perceptions), and at one point Wenders composes a group of them talking and smoking, in a way that recalls the cinema style of the thirties and early forties.

This sequence follows Cassiel's car ride through Berlin, during which old footage of the last months of the war and the rubble of bombing raids (recalling the postwar *Trümmerfilm* in which the urban rubble of postwar Europe set the background for narratives of displaced people and broken families). Cassiel sees past and present, and in voice-over he meditates upon history and the German spirit, its lack of individuality and sense of spiritual community. But the connection of these scenes – the old cinematic trick of intercutting old and recent footage, the uncanny movie set that looks like a Nazi prison, the compositions that imitate films of the period – causes history to become a scene for nostalgic encounter mediated by the apparatus of angels, a television celebrity, and filmmaking. The film seems to be searching for ways that will give the past significance, but in the process runs the danger of reducing the significance to the status of special effects and set design.

Wenders, who so much values the authentic image, cannot seem to pull away from the traps of postmodern pastiche. On one level, he would appear to be commenting upon the degradation of history through mass-mediated representations, particularly in the sequence of Falk and the movie set. But if this is so, why is he so affectionate about Peter Falk and his musings about "extra people" and their expendability in the process of history? Are we to read Falk as an ironic commentator on the scene in front of him, the detective wiser than his bumbling presence would lead us to believe because he was once an angel? But Falk is himself a mediated figure, a man who exists only as his television image; nothing in the film adequately addresses the counterpoint of actor, character, and personality. Is the "documentary" footage of the end-of-war rubble meant to play against the trifling re-creations of the movie set? But as we said, the footage is itself evident movie trickery, and within the space of the film, it is meant to represent the time perceptions of an "angel," a fantasy figure who exists only in film.

History is fragmented and devitalized by all of this, presented with an only half-formed irony that glosses over the burden of the past until past and present lose their sense of difference. Falk jokes with a child about the myth of Hitler's double; voices of the extras intermingle with Damiel as they speculate on whether the people acting in the film actually are concentration camp survivors or not. What might have been a multilayered mise-en-scène, mixing history and its myths, a time capsule of the uncanny where present-day makers of images of the Nazi past confront the viewer with the need for more accurate knowledge of history, becomes more puzzle than inquiry, more trick than insight. The image of Bruno's girlfriend, cradling the Hitler candle in her arm in *Kings of the Road,* had more weight. Finally, history subsides completely into the recesses of memory, and is all but forgotten under the weight of the film's many mediations and its ultimate diversion into romantic redemption.

Damiel's infatuation with human existence and his longing for sexual and spiritual union come to exemplify – as the universalist longings of the film would suggest – the innate desires of all humankind. And it is at this narrative crux, when Falk and Marion enter the story, when fantasy, history, and romantic love curl around each other and history is finally subdued, where the film desires an ascent to lofty heights as its central figure falls to earth, that it falls into bathos. In the end, romance itself must take on mythic, universal proportions, first absolve and then divorce itself from history, and redeem all of humankind. In so doing, it reduces the realities of humans and their history to melodramatic gestures.

Damiel's movement down to earth is consummated when he meets a

The angel with "chicken feathers": Marion's circus act as a metaphor for the swing to heaven, from *Wings of Desire*.

woman who is heading heavenward. Marion is a trapeze artist – a French woman in a German circus ("I'm someone who has no roots, no story, no country," she says, echoing Friedrich in *The State of Things*) – who would be angel, sprouting wings on her costume as she practices on her swing in the Circus Alekan (named after the film's cinematographer, Henri Alekan, who photographed *The State of Things* and, many years ago, Cocteau's *Beauty and the Beast*). The circus, like the movie house filled with children in *Kings of the Road,* starts as a place of respite for the angels, a counterbalance to the dark abyss of the past, but becomes the scene of Damiel's transfixion and transition. Damiel becomes infatuated with Marion and is able to act out his desire through a most remarkable realization of male fantasy. He becomes a voyeur.[15] Nervous about her act, herself thinking of changing her life, Marion seeks refuge in her trailer. Lounging on her bed, undressing, and singing along with a record ("Your Funeral, My Trial" by the progressive rock singer Nick Cave, who will appear later in the film when the newly fleshed Damiel happily enjoys his first rock concert before his meeting with Marion), Damiel looks on in a scene that borders on sexual invasion. He caresses the egg-shaped object on her desk and then her bare shoulder. In a later bedroom scene, under similar angelic circumstances, Damiel, like a homunculus, comes to Marion in a dream, in full angelic armor – reminiscent of Eric Rohmer's *The Marquise of O.,* in which Bruno Ganz appears to a woman as if in a dream and rapes her to begin the consummation of their love.

The fact that the romantic episodes in *Wings of Desire* can be reduced not merely to absurdity, but to a more ineffectual and humiliating mode of male voyeurism, speaks badly about the continuing inability of Wenders' films to address sexuality and gender. Clearly, Wenders wishes *Wings of Desire* to express the profound interactions of eros and thanatos, of history and personality. His angel is moved by large forces of worldly desire greater than the merely intangible intimacies he can provide as an angel; he desires erotic fulfillment. Against the recurring theme of history's abyss, Damiel retreats into the inner space of humankind by pursuing his fascination with Marion's body. Her own search for inner peace and her quest for companionship add to the attraction and their interaction. But their mutual desire to create a "story" for themselves leads to a rite of passage into the most mundane, even puerile, movie conventions that appear greater than they are because of the heightened visual and verbal language in which they are presented. The poetic apotheosis of human passion and domestic need that ends the film trivializes its high concerns and endangers the complexity Wenders set out to construct.

Here, indeed, one is tempted to blame Handke, for the poetic declamation of the final dialogue between Damiel and Marion is pompous and operatic. Earlier in the film, in front of a sausage stand in a ruined part of the city, Falk speaks to Damiel about the ordinariness of human existence, about coffee and cigarettes, the pleasures of drawing and of rubbing hands together when they are cold (the sequence plays out the old movie convention of a "live" person talking to a "ghost," whom only he – and the viewer – can see; the owner of the sausage stand looks on with incomprehension as Falk speaks to "nobody"). It is a tender scene about the everyday. When Marion and Damiel finally meet, "in the flesh," in the bar of the rundown Hotel Esplanade (a favorite meeting place for the upper-echelon Nazis during the Third Reich), the everyday is replaced by a postmodern dawn of the gods.

Marion accepts a glass of wine that Damiel ceremoniously presents to her as if it were a mythic love potion or an act of Communion. She then assumes the role of seer and prophet with a speech that presents the woman as philosopher, mediator, and redeemer of self, history, and utopian ideals. Marion's annunciation is that of a biblical millennium achieved not through

The detective and his "ghost": Peter Falk, alias Columbo, former angel and member of the spiritual realm, tries to greet his *compañero* and win him for the world of the ordinary, from *Wings of Desire.*

divine intervention but through extraordinary human endeavor. While progressive rock dominates the locale that used to be a staging ground for Nazi hopes, Marion, standing next to the swooping line of the bar, announces her metaphysics of human happiness and progress in history. This potentially subversive moment of female intervention is subverted, however, by Handke's stilted and artificial language, reverberating with the images and slogans of the Great Revolution and the language of a new mythology that reappropriates Promethean grandeur while coming dangerously close to crypto-fascist fantasies.

The earth angel in the carnal red dress with earrings of silver wings displays the overt symbolism of a mercurial herald of utopian messages. With the self-assurance of an emancipated spirit, she reflects on her personal evolution, about chance and destiny in one's life, about solitude not as isolation but as togetherness, wholeness, oneness of the self. This elaborate Handkean meditation on the existential benefits of supreme individualism and monadic existence shifts to a bold proclamation of determination and decisive action. Seeing their romantic union a reflection of the "new moon of decision," Marion would cast away all elements of chance. She invites her former angel to share a vision of a public square filled with people of which

The mediation of eros and history: the new titans of humankind plan the future of history in a Berlin bar, from *Wings of Desire*.

she and Damiel are at the same time a part and representatives: "Entscheide dich! Wir sind jetzt die Zeit." ("Decide! We are now the time.") The activism she calls for rings with the sounds of leftist songs of the twenties when Mayakovsky in the Soviet Union and Hanns Eisler in Germany created revolutionary songs envisioning the proletariat as harbingers of a new age. "There is no greater story than ours, of man and woman," she says.

While Damiel is challenged by the woman he loves to make up his mind, she employs Handke's favorite trope of play. "We are deciding everyone's game," she says. "Nun bist du dran. Du hast das Spiel in der Hand. Jetzt oder nie." ("Now it's your turn. You are in charge of the game. It's now or never!") Gender reversal reverts! Marion gives the power back to Damiel and proclaims the recuperation of a lost hope for the future by suggesting a re-creation of the human race: "eine Geschichte von Riesen" ("a story of giants"), which, invisible and absorbing all individuals, become the titans, the new ancestors of humankind.

The words of the Left ring with Promethean and revolutionary resolve and then veer in the opposite direction. A neoconservative tinge discolors the utopian rhetoric, allowing images of Nazi racial superiority to creep in. When this female philosopher of self-realization and utopian fantasy, mediator of eros and history, and redeemer of male desire and human destiny finally embraces her former angel and child-man before the empty bar, the camera moves up to an elevated, distant vantage point. No longer an angelic perspective, it is now the point of view of a superior breed of lovers, a new master race.

Wings of Desire does not end with this aberrant proclamation of union and prophecy of a master race. A carefully composed coda reveals the need for concrete work that will make the rhetorical flashes of language a living reality. But after all, it is not the concrete everyday that Wenders seems most interested in. While Marion and Damiel have experienced the pleasures of the libido, the fruit of their union is not flesh and blood, but knowledge of conquering a mere mortal sexuality. As if the Fall in Genesis had to be retold and reversed, carnal knowledge leads Damiel to a new vision of self and human existence. Instead of procreating a mortal child, the creation of a unifying immortal race of giants is promised. It is the image that Damiel claims will stay with him until death. Supporting Marion on the rope as she practices her act (which now has become a meditation between heaven and earth), Damiel proclaims his humanness and suggests that he has overcome the history of patriarchal maleness. But given the utopian pomposity of all that has been said, this is too simple a conclusion for the film to make. Wenders must apostrophize the couple further, turn sex into apocalyptic redemption, and make the couple the image of eternity.

At the end, Marion's function as artiste and angelic-mythological icon is reinscribed as Wenders composes the shadow of her airborne body against the figures of gracefully dancing couples painted on the wall behind her. (Marion's body forms a shadowy bow and arrow reminiscent of the mythic Diana while one of the dancing couples configures the mythical image of death and the maiden.)[16] Cassiel looks on (in black and white), mournfully, protectively. Damiel continues the story of his knowledge, inscribing in his journal, which he reads and which we see on the screen: "The amazement about man and woman . . . made a human being of me . . . I know what no angel knows." Homer is seen one more time, from behind, walking toward the Berlin Wall, imploring his audience to attend to their storyteller and spiritual guide, while Cassiel takes refuge on the shoulder of Victoria's stat-ue. He says in French, as the camera observes the sky over Berlin, "We have begun" ("Nous sommes embarqués"); and a title offers a promise: "Fort-setzung folgt" ("To be continued").

So not only will this angelic love shape eternity, but it will be the source of a sequel. The language of the movie business becomes too overpowering in its banality. Perhaps "To be continued" was meant, with Wenders' sincerity, to indicate the high purpose of the film and the love of its characters while, at the same time, making an ironic reference to the ways movies reproduce themselves. However, the possibility of a saving irony – the suggestion that movies diminish the realities of romance while, at the same time, speaking to our most profound desires – comes apart. The fantasies of romance seem to have closed all outlets to the everyday world suspended between heaven and earth.

Within a few years of the release of *Wings of Desire,* the Berlin Wall came down; but it was not an event promoted by archaic myth – universal love, a race of giants, or an ancient storyteller. Politics, economics, and the leveling force of media images drove the people into the streets. A yearning for freedom, desire for the West and consumer goods, and fatigue with oppressive standards of living changed the demarcations of postwar Europe. Wenders thinks about these things in this film, but cannot quite deal with them, because, finally, they are too earthbound. His is the realm of images, the imaginary of cinema, the transcending power of redemptive vision. The king of the road wants to mount the stairway to heaven.

7
Conclusion
A Stranger in *Heimat*

"I'm at home nowhere, in no house, in no country."
Friedrich Munro, in *The State of Things*

I am at home in no house and in no country.
Friedrich Wilhelm Murnau, in a letter
to his mother from Tahiti in 1929.[1]

Wenders, through his characters, their narratives, and his own acts as itinerant filmmaker, lives out the peculiarly Germanic state of postwar rootlessness. He makes homelessness a virtue, an aesthetic. While the characters of American film, from Dorothy in *The Wizard of Oz* to E.T., the extraterrestrial, seek home as safe haven and reaffirmation of self, as comfort and closure – the realm built against the threats of modernity – and while late-twentieth-century Western culture stands paralyzed in guilt and revulsion over the actual homelessness of dispossessed classes, Wenders finds his own affirmation in the negation of home. The wanderer, finally, finds his redemption not in the end point, not in the return, but in the act of moving on. Ethan Edwards returns to the desert. Walter Benjamin dies on the Spanish border. Fritz Lang dies in Hollywood. Lotte Eisner (to whom Wenders dedicates *Paris, Texas*) remained in Paris. Bruno Winter tears up his itinerary but stays in his truck. Travis recreates a domestic space and then drives off in his car. Damiel and Marion's proclamation of love occurs not within the fantasy of home, but in a public space, full of the promise of godlike transcendence beyond the domestic.

Wenders lives within modernity and is fully equipped to pass through it to its sequel, the postmodern. Like Benjamin, Brecht, Duras, Joyce, Fassbinder, Godard, and so many other modernists, he looks to the city and takes to the road. He turns to images of production, consumption, and evasion, the painful conflict of signifiers whose only meaning lies in their spectacular conflict. He slips out of his modernist legacy and enters the postmodern with ease, moving past doubts of subjectivity into its denial. He begins to think in terms other than self. And while he laments the loss of history, while the figure of the frail Homer among the ruins of Berlin evokes a sentiment for man's home (woman is elsewhere, on the trapeze or in a spaceship, seeking heaven), his angel gives up the suffocating certainty of his celestial self to become the earthly spirit of archetypal, mythic lover. If romanticism opened the door to modernism, postmodernism searches again for the entrance to the romantic space, where the subject, always aware of its fragility, can shift the anxiety of dissolution into desire.

In his initial modernist enterprise of reconfiguring history through the aesthetics of perception and motion, Wenders hoped that the structures of cinema would represent the lost stability of the subject. Having failed in this endeavor, he responds to the German fantasy of *Heimat* with the postmodern urge to give up meaning, search, and closure, to indulge in the fantasy of the image and the ahistorical proclamation of a mythologized self. At the same time, he responds to postmodernism with the romantic's assertion that desire will redeem the self. Representations of motion and transit in the earlier films suggested excitement and escape; motion on the road was preferable to a despairing stasis. The school films and the early theatrical features are marked by the despair of stability. Inaction and immobility move the characters into pathological states, unmoor them almost against their will. Later, especially in *Kings of the Road,* movement becomes a means of learning, a variation on the classical bildungsroman, where the traveling adolescent creates an idea of self through exposure to a variety of other individuals. Although *Wrong Move* is based on a classic bildungsroman by Goethe, it becomes deformed with modernist angst; in *Kings of the Road,* despair is foreshortened by another modernist agent, belief in the dependable structures of art – language and cinema in this case.* When those agents prove undependable and corrupt, as they do in *Hammett* and *The State of Things,* Wenders turns to the postmodern promise of redemption outside of history, fantasized in images of domesticity and romance.

A key image in *Paris, Texas* summarizes the shifts in sensibility and temperament. Walt and Anne live in a house in the Los Angeles hills, directly

---

* Shifting the classical goal of social integration to the individual's self-centeredness and angst, Handke and Wenders created – in the spirit of the "new subjectivism" of the early seventies – a revisionist version of their classical model, in itself a postmodernist exercise.

overlooking L.A. airport. The space of domestic stability is disrupted by the constant movement just below it, planes flying in and out mark the home as a place of transition and impermanence in a way Ford's desert outposts never could. Wenders takes pains to compose shots of the house and the airport together, to show Travis sitting on the edge of the hill that makes up the backyard, watching the planes go by. The image resonates all the way back to Bruno's childhood home on the Rhine (which comes, in its turn, from Nicholas Ray's image of the lost childhood home in *The Lusty Men*). Bruno's home was a place of sadness, despair, and reawakening. Walt and Anne's house, an expensive suburban refuge, is, immediately, less fraught. It should represent a withdrawn and calm place, a secure shutting out of the world. But teetering on the edge of instability and transience, its very ideological purpose is denied. The image stands as warning that no matter how much Travis may move into the patriarchal mode, he will not be able to grasp domestic stability. That victory is saved for the spirits in *Wings of Desire*.

The desire for stability represented by Walt and Anne's house is obscured by its location overlooking the airport. At the same time, the airport – and its attendant signifieds of transitoriness – is somewhat stabilized in its relation to the house. Held within the same image, these two images form a kind of negative dialectic. They indicate the uncertain transitional point of Wenders' own position and perhaps a final response to the Fordian image of the homestead at the edge of the wilderness. For Ford, the reproduction of European and East Coast hegemony is assured by the movement west. The European middle class reestablishes its home there, claims the land, and perhaps rediscovers *Heimat*. But the house overlooking the airport recalls the antimodernism that *Heimat* was all about. The concept of the simple, country spirit was invented to show urbanism as evil and to manufacture mass-mediated images of rural stability to deflect the culture from the fears of social progress.[2] In all of his films, Wenders shows clearly that *Heimat* is not home. But in *Paris, Texas* he begins to waver, and in *Wings of Desire* a new *Heimat* is aborning, only to be reconfigured once again in *Until the End of the World*.

In this film, the quest for *Heimat* collapses, implodes upon itself. Searching the world for images that will give his blind mother sight, pursued by a variety of detectives and lowlifes, accompanied by Claire (played by Solveig Dommartin, the trapeze artist of *Wings of Desire*), Sam, an American, comes home to his family in the Australian aboriginal outback, where they all await the atom blast that will end time. The end doesn't come, for here climactic moments are avoided, or misdirected. In place of apocalypse, the wanderers become addicted to dream images of their childhood manufactured for them by Sam's father Henry (an American, who is ultimately imprisoned by his own government for stealing technology). The comic melodrama of *Heimat* at the end of the world seems to confuse happiness and escape, old and new, dream and technology. Even its allusions to other films no longer provide the security of communal images and stories. Finally, everything is misaligned with history.

Until the End of the World is a film of uncertainty in which redemption is reaction. The figure who survives most intact is a cuckolded husband, a writer who loses his computer files and re-creates his novel on an old-fashioned typewriter in the Australian outback. His wife flies around the earth in a satellite, scanning earth for ecological disasters. Modernity has been reduced, awkwardly, to the romantic, the adorable, and the politically banal, while visions of technology are condemned and the old ways of storytelling are celebrated in retrospect and, perhaps, in bad faith. The imagination seeks *Heimat* in a heap of images, old and new, masquerading as postmodernity.

Are we suggesting that Wenders' films have pursued an ultimately re-gressive, perhaps even reactionary course? We might rather suggest that they have always been conservative, always pulled back from the large social issues of history and class pursued by Fassbinder. In his earlier films, Wen-ders joined in the movement that rebuked *Heimat,* at least in its cinematic forms. The celebration of the peasant and petit bourgeois rural life in *Heimatfilm* – a disingenuous representation of defeated and exhausted cul-tural practice – was a major target of the New German Cinema.[3] *The Goalie's Anxiety at the Penalty Kick* was one of a number of anti-*Heimat* films that portrayed rural life as less than moral, pure, and rejuvenating. But the anti-*Heimat* film itself came under question during the growing neocon-servatism of West Germany in the seventies and eighties, and the form was reappropriated. Edgar Reisz' television series, called, simply, *Heimat,* repre-sented, in an apologetic and unproblematic way, the evolution of a country town and its inhabitants in a linear progression from World War I, through Nazism, World War II, and into the fifties, replete with an aura of innocent recuperation of the past that could be interpreted as denying that past at the very moments of its telling.[4] While Wenders never attempts such a recupera-tion of German history, he does seek a recuperation of the individual into a more secure, less anxiety-producing state of domesticity. But finally he gives up homesteading. He seeks the heimatization of the self.

This becomes clearer when we attempt to find the more conventional oppositions of city and country, the urban "cosmopolitan" and rural peas-ant or petit bourgeois in his films. The city, a place of fascination for Wenders, has also been a place of discomfort, if not dread. He seems nostalgic not for the green world, but for the road outside the city, the interurban road that skirts the country and provides quick exit and entrance to the town. He laments the deindividuation of the city. The Paris, Hamburg, and New York of *The American Friend* and the Tokyo of *Tokyo-Ga* appear occasionally monstrous in the sameness of architecture and the deadening effects Wenders imagines they have upon the individual. (In *Hammett*, set in the thirties, the city takes on a more generic quality as the place of corruption figured as immoral, criminal behavior; in *Until the End of the World*, set in the near future, the cities of the world fall away to backdrops, decayed, corrupt, existing only as places to leave.) He is appalled by the technology of the modern city and its inauthentic images. In short, he invokes the longtime conservative notion of urbanism as corruption, but without a corresponding image of purity and innocence. The city is *unheimlich* (though the Los Angeles of *Paris, Texas* is less threatening than the science fiction nightmare Los Angeles of *The State of Things*; in *Paris, Texas*, it is Houston that is the uncanny city). There is, finally, no *Heimat* to return to in the sense of a real place, for *Heimat* is and remains that "which shines into everyone's childhood," as the philosopher Ernst Bloch once remarked.[5] Philip Winter finds this out in *Alice in the Cities*. Bruno discovers it to his sorrow in *Kings of the Road*. Travis discovers it at every step in *Paris, Texas*. When they discover it, the characters of *Until the End of the World* need to flee the earth or retreat into the past in order to regain their sanity.

Throughout his work, Wenders attempts to account for Germany's appalling past by exploring the cultural and personal lacunae in its present, by using restlessness and motion as a metaphor for the inability to stay still and remember. But within his efforts to come to grips with the situation at hand, there is, finally, an element of nostalgia and the hope for simplicity. This desire for the uncomplicated and natural comes from a stance of remoteness that, time and again, is subject to the temptation to simply run away and escape from the prevailing burdens. At its best, Wenders' longing for more imagination, innovation, and movement manifests itself in the calling forth of cinema to act as a lever for further exploration and clearer expression. On a more banal level, it appears in the love of rock and roll music and the adolescent desire for security and individuality through a song and a road of one's own. At its worst, in *Wings of Desire* and *Until the End of the World*, it appears as a mythologizing of romance, an apotheosis of the static, eternal couple, a home for the heart, a return to the simple life and good works.

The movement of Wenders' films turns out, finally, to be a long drive toward stability and stasis. The apotheosis of the lovers at the end of *Wings of Desire,* pledging the eternity of their romance safely within the confines of an old Nazi hotel bar, surrounded by mythological, theological, utopian, and finally cryptofascist trappings, or Claire traveling far above the earth at the end of *Until the End of the World,* are far removed from the displaced travelers who people his earlier films – those escapees from eternity, the wanderers on the roads of the present. Wenders' discovery of a secure place, an illusion of desire fulfilled within the embrace of subjectivity, parallels the movement of cinema itself during the period of his most creative work. The modernism into which he entered in the late sixties disavowed the secure place of cinematic conventions and codes that seemed so permanently installed. The installation was questioned, the home ground dug up by Godard, Antonioni, Straub and Huillet, by the young Bertolucci, the always already old Fassbinder, the wanderer Tarkovsky, and, for a moment, by Wenders.

Cultural practice moves in cycles, and the end of any cycle seems inevitably to go back to a regressive point. The longing for stability in cultural and political ideologies is as irresistible as desire itself. It may be desire itself. The postmodern condition claimed an exhaustion with the avant-garde and a sickness unto death with the history that modernism kept insisting was the real signified of the text. Postmodernism has reset the signs and – as far as they point to anything beyond themselves – directed them back to home, though this time not a comforting place: one filled with violence and instability, denied meaning and subjective certainty, a place of emotional and intellectual fatigue. That's why *Wings of Desire* seems, at last, such a conflicted work that shows the signs of an imagination confronted with its own exhaustion and why *Until the End of the World* is a film in which uncertainty and exhaustion seem to collide. Wenders gives up the angelic freedom of the wanderer for the flesh and blood of the lover and expresses a sudden fear of the complex, articulate image of the road. In so doing, he comes home to the banality of the unsurprising and the undesiring. Love as *Heimat* is created by a desire that is superior to the forces that forever oppress the ordinary. Desire takes wing and leaves behind the road to the city of dreadful night.

Notes

1. The Boy with the Movie Camera

1. Jan Dawson, *Wim Wenders,* trans. Carla Wartenberg (New York: Zoetrope, 1976), p. 12.

2. Michel Boujut, *Wim Wenders,* 3d ed. (Paris: Edilig, 1986), p. 8.

3. See Boujut, *Wenders,* p. 8, and Uwe Küntzel, *Wim Wenders. Ein Filmbuch,* 3d, enl. ed. (Freiburg i. Br.: Dreisam, 1989), p. 12.

4. "Warum filmen Sie? Antwort auf eine Umfrage," in Wim Wenders, *Die Logik der Bilder. Essays und Gespräche,* ed. Michael Töteberg (Frankfurt/Main: Verlag der Autoren, 1988), p. 9 (English translation by Peter Beicken). See also an English version, "Why Do You Make Films?" in Wim Wenders, *The Logic of Images, Essays and Conversations,* trans. Michael Hofmann (London: Faber & Faber, 1991), pp. 39–50.

5. Wenders, *Die Logik der Bilder,* p. 10.

6. Ibid., p. 9.

7. Ibid.

8. "From Dream to Nightmare: The Terrifying Western *Once Upon a Time in the West,*" in Wim Wenders, *Emotion Pictures: Reflections on the Cinema,* trans. Sean Whiteside in association with Michael Hofmann (London: Faber & Faber, 1989), p. 24.

9. Wenders, *Die Logik der Bilder,* p. 9.

10. Ibid., p. 10.

11. For the reference to his father as fascist, see Tom Farrell, "Nick Ray's German Friend Wim Wenders," *Wide Angle* 5 (1983), no. 4, p. 62.

12. Dawson, *Wim Wenders,* p. 18.

13. Ibid.

14. Frederic Jameson, *Postmodernism or, The Logic of Late Capitalism* (Durham, N.C.: Duke University Press, 1991), pp. 26–7.

15. Wim Wenders, "Jukebox Kino," *Filme* 2 (1981), no. 12, p. 38.

16. Dawson, *Wim Wenders,* p. 20.

17. For this and the Paris years, see Kathe Geist, *The Cinema of Wim Wenders, From Paris, France, to Paris, Texas* (Ann Arbor: UMI Research Press, 1988), p. 5.

18. Ibid.
19. Dawson, *Wim Wenders*, p. 10.
20. Ibid., p. 11.
21. Ibid., p. 12.
22. See the groundbreaking study by German sociologist Helmut Schelksy, *Die skeptische Generation. Eine Soziologie der deutschen Jugend* (Frankfurt/Main, Berlin: Ullstein, 1975).
23. Dawson, *Wim Wenders*, p. 11.
24. Ibid., p. 12.
25. Ibid.
26. Ibid., p. 11.
27. Ibid., p. 12.
28. Ibid.
29. Geist, *The Cinema of Wim Wenders*, p. 14.
30. Wenders, *Emotion Pictures*, p. vii.
31. Ibid., p. 24.
32. Ibid.
33. Ibid., p. 38.
34. Ibid.
35. Ibid., p. 127.
36. "*Three Rivals. The Tall Men*," ibid., p. 21.
37. Ibid., p. 22.
38. "Terror of the Outlaws," ibid., p. 19.
39. Ibid., pp. 1–3.
40. Ibid.
41. For the source of the music, see Geist, *The Cinema of Wim Wenders*, p. 9.
42. Ibid.
43. Ibid., p. 10.
44. Dawson, *Wim Wenders*, p. 18.
45. Cf. Tony Rayns, "Forms of Address: Interviews with Three German Film-makers," *Sight and Sound* 44 (Winter 1974–5), no. 1, p. 5.
46. "*Easy Rider, a Film Like Its Title*," in Wenders, *Emotion Pictures*, p. 27.
47. An important study of the malaise of the modern city in postwar Germany can be found in Alexander Mitscherlich, *Die Unwirtlichkeit unserer Städte. Anstiftung zum Unfrieden* (Frankfurt/Main: Suhrkamp, 1965).

2. On the Road

1. This argument is eloquently presented by Anton Kaes, *From Heimat to Hitler* (Cambridge, Mass.: Harvard University Press, 1989), pp. 3–35. Our discussion follows closely upon his.
2. Quoted in Thomas Elsaesser, *New German Cinema, A History* (New Brunswick, N.J.: Rutgers University Press, 1989), pp. 20–1.
3. Elsaesser also talks about the problems and aesthetics of reception of the New German Cinema; see ibid., pp. 117–206.
4. Quoted in J. C. Franklin, "The Films of Fassbinder: Form and Formula," *Quarterly Review of Film Studies* 5 (Spring 1980), no. 2, p. 169.

5. Wenders, *Emotion Pictures,* p. 94. In addition, for Wenders and many of his colleagues, the distaste for the images of German cinema is linked to a hatred for the patronizing and disrespectful business of German film, particularly in the sixties. See Wenders, "Despising What You Sell," *Emotion Pictures,* pp. 36–7.

6. *See* "Death Is No Solution: The German Director Fritz Lang," Wenders, *Emotion Pictures,* pp. 104–8.

7. *"Easy Rider,"* ibid., p. 26.

8. "The American Dream," ibid., p. 133.

9. See Daniel Dyan, "The Tutor-Code of Classical Cinema," in Bill Nichols, ed., *Movies and Methods,* Vol. 1 (Berkeley & Los Angeles: University of California Press, 1976), pp. 438–51.

10. See the screenplay, Wim Wenders & Fritz Miller-Scherz, *Im Lauf der Zeit* (Frankfurt/Main: Zweitausendeins, 1976), p. 262. The title of the book is all but invisible in the film itself.

3. Kings of the Road

1. Quoted in Dawson, *Wim Wenders,* p. 24.

2. Cf. Peter Brunette & David Wills, *Screen/Play* (Princeton, N. J.: Princeton University Press, 1989), pp. 43–5.

3. Roland Barthes, "Rhetoric of the Image," *Image, Music, Text,* trans. Stephen Heath (New York: Hill & Wang, 1977), pp. 38–9.

4. The concept belongs to Thierry Jutel.

5. Barthes, "Rhetoric of the Image," p. 45.

6. For a good summary of the structures and tonalities of conventional melodrama, see Thomas Elsaesser, "Tales of Sound and Fury: Observations on the Family Melodrama," in Bill Nichols, ed., *Movies and Methods,* Vol. 2 (Berkeley & Los Angeles: University of California Press, 1985), pp. 165–89.

7. See Alexander Mitscherlich and Margarete Mitscherlich, *The Inability to Mourn,* trans. Berverly R. Placzek (New York: Grove, 1975).

8. See Wenders' essay, "Death Is No Solution," pp. 104–8.

9. Elsaesser, *New German Cinema,* p. 67.

10. The concept of the homosocial is dealt with by Eve Kosofsky Sedgwick, *Between Men* (New York: Columbia University Press, 1985) and Angela Della Vache, *The Body in the Mirror: Shapes of History in Italian Cinema* (Princeton, N.J.: Princeton University Press, 1992).

11. Hans C. Blumenberg, "Die Angst des Kinos vor dem Kino. Identitätsprobleme vor und auf der Leinwand: Altman, Wenders, die Tavianis und andere: Filmfestspiele Cannes 1977," *Die Zeit* (June 10, 1977), no. 24, p. 11.

12. Reinhold Rauh, *Wim Wenders und seine Filme* (Munich: Heyne, 1990), p. 26.

4. The State of Things

1. In this he follows Roland Barthes; see *The Empire of Signs,* trans. Richard Howard (New York: Hill & Wang, 1982).

2. See Timothy W. Luke, *Screens of Power* (Urbana: University of Illinois Press,

1982), p. 22. Jameson, *Postmodernism,* has many insights into the transition of modernism to postmodernism.

3. See Geist, *The Cinema of Wim Wenders,* p. 84. Wim Wenders & Chris Sievernich, *Nick's Film: Lightning over Water* (Frankfurt/Main: Zweitausendeins, 1981). Rauh, *Wim Wenders,* p. 78.

4. See Harold Bloom, *The Anxiety of Influence* (New York: Oxford University Press, 1973).

5. Wenders, *Emotion Pictures,* p. vii.

6. For production history, see Geist, *The Cinema of Wim Wenders,* pp. 81–3, 90, 100–103; a fuller story is offered in German: Rauh, *Wim Wenders,* pp. 68–73. For the story from Coppola's point of view, see Peter Cowie, *Coppola* (New York: Scribners, 1990), pp. 152–4.

7. Kenneth Michael Mashon, "The Search for Identity," unpublished paper.

8. Details from Michel Ciment, "Entretien avec Wim Wenders," *Positif* (November 1982), no. 261, pp. 17–23.

9. Ibid., p. 20.

10. Ibid., pp. 21–2.

11. Geist, *The Cinema of Wim Wenders,* p. 100, suggests that the computer is a reference to Coppola's fascination with the technologies of film.

12. Mashon suggests that the last part of the film adopts many of the conventions common to the classical Hollywood style that were denied in the Portuguese section.

13. Max Horkheimer and Theodor W. Adorno, *Dialectic of Enlightenment,* trans. John Cumming (New York: Herder & Herder), 1972, pp. 153–4.

5. Paris, Texas

1. Katherine Dieckmann, "Wim Wenders: An Interview," *Film Quarterly* 38 (Winter 1984–5), no. 2, p. 7. See also Mas'ud Zavarzadeh, "Biology and Ideology: The 'Natural' Family in *Paris, Texas,*" *CineAction* (Spring 1987), no. 8, pp. 25–30.

2. See Robert Phillip Kolker, *A Cinema of Loneliness,* 2d ed. (New York: Oxford University Press, 1988), pp. 151–8.

3. This generalization of the Lacanian–Althusserian model is explained more fully in Louis Althusser, "Freud and Lacan," in *Lenin and Philosophy,* trans. Ben Brewster (New York: Monthly Review Press), pp. 190–219.

4. Zavarzadeh, "Biology and Ideology," p. 29.

5. Thierry Jutel pointed out the significance of the billboard.

6. Geist points out the allusion to the confessional in *The Cinema of Wim Wenders,* p. 121.

6. Wings of Desire

1. The ideas on perception in *Wings of Desire* are suggested, in part, by Ruth Perlmutter, "Wenders Returns Home on Wings of Desire," *Studies in Humanities* (forthcoming).

2. In a 1989 documentary film, "Motion and Emotion," by Peter Don and Tony Larson.

3. See Andrei Tarkovsky, *Sculpting in Time,* trans. Kitty Hunter-Blair (Austin: University of Texas Press, 1989), pp. 176–89.

4. Ibid., pp. 63–80.

5. See Ruth Perlmutter, "Wenders Returns Home."

6. John Willett, *Art and Politics in the Weimar Period* (New York: Pantheon, 1978), pp. 95–117.

7. Wenders, *Die Logik der Bilder,* p. 134.

8. See Peter Brunette, "Filming Words: Wenders' *The Goalie's Anxiety at the Penalty Kick* (1971)," in *European Film and the Art of Adaptation,* ed. Andrew Horton and Joan Magretta (New York: Ungar, 1981), pp. 188–202.

9. See Peter Handke, *Falsche Bewegung* (Frankfurt/Main: Suhrkamp, 1972).

10. See Rauh, *Wim Wenders,* p. 117.

11. Wenders, *Die Logik der Bilder,* p. 136.

12. Xavier Vila and Alice Kuzner, "Witnessing Narration in *Wings of Desire,*" *Film Criticism,* 16 (Spring 1992), no. 3, pp. 53–65.

13. The comment about the vertical road movie can be found in Coco Fusco, "Angels, History and Poetic Fantasy: An Interview with Wim Wenders, *Cineaste* 4 (1988), no. 4, p. 16.

14. See David Caldwell and Paul W. Rea, "Handke's and Wenders' *Wings of Desire:* Transcending Postmodernism," *German Quarterly* 64 (Winter 1991), no. 1, p. 49.

15. Bell Hooks, "Representing Whiteness. Seeing *Wings of Desire.*" *Yearning: Race, Gender, and Cultural Politics* (Boston: West End Press, 1990), pp. 165–71.

16. Simon Richter made this observation.

7. Conclusion

1. Lotte Eisner, *Murnau* (Berkeley & Los Angeles: University of California Press, 1973), p. 13.

2. For a good reading of late-nineteenth-century German antimodernism, see Fritz Stern, *The Politics of Cultural Despair* (Berkeley & Los Angeles: University of California Press, 1961).

3. See Eric Rentschler, *West German Film in the Course of Time* (Bedford Hills, N.Y.: Redgrave, 1984), pp. 103–28, and Elsaesser, *New German Cinema,* pp. 141–50.

4. See Ruth Perlmutter, "German Revisionism: Edgar Reitz's *Heimat,*" *Wide Angle 9* (1987), no. 3, pp. 21–37.

5. Ernst Bloch, *Das Prinzip Hoffnung* (Frankfurt/Main: Suhrkamp, 1959).

Filmography

1966–7
Schauplätze
Producer, director, cinematographer, editor: Wim Wenders
Music: Rolling Stones
(B&W, 16mm, 10 min.; no prints exist; two shots appear at the beginning of *Same Player Shoots Again*)

1967
Same Player Shoots Again
Producer, director, screenwriter, cinematographer, editor: Wim Wenders
Music: "Mood Music"
Cast: Hanns Zischler
(B&W negative, colored, 16mm, 12 min.)
Premiered: Oct. 11, 1967

1968–9
Silver City
Producer, director, screenwriter, cinematographer, editor: Wim Wenders
Music: "Mood Music"
(Eastmancolor, 16mm, 25 min., recut as *Silver City Revisited*)
Premiered: Mar. 7, 1969

1969
Alabama: 2000 Light Years
Director, screenwriter, editor: Wim Wenders
Cinematographers: Robby Müller, Wim Wenders
Music: Rolling Stones, Jimi Hendrix, Bob Dylan, John Coltrane
Cast: Paul Lys (hero), Peter Kaiser, Werner Schröter, Schrat, Muriel Werner, King Ampaw, Christian Friedel (friends)
Producer: Wim Wenders
Production company: Hochschule für Fernsehen und Film, Munich
(B&W, 35mm, 21 min.)
Premiered: May 18, 1969

1969
3 American LPs (*3 amerikanische LPs*)
Screenplay: Peter Handke
Director, cinematographer, editor: Wim Wenders
Music: Van Morrison, Creedence Clearwater Revival, Harvey Mandel
Cast: Peter Handke, Wim Wenders
Producer: Wim Wenders
Production company: Hessischer Rundfunk (HR), Frankfurt/Main
(Eastmancolor, 16mm, 13 min.)
Premiered: Nov. 18, 1989 (TV, HR 3)

1969
Polizeifilm (*Film about the Police*)
Screenplay: Albrecht Göschel, Wim Wenders
Director, cinematographer, editor: Wim Wenders
Cast: Jimmy Vogler (demonstrator), Kasimir Esser (policeman)
Producer: Wim Wenders
Production company: Bayerischer Rundfunk, Munich
(B&W, 16mm, 11 min.)
Premiered: May 16, 1969

1971
Summer in the City (dedicated to the Kinks)
Screenplay: Wim Wenders
Director: Wim Wenders
Cinematographer: Robby Müller
Editing: Peter Przygodda
Music: The Kinks, Lovin' Spoonful, Chuck Berry, The Troggs, Gene Vincent, Gustav
Mahler
Cast: Hanns Zischler (Hans), Gerd Stein (gang member who picks Hans up outside
prison), Muriel Werner (gang member), Helmut Färber (himself), Edda Köchl (friend
in Munich), Wim Wenders (friend at pool hall), Schrat (Christian, the rock musician),
Libgart Schwartz (girlfriend in Berlin), Marie Bardischewski (friend in Berlin)
Producer: Wim Wenders
Production company: Hochschule für Fernsehen und Film, Munich
(B&W, 16mm, 125 min.)
Premiered: June 2, 1972

1972
The Goalie's Anxiety at the Penalty Kick (*Die Angst des Tormanns beim Elfmeter*)
Screenplay: Wim Wenders, from the novel by Peter Handke
Dialogue: Wim Wenders, Peter Handke
Director: Wim Wenders
Assistant director: Klaus Badekerl, Veith von Fürstenberg
Cinematographer: Robby Müller
Assistant cinematographer: Martin Schäfer
Design: R. Schneider, Burghard Schlicht

Editing: Peter Przygodda
Music: Jürgen Knieper; songs by Johnny and the Hurricanes, Roy Orbison, Tokens, Ventures
Cast: Arthur Brauss (Josef Bloch), Erika Pluhar (Gloria), Kai Fischer (Hertha Gabler), Libgart Schwartz (Anna, hotel maid), Rüdiger Vogler (village idiot), Edda Köchl (pickup in Vienna), Marie Bardeschewski (Maria, Hertha's waitress), Rudi Schippel (cashier in Vienna), Rosl Dorena (woman on bus), Mario Kranz (school janitor), Ernst Meister (tax assessor), Monika Pöschel and Sybille Danzer (hairdressers), Karl Krittle (castle gatekeeper), Maria Engelstorfer (shopkeeper), Otto Hoch-Fischer (innkeeper), Michael Troost (salesman at soccer match), Bert Fortell (policeman), Wim Wenders (walks through Vienna bus station), Ernst Koppens, Gerhard Totschinger, Liane Gollé, Brigitte Svoboda, Paul Hör, Ottilie Iwald, Achim Kaden, Alexandra Back, Ina Geneé, Eberhard Maier, Ernst Essel, Josef Menschik, Norma Mayer, Ulli Stenzel, Hans Premmer
Producer: Peter Genée, Thomas Schamoni
Production company: Filmverlag der Autoren (PIFDA), Munich; Osterreichische Telefilm AG, Vienna; Westdeutscher Rundfunk, Cologne
(Eastman color, 35mm, 100 min.)
Premiered: Feb. 29, 1972 (ARD)

1973
The Scarlet Letter (*Der Scharlachrote Buchstabe*)
Screenplay: Bernardo Fernandez, Wim Wenders, adapted from a script by Tankred Dorst and Ursula Ehler, "Der Herr klagt über sein Volk in der Wildnis Amerika," ("The Lord Bemoans His People in the American Wilderness"), based on *The Scarlet Letter* by Nathaniel Hawthorne
Director: Wim Wenders
Cinematographer: Robby Müller
Assistant cinematographer: Martin Schäfer
Design: Manfred Lütz, Adolfo Cofino
Editing: Peter Przygodda
Assistant editor: Barbara von Weitershausen
Music: Jürgen Knieper
Cast: Senta Berger (Hester Prynne), Hans Christian Blech (Chillingworth), Lou Castel (Dimmesdale), Yelena Samarina (Hibbins), Yella Rottländer (Pearl), Rüdiger Vogler (sailor), William Layton (Bellingham), Alfredo Mayo (Fuller), Angel Alvarez (Wilson), Rafael Albaicin (Indian), Laura Currie (Sarah), Tito Garcia (beadle), Lorenzo Robledo (ship captain), José Villasante (shopkeeper)
Producers: Primitivo Alvarez, Peter Genée
Production company: Filmverlag der Autoren (PIFDA), Munich; Westdeutscher Rundfunk (WDR), Cologne; Elias Querejeta P.C., Madrid
(Kodachrome, 35mm, 90 min.)
Premiered: Mar. 13, 1973 (ARD)

1974
Alice in the Cities (*Alice in den Städten*)
Screenplay: Veith von Fürstenberg, Wim Wenders

Director: Wim Wenders
Cinematographer: Robby Müller
Assistant cinematographer: Martin Schäfer
Editing: Peter Przygodda
Music: Can, Chuck Berry, Canned Heat, Deep Purple, Count Five, Stories, Gustav Mahler
Cast: Rüdiger Vogler (Philip Winter), Yella Rottländer (Alice), Lisa Kreuzer (Lisa, Alice's mother), Edda Köchl (Angela, girlfriend in New York), Didi Petrikat (woman at the beach), Hans Hirschmüller (policeman who finds Alice), Sam Presti (used-car dealer), Ernst Böhm (writers' agent), Mirko (boy at jukebox), Lois Moran (ticket agent), Sibylle Baier (woman), Wim Wenders (man standing at jukebox)
Producer: Peter Genée
Production company: PIFDA, Produktion 1 im Filmverlag der Autoren, Munich; Westdeutscher Rundfunk (WDR), Cologne
(B&W, 16mm, 110 min.)
Premiered: Mar. 3, 1974

1974
Aus der Familie der Panzerechsen and **Die Insel** (*The Crocodile Family* and *The Island*) ninth & tenth parts of TV series "Ein Haus für Uns" ("A House for Us")
Screenplay: Philippe Pilliod
Director: Wim Wenders
Cinematographer: Michael Ballhaus
Editing: Lilian Seng
Cast: Lisa Kreuzer (Monica), Katya Wulff (Ute), Nicolas Brieger & Helga Trümper (Ute's parents), Marquard Bohm (zookeeper), Thomas Braut, Hansjoachim Krietsch
Producer: Eva Mieke
Production company: Bavaria-Atelier, Munich; Westdeutsches Werbefernsehen GmbH (WWF), Cologne
(color, 16mm, 25 min. each)
Premiered: July 26, 1977

1975
Wrong Move (*Falsche Bewegung*)
Screenplay: Peter Handke, after Goethe's *Wilhelm Meister's Apprenticeship*
Director: Wim Wenders
Cinematographer: Robby Müller
Assistant cinematographer: Martin Schäfer
Design: Heide Lüdi
Editing: Peter Przygodda
Assistant editor: Barbara von Weitershausen
Music: Jürgen Knieper, Troggs
Cast: Rüdiger Vogler (Wilhelm Meister), Hanna Schygulla (Thérèse), Hans Christian Blech (Laertes), Nastassja Kinski (Mignon), Peter Kern (Bernhard Landau), Marianne Hoppe (Wilhelm's mother), Ivan Desny (industrialist), Lisa Kreuzer (Janine), Adolf Hansen (conductor), Wim Wenders (man in dining car)
Producer: Bernd Eichinger

Production company: Solaris Film and TV Production, Munich; Westdeutscher Rundfunk (WDR), Cologne
(Eastman color, 35mm, 103 min.)
Premiered: Mar. 14, 1975

1976
Kings of the Road (*Im Lauf der Zeit*)
Screenwriter: Wim Wenders
Director: Wim Wenders
Assistant director: Martin Henning
Cinematographer: Robby Müller
Assistant cinematographer: Martin Schäfer
Design: Heide Lüdi, Bernd Hirskorn
Editing: Peter Przygodda
Music: Axel Linstädt, Improved Sound Ltd., Chris Montez, Chrispian St. Peters, Heinz, Roger Miller
Cast: Rüdiger Vogler (Bruno Winter), Hanns Zischler (Robert Lander), Marquard Bohm (man whose wife commits suicide), Rudolf Schündler (Robert's father), Lisa Kreuzer (Pauline), Dieter Traier (Robert's friend), Franziska Stömmer (female theater owner), Peter Kaiser (projectionist in Pauline's theater), Patrick Kreuzer (boy at railway station), Wim Wenders (spectator at Pauline's theater)
Producer: Michael Wiedemann
Production company: Wim Wenders Produktion, Munich
(B&W, 35mm, 176 min.)
Premiered: Mar. 4, 1976

1977
The American Friend (*Der amerikanische Freund*)
Screenplay: Wim Wenders, adapted from the novel *Ripley's Game* by Patricia Highsmith
Director: Wim Wenders
Assistant directors: Fritz Müller-Scherz, Emmanuel Clot, Serge Brodskis
Cinematographer: Robby Müller
Assistant cinematographers: Martin Schäfer, Jacques Steyn, Edward Lachman
Design: Heide Lüdi, Toni Lüdi
Editing: Peter Przygodda
Assistant editors: Barbara von Weitershausen, Gisela Bock
Music: Jürgen Knieper, Kinks
Cast: Bruno Ganz (Jonathan Zimmermann), Dennis Hopper (Tom Ripley), Lisa Kreuzer (Marianne Zimmermann), Gerard Blain (Raoul Minot), Nicholas Ray (Derwatt/Pogash), Samuel Fuller (Mafia boss), Peter Lilienthal (Marcangelo, killed on train), Daniel Schmid (Ingraham, killed in Métro), Jean Eustache (man in Arab restaurant), Sandy Whitelaw (American doctor in Paris), Lou Castel (Rodolphe), Andreas Dedecke (Daniel), David Blue (Allan Winter), Stefan Lennert (auctioneer), Rudolf Schündler (Gantner), Gerty Molzen (old lady), Heinz Joachim Klein (Dr. Gabriel), Rosemarie Heinikel (Mona), Heinrich Marmann (man in train with dog),

Satya de la Manitou (Angie), Axel Schiessler (Lippo), Adolf Hansen (conductor), Wim Wenders (figure wrapped in plaster bandages in ambulance)
Producers: Michael Wiedemann, Pierre Cottrell
Production company: Road Movies Filmproduktion, Berlin; Les Films du Losange, Paris; Wim Wenders Produktion, Munich; Westdeutscher Rundfunk (WDR), Cologne
(Eastmancolor, 35mm, 123 min.)
Premiered: May 26, 1977

1980
Lightning over Water (*Nick's Film*)
Screenplay: Wim Wenders, Nicholas Ray
Director: Nicholas Ray, Wim Wenders
Assistant director: Pat Kirck
Cinematographer: Edward Lachman
Assistant cinematographers: Martin Schäfer, Mitch Dubin, Tim Ray
Video: Tom Farrell
Editing: Peter Przygodda (first version), Wim Wenders (second version)
Assistant editor: Barbara von Weitershausen
Music: Ronee Blakley
Cast: Gerry Bamman, Ronee Blakley, Pierre Cottrell, Stefan Czapsky, Mitch Dubin, Tom Farrell, Becky Johnston, Maryte Kavaliauskas, Martin Müller, Craig Nelson, Nicholas Ray, Susan Ray, Martin Schäfer, Chris Sievernich, Wim Wenders (as themselves)
Producers: Pierre Cottrell, Chris Sievernich
Production company: Road Movies Filmproduktion, Berlin; Wim Wenders Produktion, Berlin; Viking Film, Stockholm
(Eastmancolor, 35mm, 90 min.)
Premiered: Nov. 1, 1980

1978–82
Hammett
Screenplay: Ross Thomas, Dennis O'Flaherty, from an adaptation by Thomas Pope of the novel *Hammett* by Joe Gores
Director: Wim Wenders
Assistant director: Arne Schmidt
Cinematographers: Philip Lathrop, Joseph Biroc
Design: Dean Tavoularis, Eugene Lee
Editing: Barry Malkin, Mark Laub, Robert Q. Lovett, Randy Roberts, Andrew London
Music: John Barry
Cast: Frederic Forrest (Hammett), Peter Boyle (Jimmy Ryan), Marilu Henner (Kit Conger, Sue Alabama), Roy Kinnear (Eddie Hagedorn), Elisha Cook (Eli, the taxi driver), Hank Worden (poolhall employee), Lydia Lei (Crystal Ling), R. G. Armstrong (Lt. Pat O'Mara), Richard Bradford (Det. Tom Bradford), Michael Chow (Fon Wei Tau), David Patrick Kelly (the punk), Sylvia Sidney (Donaldina Cameron), Jack Nance (Gary Salt), Elmer L. Kline (Doc Fallon), Royal Dano (Pops), Samuel

Fuller (old billiard player), Lloyd Kino (barber), Fox Harris (Frank), Rose Wong (laundress), Liz Robertson (woman in the library), Jean François Ferreol (French sailor), Alison Hong (girl), Patricia Kong (girl at Fong's), Lisa Lu (Miss Cameron's assistant), Andrew Winner (bank guard), Kenji Shibuya (Chinese bouncer), James Quinn (Fong's bodyguard), Mark Anger (barman), James Devney (projectionist), Cicely Rush and Christopher Day (neighborhood children), Christopher Alcaide, James Brodhead, John Hamilton, Ben Breslauer, John T. Spiotta, and Ross Thomas (men in the council chamber)
Producers: Fred Roos, Ronald Colby, Donald Guest
Executive producer: Francis Ford Coppola
Production company: Orion Films and Zoetrope Studios
(Technicolor, 35mm, 94 min.)
Premiered: May 22, 1982

1982
The State of Things (*Der Stand der Dinge*)
Screenplay: Robert Kramer, Wim Wenders
Director: Wim Wenders
Assistant director: Carlos Santana
Cinematographers: Henri Alekan, Fred Murphy
Assistant cinematographers: Agnès Godard, Steve Dubi
Design: Ze Branco
Editing: Barbara von Weitershausen; consultant, Peter Przygodda
Assistant editors: Jon Neuburger, Danny Fischer
Music: Jürgen Knieper
Cast: Patrick Bauchau (Friedrich Munro), Allen Goorwitz (Gordon), Isabelle Weingarten (Anna), Samuel Fuller (Joe), Paul Getty III (Dennis), Viva Auder (Kate), Monty Bane (Herbert), Geoffrey Carey (Robert), Roger Corman (Jerry), Jeffrey Kime (Mark), Rebecca Pauly (Joan), Alexandra Auder (Jane), Camila Mora (Julia), Arturo Semedo (crew member, producer), Francisco Baiao (crew member, sound), Martine Getty (secretary), Janet Rasak (Karen), Judy Moradian (waitress)
Producer: Chris Sievernich
Production company: Gray City, Inc., New York; Road Movies, Berlin; V.O. Films, Lisbon
(B&W, 35mm, 123 min.)
Premiered: Oct. 29, 1982

1982
Reverse Angle: NYC March '82 (*Lettre d'un cinéaste; quand je m'éveille*)
Screenwriter, commentator: Wim Wenders
Director: Wim Wenders
Cinematographer: Liza Rinsler
Editing: Jon Neuburger
Music: Allen Goorwitz, Del Byzanteens, Echo and the Bunnymen, Martha and the Muffins, Public Image Ltd.
Cast: Wim Wenders, Isabelle Weingarten, Barry Malkin, Mark Laub, Bob Lovett, Francis Ford Coppola, Tony Richardson, Louis Malle (in a television talk show)

Producer: Lilyan Sievernich
Production company: Gray City, Inc., New York; Antenne 2, Paris
(Color, 16mm, 17 min.)
Premiered: Mar. 16, 1982 (Antenne 2)

1982
Chambre 666 (Cannes, May 1982)
Screenwriter, commentator: Wim Wenders
Director: Wim Wenders
Cinematographer: Agnès Godard
Editing: Chantal de Vismes
Music: Jürgen Knieper, Bernd Herrmann
Cast: Jean-Luc Godard, Paul Morrissey, Mike De Leon, Monte Hellman, Romain
Goupil, Susan Seidelman, Noel Simsolo, Rainer Werner Fassbinder, Werner Herzog,
Robert Kramer, Ana Carolina, Mahroun Baghbadi, Steven Spielberg, Michelangelo
Antonioni, Wim Wenders, Yilmaz Güney (voice only)
Producer: Chris Sievernich
Production company: Gray City, Inc., New York; Antenne 2, Paris
(Fujicolor, 16mm, 45 min.)
Premiered: June 2, 1982 (Antenne 2; 21 min. television version)

1984
Paris, Texas
Screenplay: Sam Shepard, adapted by L. M. Kit Carson
Director: Wim Wenders
Cinematographer: Robby Müller
Assistant cinematographers: Agnès Godard, Pim Tjujerman
Design: Kate Altman
Editing: Peter Przygodda
Assistant editor: Anne Schnee; with the help of Barbara von Weitershausen
Music: Ry Cooder, David Lindley, Jim Dickinson
Cast: Harry Dean Stanton (Travis Henderson), Nastassja Kinski (Jane), Dean Stock-
well (Walt A. Henderson), Hunter Carson (Hunter), Aurore Clément (Anne),
Bernhard Wicki (Dr. Ulmer), John Lurie ("Slater"), Sally Norvell (Nurse Bibs), Tom
Farrell (screaming man), Claresie Mobley (car rental woman), Socorro Valdez (Car-
melita), Viva Auder (woman on television), Sam Berry (gas station attendant), Ed-
ward Fayton (Hunter's friend), Justin Hogg (Hunter, age 3), Sharon Menzel (comedi-
enne), Jeni Vici, The Mydolls (band)
Producer: Don Guest
Executive producer: Chris Sievernich
Production company: Road Movies, Berlin; Argos Films, Paris; WDR, Cologne;
Channel 4, London; Pro-ject Filmproduktion im Filmverlag der Autoren, Munich
(Color, 35mm, 145 min.)
Premiered: May 19, 1984

1985
Tokyo-Ga
Scriptwriter, commentator: Wim Wenders
Director: Wim Wenders
Cinematographer: Edward Lachman
Editing: Wim Wenders, Solveig Dommartin, Jon Neuburger
Music: "Dick Tracy," Loorie Petitgand, Meche Mamecier, Chico Rojo Ortega
Cast: Chishu Ryu, Yuharu Atsuta, Werner Herzog
Producer: Chris Sievernich
Production company: Gray City, Inc., New York; Wim Wenders Produktion, Berlin; Chris Sievernich Produktion, Berlin; WDR, Cologne
(Color, 16mm, 92 min.)
Premiered: Apr. 24, 1985

1987
Wings of Desire (*Der Himmel über Berlin*)
Screenplay: Wim Wenders, Peter Handke
Director: Wim Wenders
Assistant directors: Claire Denis, Knut Winkler, Carola Hochgräf
Cinematographer: Henri Alekan
Assistant cinematographers: Louis Cochet, Agnès Godard, Achim Poulheim, Peter Ch. Arnold, Martin Kukula, Frank Blasberg, Peter Braatz, Klemens Becker, Klaus Krieger
Design: Heide Lüdi
Editing: Peter Przygodda
Assistant editors: Anne Schnee, Leni Savietto-Pütz
Music: Jürgen Knieper, Laurent Petitgand, Laurie Anderson, Crime and the City Solution, Nick Cave and the Bad Seeds, Sprung aus den Wolken, Tuxedomoon, Minimal Compact
Cast: Bruno Ganz (Damiel), Solveig Dommartin (Marion), Otto Sander (Cassiel), Curt Bois (Homer), Peter Falk (himself), Hans Martin Stier (dying man), Elmar Wilms (sad man), Sigurd Rachman (suicide man), Beatrice Mankowski (street prostitute); in the circus: Lajos Kovacs (Marion's coach), Laurent Petitgand (musician), Dominique Rojo (percussion), Otto Kuhnle, Christoph Merg (jugglers), Peter Werner (manager), Susanne Vierkötter, Paul Busch, Karin Busch, Irene Mössinger, Franky; angels in the library: Teresa Harder, Bernd Eisenschitz, Didier Flamand, Rolf Henke, Scott Kirby, Franck Glémin; in the air raid shelter: Jerry Barrish (director), David Crome (assistant director), Jeanette Pollak (costumes), Christian Bartels (Hitler youth), Käthe Fürstenwerth, Werner Schönrock, Bernd Ramien, Erika Rabau, Silvia Blagojeva Itscherenska, Sultan Metal, Olivier Picot, Jochen Gliscinsky, Erich Schupke; in the apartments: Margarete Hafner, Oliver Herder, Margitta Haberland, Jürgen Heinrichs, Ralf Strathmann, Walter Ratayszak, Charlotte Oberberg, Lubinka Kostiç; on the highway: Gisela Westerboer, Andreas Valentin, Anne Gerstl, Dirk Vogeley, Ruth Rischke, family Aik; Simon Bonney and "Crime and the City Solution," Nick Cave and the Bad Seeds, Kid Congo; with the children: Denis Rodriguez, Dieta von Aster, Gustav, Paul Geisler, Lorenz Geisler, Sladjana Kostiç, Benedikt Schumann,

Nicolas Roth, Marcus Stenzel, Benjamin Ferchow, Mario Meyer, Mark Leuschner, Tibor Dahlenburg, Lia Harder, Mascha Noak, Vera Butzek, Donald Behrendt, Patrick Kreuzer, Simone Säger, Gerdi Hofmann, Ulrike Schirm, Hans Marquard, Heimke Carl, Klaus Mausolf, Özyer Hüsinye, Jean-Claude Lézin, Thierry Noir, Matthias Maass, Henry Luckow
Producers: Wim Wenders, Anatole Dauman
Associate producer: Pascale Dauman
Production company: Road Movies, Berlin; Argos Films, Paris; Westdeutscher Rundfunk, Cologne
(B&W, color, 35mm, 127 min.)
Premiered: May 17, 1987

1989
Notebooks on Clothes and Cities (*Aufzeichnungen zu Kleidern und Städten*)
Scriptwriter: Wim Wenders
Director: Wim Wenders
Cinematographer: Robby Müller, Muriel Edelstein, Uli Kudicke, Wim Wenders, Musatocki Nakajima, Masasai Chikamori
Editing: Dominique Auvray, Lenie Savietee, Anne Schnee
Music: Laurent Petitgand
Cast: Yashiro Yamamoto, Wim Wenders
Producer: Ulrich Felsberg
Production company: Road Movies Filmproduktion, Berlin; Centre National d'Art et de Culture Georges Pompidou, Paris
(Eastmancolor, 35mm, video, 79 min.)
Premiered: Dec. 20, 1989

1991
Until the End of the World (*Bis ans Ende der Welt*)
Screenplay: Peter Carey, Wim Wenders after an idea of Wim Wenders, Solveig Dommartin
Director: Wim Wenders
Cinematographer: Robby Müller
Design: Thierry Flamand
Editing: Peter Przygodda
Costumes: Montserrat Casanova
HDTV-Design: Sean Naughton
Music: Graeme Revell, songs by U2, Lou Reed, Talking Heads, Peter Gabriel, Elvis Costello, R.E.M., Depeche Mode, Patti Smith, Nick Cave, and others.
Cast: Solveig Dommartin (Claire Tourneur), William Hurt (Sam Farber alias Trevor McPhee), Rüdiger Vogler (Philip Winter), Sam Neill (Eugene Fitzpatrick), Jeanne Moreau (Edith Farber, neé Eisner), Max von Sydow (Henry Farber), Ryu Chishu, Chick Ortega (Chico), Eddy Mitchell (Raymond), Ernie Dingo, Allen Garfield (Goorwitz)
Producers: Anatole Daumann, Jonathan Taplin, Wim Wenders
Executive producer: Ulrich Felsberg

Production company: Road Movies Filmproduktion, Berlin; Argos Films, Paris; Village Roadshow, Sidney.
(Color, 35mm, 179 min.)
Premiered: Sept. 10, 1991

Additional Films Cited

Aguirre: Wrath of God (Aguirre: Gottes Zorn), dir. Werner Herzog (Germany, 1972)
Alphaville, dir. Jean-Luc Godard (France, 1965)
Apocalypse Now, dir. Francis Coppola (USA, 1979)
Bagdad Cafe, dir. Percy Adlon (USA, 1987)
Battle of Chile (La battala de Chile), dir. Patricio Guzmán (Chile, 1975–9)
Beauty and the Beast, dir. Jean Cocteau (France, 1946)
Berlin Alexanderplatz, dir. Rainer Werner Fassbinder (Germany, 1980)
Berlin: Symphony of a Great City (Berlin. Die Sinfonie der Grosstadt), dir. Walter Ruttmann (Germany, 1927)
Beware of a Holy Whore (Warnung vor einer heiligen Nutte), dir. Rainer Werner Fassbinder (Germany, 1970)
Bigger Than Life, dir. Nicholas Ray (USA, 1956)
Bonnie and Clyde, dir. Arthur Penn (USA, 1967)
Celeste, dir. Percy Adlon (Germany, 1981)
Citizen Kane, dir. Orson Welles (USA, 1941)
Contempt (Le mépris), dir. Jean-Luc Godard (France, 1964)
Das Boot, dir. Wolfgang Petersen (Germany, 1981)
Day for Night (La nuit américaine), François Truffaut (France, 1973)
The Day the World Ended, dir. Roger Corman (USA, 1956)
Death of a Salesman, dir. Volker Schlöndorff (USA, 1985)
Dr. Mabuse (Dr. Mabuse der Spieler), dir. Fritz Lang (Germany, 1922)
Easy Rider, dir. Dennis Hopper (USA, 1969)
Enemy Mine, dir. Wolfgang Petersen (USA, 1985)
The Exterminating Angel (El Ángel Exterminador), dir. Luis Buñuel (Mexico, 1962)
Ghost, dir. Jerry Zucker (USA, 1990)
A Guy Named Joe, dir. Victor Fleming (USA, 1943)
The Handmaid's Tale, dir. Volker Schlöndorff (USA, 1989)
Heimat, dir. Edgar Reitz (German Television, 1984)
Here Comes Mr. Jordan, dir. Alexander Hall (USA, 1941)
In a Lonely Place, dir. Nicholas Ray (USA, 1950)
It's a Wonderful Life, dir. Frank Capra (USA, 1946)
Johnny Guitar, dir. Nicholas Ray (USA, 1954)
Kuhle Wampe, dir. Slatan Dudow (Germany, 1932)
The Last Emperor, dir. Bernardo Bertolucci (Great Britain, 1987)
The Left-Handed Woman, dir. Peter Handke (Germany, 1977)
Lili Marleen, dir. Rainer Werner Fassbinder (Germany, 1980)
The Lusty Men, dir. Nicholas Ray (USA, 1952)
M, dir. Fritz Lang (Germany, 1931)
The Maltese Falcon, dir. John Huston (USA, 1941)

The Man Who Shot Liberty Valance, dir. John Ford (USA, 1962)
The Marquise of O., dir. Eric Rohmer (Germany, France, 1976)
Metropolis, dir. Fritz Lang (Germany, 1926)
Most Dangerous Man Alive, dir. Allan Dwan (USA, 1961)
My Darling Clementine, dir. John Ford (USA, 1946)
Night of the Riding Corpses (Die Nacht der Reitenden Leichen)
Nosferatu (Nosferatu, eine Symphonie das Grauens), dir. F. W. Murnau (Germany, 1922)
Not Reconciled (Nicht Versöhnt), dir. Jean-Marie Straub and Danièle Huillet (Germany, 1965)
Once Upon a Time in the West, dir. Sergio Leone (Italy, 1969)
On Dangerous Ground, dir. Nicholas Ray (USA, 1951)
Pierrot le fou, dir. Jean-Luc Godard (France, 1965)
Psycho, dir. Alfred Hitchcock (USA, 1960)
Railway (Eisenbahn), dir. Lutz Mommartz (Germany, n.d. available)
Rebel Without A Cause, dir. Nicholas Ray (USA, 1955)
Red Sun (Rote Sonne), dir. Rudolf Thome (Germany, 1969)
Rosalie Goes Shopping, dir. Percy Adlon (USA, 1990)
The Sacrifice, dir. Andrei Tarkovsky (Sweden, 1986)
Sauve qui peut (La Vie), dir. Jean-Luc Godard (France, 1980)
The Searchers, dir. John Ford (USA, 1956)
The Sheltering Sky, dir. Bernardo Bertolucci (USA, 1991)
Stairway to Heaven (A Matter of Life and Death), dir. Michael Powell and Emeric Pressberger (Great Britain, 1946)
Stalker, dir. Andrei Tarkovsky (USSR, 1979)
Sugarbaby (Zuckerbaby), dir. Percy Adlon (Germany, 1983)
The Tall Men, dir. Raoul Walsh (USA, 1955)
The Territory, dir. Raoul Ruiz (France, 1981)
They Live By Night, dir. Nicholas Ray (USA, 1949)
Three Godfathers, dir. John Ford (USA, 1948)
The Tin Drum (Die Blechtrommel), dir. Volker Schlöndorff (Germany, 1979)
Wavelength, dir. Michael Snow (USA, 1967)
The Wizard of Oz, dir. Victor Fleming (USA, 1939)
Yesterday Girl (Abschied von Gestern), dir. Alexander Kluge (Germany, 1966)
Young Törless (Der junge Törleß), dir. Volker Schlöndorff (Germany, 1966)
Zabriskie Point, dir. Michelangelo Antonioni (USA, 1970)

Bibliography

Althusser, Louis. "Freud and Lacan." *Lenin and Philosophy.* Trans. Ben Brewster. New York: Monthly Review Press, 1972, pp. 190–219.

Barthes, Roland. "Rhetoric of the Image." *Image, Music, Text.* Trans. Stephen Heath. New York: Hill & Wang, 1977.

The Empire of Signs. Trans. Richard Howard. New York: Hill & Wang, 1982.

Bloch, Ernst. *Das Prinzip Hoffnung.* Frankfurt/Main: Suhrkamp, 1959.

Bloom, Harold. *The Anxiety of Influence.* New York: Oxford University Press, 1973.

Blumenberg, Hans C. "Die Angst des Kinos vor dem Kino. Identitätsprobleme vor und auf der Leinwand: Altman, Wenders, die Tavianis und andere: Film-festspiele Cannes 1977." *Die Zeit* (June 10, 1977), no. 24, p. 11.

Boujut, Michel. *Wim Wenders.* 3d ed. Paris: Edilig, 1986.

Brunette, Peter. "Filming Words: Wenders' *The Goalie's Anxiety at the Penalty Kick (1971).*" *European Film and the Art of Adaptation.* Ed. Andrew Horton & Joan Magretta. New York: Ungar, 1981, pp. 188–202.

Brunette, Peter, & David Wills. *Screen/Play.* Princeton, N.J.: Princeton University Press, 1989.

Brunow, Jochen. *Schreiben für den Film. Das Drehbuch als eine andere Art des Erzählens.* Munich: edition text+kritik, 1989.

Buchka, Peter. *Augen kann man nicht kaufen. Wim Wenders und seine Filme.* Munich: Hanser, 1983. 2d ed. Frankfurt/Main: Fischer Taschenbuchverlag, 1985, no. 4457.

Cahiers du Cinéma. *Wim Wenders.* vol. 400 (Oct. 1987).

Wim Wenders. Le Souffle de l'Ange. (Paris): Cahiers du Cinéma, 1988.

Caldwell, David, & Paul W. Rea. "Handke's and Wenders' *Wings of Desire:* Transcending Postmodernism." *German Quarterly* 64 (Winter 1991), no. 1, pp. 46–60.

Camera/Stylo. *Wim Wenders.* New enlarged ed. Paris: Ramsay Poche Cinéma, 1987, nos. 49–50.

Ciment, Michel. "Entretien avec Wim Wenders." *Positif* (Nov. 1982), no. 261, pp. 17–23.

Coates, Paul. *The Gorgon's Gaze: German Cinema, Expressionism, and the Image of Horror.* Cambridge University Press, 1991.

Corrigan, Timothy. "The Realist Gesture in Films of Wim Wenders: Hollywood and the New German Cinema." *Quarterly Review of Film Studies* 5 (Spring 1980), no. 2, pp. 205–16.

"Wenders' *Kings of the Road:* The Voyage from Desire to Language." Corrigan, *New German Film: The Displaced Image*. Austin: University of Texas Press, 1983, pp. 24–41.

Covino, Michael. "Wim Wenders: A Worldwide Homesickness." *Film Quarterly* 31 (Winter 1977–8), no. 2, pp. 9–19.

Cowie, Peter. *Coppola*. New York: Scribners, 1990.

cult movie. Wenders/Ray. vol. 3 (Feb.–Mar. 1982), no. 8.

Dawson, Jan. *Wim Wenders*. Trans. Carla Wartenberg. New York: Zoetrope, 1976.

"A Labyrinth of Subsidies: The Origins of the New German Cinema." *Sight and Sound* 50 (Winter 1980–1), no. 1, pp. 14–20.

Della Vacche, Angela. *The Body in the Mirror: Shapes of History in Italian Cinema*. Princeton, N.J.: Princeton University Press, 1992.

Devillers, Jean-Pierre. *Wim Wenders: Berlin, L.A., Berlin*. Paris: Samuel Tastet Editeur, 1985.

Dieckmann, Katherine. "Wim Wenders: An Interview." *Film Quarterly* 38 (Winter 1984–5), no. 2, pp. 2–7.

Dyan, Daniel. "The Tutor-Code of Classical Cinema." *Movies and Methods*. Ed. Bill Nichols. vol. 1. Berkeley & Los Angeles: University of California Press, 1976, pp. 438–51.

Eisner, Lotte. *Murnau*. Berkeley & Los Angeles: University of California Press, 1973.

Elsaesser, Thomas. "Tales of Sound and Fury: Observations on the Family Melodrama." *Movies and Methods*. Ed. Bill Nichols. vol. 2. Berkeley & Los Angeles: University of California Press, 1985, pp. 165–89.

New German Cinema: A History. New Brunswick, N.J.: Rutgers University Press, 1989.

Farrell, Tom. "Nick Ray's German Friend Wim Wenders." *Wide Angle* 5 (1983), no. 4, pp. 15–21.

Farrell, Tom, & Jost, Jon. "Nicholas Ray: The Last Movies." *Sight and Sound* 50 (1981), no. 2, pp. 92–7.

Franklin, James. *New German Cinema: From Oberhausen to Hamburg*. Boston: Twayne, 1983.

Franklin, J. C. "The Films of Fassbinder: Form and Formula." *Quarterly Review of Film Studies* 5 (Spring 1980), no. 2, pp. 169–81.

Frisch, Shelley. "The Disenchanted Image: From Goethe's *Wilhelm Meister* to Wenders' *Wrong Movement*." *Literature/Film Quarterly* 7 (1979), no. 3, pp. 208–14.

Fusco, Coco. "Angels, History and Poetic Fantasy, An Interview with Wim Wenders." *Cineaste* 16 (1988), no. 4, pp. 14–17.

Gallagher, John Andrew. "Wim Wenders." *Filmdirectors on Directing: Twenty-one Filmmakers Talk about Their Craft*. New York: Praeger, 1989, pp. 269–77.

Geist, Kathe. *The Cinema of Wim Wenders: From Paris, France to Paris, Texas*. Ann Arbor, Mich.: UMI Research Press, 1988.

Goodwin, Michael, & Naomi Wise. *On the Edge: The Life and Times of Francis Coppola*. New York: Morrow, 1989.

Grob, Norbert. *Wenders. Die frühen Filme. Die Formen des filmischen Blicks.* Berlin: Edition Filme, 1984.

"Wim Wenders." *Cinegraph.* Lexikon zum deutschsprachigen Film. Ed. Hans-Michael Bock. Munich: edition text+kritik, 1988.

Wenders. Berlin: Edition Filme, 1991.

Grob, Norbert, & Manuela Reichart (eds.). *Ray.* Berlin: Edition Filme, 1989.

Handke, Peter. *Falsche Bewegung.* Frankfurt/Main: Suhrkamp, 1972.

The Goalie's Anxiety at the Penalty Kick. New York: Farrar, Straus & Giroux, 1972.

Hooks, Bell. "Representing Whiteness. Seeing *Wings of Desire.*" *Yearning: Race, Gender, and Cultural Politics.* Boston: West End Press, 1990, pp. 165–71.

Horkheimer, Max, & Theodor W. Adorno. *Dialectic of Enlightenment.* Trans. John Cumming. New York: Herder & Herder, 1972.

Horton, Andrew. "Wim Wenders' *Alice in the Cities:* Song of the Open Road." *Ideas of Order in Literature and Film.* Ed. Peter Ruppert. Tallahassee: University Presses of Florida, 1980, pp. 84–93 (selected papers from the Fourth Annual Florida State University Conference on Literature and Film).

Jameson, Frederic. *Postmodernism or, The Logic of Late Capitalism.* Durham, N.C.: Duke University Press, 1991.

Johnston, Sheila (ed.). *Wim Wenders.* London: British Film Institute, 1981 (BFI Dossier, no. 10).

Kaes, Anton. *From Heimat to Hitler.* Cambridge, Mass.: Harvard University Press, 1989.

Kanzog, Klaus (ed.). *Der erotische Diskurs. Filmische Zeichen und Argumente. Diskurs film: Münchner Beiträge zur Filmphilologie,* vol. 3. Munich, 1989.

Kolker, Robert Phillip. *The Altering Eye: Contemporary International Cinema.* New York: Oxford University Press, 1983.

A Cinema of Loneliness: Penn, Kubrick, Scorsese, Spielberg, Altman: 2d ed. New York: Oxford University Press, 1988.

Küntzel, Uwe. *Wim Wenders. Ein Filmbuch.* 3d ed. Freiburg i.Br.: Dreisam, 1989.

Lehmann, Peter, Robin Wood, & Edward Lachmann. "Wim Wenders. An Interview." *Wide Angle* 2 (1978), no. 4, pp. 72–9.

Luke, Timothy W. *Screens of Power.* Urbana: University of Illinois Press, 1982.

McCormick, Richard W. *Politics of the Self. Feminism and the Postmodern in West German Literature and Film.* Princeton, N.J.: Princeton University Press, 1991.

Mitscherlich, Alexander. *Die Unwirtlichkeit unserer Städte. Anstiftung zum Unfrieden.* Frankfurt/Main: Suhrkamp, 1965.

Mitscherlich, Alexander, & Margarete Mitscherlich. *The Inability to Mourn.* Trans. Beverly R. Placzek. New York: Grove, 1975.

Paneth, Ira. "Wim and His Wings," *Film Quarterly* 42 (Fall 1988), no. 1, pp. 2–8.

Perlmutter, Ruth. "German Revisionism: Edgar Reitz's *Heimat.*" *Wide Angle* 9 (1987), no. 3, pp. 21–37.

"Wenders Returns Home on Wings of Desire." *Studies in Humanities* (forthcoming).

Petit, Catherine, Philippe Dubois, & Claudine Delvaux. *Les Voyages de Wim Wenders.* Crisnée (Belgium): Editions Yellow Now, 1985.

Prinzler, Hans Helmut, & Eric Rentschler (eds.). *Augenzeugen. 100 Texte neuer deutscher Filmemacher.* Frankfurt/Main: Verlag der Autoren, 1988.

Rauh, Reinhold. *Wim Wenders und seine Filme.* Munich: Heyne, 1990.

Rayns, Tony. "Forms of Address: Interviews with Three German Filmmakers." *Sight and Sound* 44 (Winter 1974–5), no. 1, pp. 2–7.

Rentschler, Eric. *West German Film in the Course of Time.* Bedford Hills, N.Y.: Redgrave, 1984.

Rentschler, Eric (ed.). *German Film and Literature: Adaptations and Transformations.* New York: Methuen, 1986.

Ruppert, Peter. "Audience Engagement in Wenders's *The American Friend* and Fassbinder's *Ali: Fear Eats the Soul.*" *Narrative Strategies: Original Essays in Film and Prose Fiction.* Ed. Syndy M. Conger & Janice R. Welsch. Macomb: Western Illinois University Press, 1980, pp. 61–77.

Sandford, John. *The New German Cinema.* New York: Da Capo, 1980.

Schelksy, Helmut. *Die skeptische Generation: Eine Soziologie der deutschen Jugend.* Frankfurt/Main, Berlin: Ullstein, 1975.

Schlunk, Jürgen E. "The Image of America in German Literature and in the New German Cinema: Wim Wenders' *The American Friend.*" *Literature/Film Quarterly* 7 (1979), no. 3, pp. 215–22.

Sedgwick, Eve Kosofsky. *Between Men: English Literature and Male Homosocial Desire.* New York: Columbia University Press, 1985.

Shepard, Sam. *Motel Chronicles.* San Francisco: City Lights Books, 1982.

Stern, Fritz. *The Politics of Cultural Despair.* Berkeley & Los Angeles: University of California Press, 1961.

Tarkovsky, Andrei. *Sculpting in Time.* Trans. Kitty Hunter-Blair. Austin: University of Texas Press, 1989.

Vila, Xavier, and Alice Kuzner. "Witnessing Narration in *Wings of Desire.*" *Film Criticism* 16 (Spring, 1992), no. 3, pp. 53–65.

Welsh, James M. "Wim Wenders Bibliography." *Wide Angle* 2 (1978), no. 4, pp. 80–1.

Wenders, Wim. *Texte zu Filmen und Musik.* Berlin: Freunde der Deutschen Kinemathek, 1975.

Alice Dans Les Villes. Trans. Anne Quesemand. *Avant-Scène du Cinéma* (May 1, 1981), no. 267, pp. 1–74.

"Jukebox Kino." A conversation about film and music with Jochen Brunow. *Filme* 2 (Nov.–Dec. 1981), no. 12, pp. 38–9.

Emotion Pictures: Essays und Filmkritiken, 1968–1984. Frankfurt/Main: Verlag der Autoren, 1986.

Tokyo-Ga: A Filmed Diary. Berlin: Gabrev, 1986 (in English, German, & French).

Written in the West: Photographien aus dem amerikanischen Westen. Munich: Schirmer/Mosel, 1987.

Die Logik der Bilder: Essays und Gespräche. Ed. Michael Töteberg. Frankfurt/Main: Verlag der Autoren, 1988.

Emotion Pictures: Reflections on the Cinema. Trans. Sean Whiteside in association with Michael Hofmann. London: Faber & Faber, 1989.

The Logic of Images: Essays and Conversations. Trans. Michael Hofmann. London: Faber & Faber, 1991.

The Act of Seeing: Texts and Conversations. Frankfurt/Main: Verlag der Autoren, 1992.

Wenders, Wim, & Peter Handke. *Der Himmel über Berlin: Ein Filmbuch.* Frankfurt/Main: Suhrkamp, 1988.

Wenders, Wim, & Fritz Müller-Scherz. *Im Lauf der Zeit.* Photoscript, dialogues, materials. Frankfurt/Main: Zweitausendeins, 1976.

Kings of the Road. Photoscript. Trans. Christopher Doherty. Munich: Filmverlag der Autoren, 1976.

Wenders, Wim, & Sam Shepard. *Paris, Texas.* Written by Sam Shepard, adaptation by L. M. Kit Carson, ed. Chris Sievernich. Nördlingen: Greno, 1984 (dialogues in English, German, & French).

Wenders, Wim, Sam Shepard, & L. M. Kit Carson. *Paris, Texas.* Updated English language ed. New York: Ecco, 1990.

Wenders, Wim, & Chris Sievernich. *Nick's Film: Lightning over Water.* Frankfurt: Zweitausendeins, 1981.

Willett, John. *Art and Politics in the Weimar Period: The New Sobriety, 1917–1933.* New York: Pantheon, 1978.

Wim Wenders. With contributions by Frieda Grafe, Wolfgang Jacobsen, Peter W. Jansen, Stefan Kolditz, Klaus Kreimeier, and Karsten Visarius. Munich: Hanser, 1991. (Reihe Film, vol. 44.)

Zavarzadeh, Mas'ud. "Biology and Ideology: The 'Natural' Family in *Paris, Texas.*" *CineAction* (Spring 1987), no. 8, pp. 25–30.

Index

191